Praise fo
Thinking Critically

"There are more than a few 'how-to-do-college' books, but none take a deep, informative dive into what it takes for college students to thrive academically and cultivate the habits of an educated mind. Newman offers a treasure trove of helpful examples to illustrate how undergraduates need to think and what they should do to effectively meet and benefit from the range of learning challenges they will encounter during and after college."

—GEORGE D. KUH,
Chancellor's Professor Emeritus of Higher Education,
Indiana University Bloomington

"*Thinking Critically in College* fills a substantial need in higher education resources. The research is available, volumes have been written to support faculty in teaching students so that enduring learning occurs, and there are a growing number of how-to-learn courses in college. What's missing is a book that speaks directly to our students as they launch their college careers. *Thinking Critically in College* is that needed resource. It is a must-read for beginning college students. I can't think of anyone better positioned to write this book than Louis Newman."

—SUSAN SINGER,
vice president for academic affairs and provost,
Rollins College

"This book could not be more timely! At a time of increasing numbers of first-generation college students, *Thinking Critically in College* provides first-year college students with a playbook that will help them succeed in college and beyond. Newman's comprehensive approach explains what many students perceive as the 'faculty language.' He empowers his readers with language and tools to build meaningful relationships, learn valuable skills, and unpack the academic world. For those who may question the value of a college education, they will find their answer in this book! Truly a valuable guide for all college students, especially those in their first year."

—SUSANA RIVERA-MILLS,
provost and executive vice president for academic affairs,
Ball State University

"This book is an essential resource for college students, and I can't wait to assign it in my first-year courses. Drawing on decades of professional experience and the latest research, Louis Newman is the ideal guide to critical thinking—and also to learning, writing, and the other core academic experiences in college. I particularly appreciate his invitation to 'begin with questions' and his 'advice for the road ahead' that provides concrete steps toward success. All students will benefit from reading and discussing this book."

—PETER FELTON,
executive director, Center for Engaged Learning and
assistant provost for teaching and learning, Elon University

"This is the perfect high-school graduation gift for anyone going to college. It is a gift that keeps on giving, a guide to gaining the most from the undergraduate academic experience. The book is replete with practical counsel on how to think critically and communicate well. Newman not only gives wise guidance for how to learn in college, but he also provides scores of helpful examples of that guidance applied to various assignments that college students must handle. The subtitle says it all, *The Essential Handbook for Student Success*."

—THOMAS EHRLICH,
president emeritus, Indiana University;
former provost, The University of Pennsylvania

"This marvelous little book is really three books in one. Its declared aim is to help students make their college years into better, more lasting, and more rewarding learning experiences. The book is also implicitly a guide for college professors on how to make their classes and assignments more supportive of real learning. And for all of us who want to continue to learn and to grow intellectually after college, this book will help us learn how to make our informal learning time more effective and rewarding."

—MICHAEL MCPHERSON,
president emeritus, Macalester College and The Spencer Foundation

"'*Why hasn't anyone ever told me this before?*' That poignant observation by one of Newman's undergraduate students captures the superb power of this gracefully written book. Written for students, it is equally valuable for their teachers and advisors. Newman focuses on the disciplines that form the backbone of undergraduate education, how to think about them, study them, and write about them. His insights will be invaluable to students and all who work to enhance their education."

—LEE S. SHULMAN,
Charles E. Ducommun Professor of Education Emeritus, Stanford University
president emeritus, The Carnegie Foundation for the Advancement of Teaching

"Almost all colleges and universities proclaim that they instill critical thinking skills in their graduates, but they all too rarely explain to students what this actually entails. Thankfully, Louis Newman's *Thinking Critically in College* fills that yawning gap. Newman offers the wisest, most perceptive—and yet eminently practical—examination I have encountered of what critical thinking truly is, why it matters, and how students can hone these skills. A college or university whose students take Newman's smart guidance to heart, and whose faculty consciously focus on imparting his lessons, will admirably live up to its aspirations."

—STEVEN G. POSKANZER,
president emeritus, Carleton College

Thinking *Critically* in College

The Essential Handbook for Student Success

LOUIS E. NEWMAN

RADIUS BOOK GROUP
NEW YORK

Radius Book Group
A Division of Diversion Publishing Corp.
www.RadiusBookGroup.com

For more information, email info@radiusbookgroup.com.

First edition: March 2023
Trade Paperback ISBN: 978-1-63576-795-7
eBook ISBN: 978-1-63576-938-8

Manufactured in the United States of America

10 9 8 7 6 5 4 3 2 1

Cover design by Tom Lau
Interior design by Neuwirth & Associates, Inc.

For my teachers,
who taught me how to learn,

for my colleagues,
who modeled for me how to teach,

and

for my students,
who enabled me to see how learning
and teaching transforms lives.

CONTENTS

FOREWORD

Educators often talk about the importance of critical-thinking skills. What are these skills and why do they matter? Well, let me tell you a story: The social scientist Xiaodong Lin-Siegler and her colleagues once told high school students about scientists like the physicist Albert Einstein.[1] Some students were told only that Einstein was a genius.

> His thoughts were so advanced that many contemporary scientists are still working on the ideas he talked about in 450 papers he published. In 1999, *Time Magazine* named Einstein the man of the century.[2]

Others learned about Einstein's achievements but were also told about the roadblocks he faced as he developed his theories—intellectual problems he could not solve, obstacles that had him spinning his wheels, personal struggles that prompted despondency. Lin-Siegler told me that, compared to high school students who learned only that Einstein was a genius, students who learned about Einstein's struggles and failures were more likely to feel engaged with physics, to do better in the subject—and to believe that they had a future in science.

I reported on this study many years ago for NPR, and it has stayed with me ever since.[3] Why would telling high school students about Einstein's limitations be more inspiring, more motivating, and more engaging than just telling them about his achievements? Well, for one thing, students could relate better to Einstein when they learned his marvelous insights didn't just pop into his head. Those discoveries took hard work and persistence—traits they could develop themselves. Humanizing Einstein undoubtedly made him more interesting.

But I believe there is a deeper truth here.

We often imagine that the purpose of education is to transfer information from teacher to student, from expert to apprentice. So much of education, even in college, takes the form of one person lecturing to others. But all of us who are a few years removed from college know that we have forgotten most of what we learned in college, and the little we remember is often rendered out of date by the progress of research. Students who learned about coronaviruses before 2019 might have to go back to school to learn all that we have learned *since* 2019 about the kind of virus that caused the COVID-19 pandemic. If the information we learn in school is quickly forgotten or rendered obsolete, what exactly is the point of going to school?

I believe Lin-Siegler's study hints at the answer: When we engage in the *backstory* of the ideas we learn, when we start to understand not just the facts, but *how* the facts were developed and *why* they look the way they do, this changes our relationship to what we study. When we learn about the struggle it took to create new ideas, we better understand how precious and hard-won ideas are. But it's more than that: learning how facts came together, observing the missteps and mistakes, the dead-ends and false starts, is like the difference between watching a play unfold on a stage and being invited backstage. Sitting in a theater, we see only the finished play—neatly packaged, beautifully produced, and coherent. When we go backstage, however, we see how direction and acting shape the play, how lighting and sound design create moods, how *choices* the playwright made produce the story we hear. We start to understand that the play we are watching is *only one of an infinite number of plays that could have been produced*. This is a moment of revelation. In that moment, we start to ask ourselves, "What if the playwright had made different choices? What if the director had the lead character portrayed by a woman instead of a man? Is this really a comedy or a tragedy?" Being invited backstage allows us to see the series of steps that led to the play and to see how different steps could lead to different plays. We start to realize that *we might create our own plays*. In the case of education, when we are invited to understand the backstory of ideas—and this is true whether we are talking about physics or anthropology, history or neuroscience—*we see how we might become explorers, not just followers*. We start to perceive that we could become Einsteins ourselves.

This, then, is our answer to our conundrum: Yes, most of what we learn in college is soon forgotten, and what we learn can be quickly rendered obsolete. Our choice to major in engineering may be supplanted in a few years by life and career changes that cause us to become journalists (my own story). But if we focus our college years not on merely learning information and studying facts, but spending time "backstage"—understanding *how* knowledge was created—then it doesn't really matter if we forget the facts. We have picked up something much more important: the real question is not "will you remember what you learned in college?" but "will you be able to rediscover what you have forgotten and be able to sift good information from bad?" If the apocalypse were to arrive tomorrow, would you and the small band of surviving humans have the ingenuity to rediscover what was lost?

Most of us, I hope, won't have to deal with the apocalypse. But most of us—and nearly everyone who is in college today—will have multiple careers. Each of those careers will likely require not only different skills than the ones we learned in college but skills that we didn't learn in our *previous* careers. Increasingly and urgently, the question we will be asked in each new career is whether we can get up to speed and make contributions of our own. If the world we formerly lived in required people to learn only a few skills and then use them throughout their lives, the world we live in today demands we repeatedly reinvent ourselves.

What are the skills, the habits of mind, that allow such reinvention? Many of them fall under the broad rubric of critical-thinking skills, which is really a fancy way of saying you know how to think for yourself. When people tell you things, you can interrogate what they say. When a manager at a new company tells you that this is the way the organization has always been run, you are able to learn the company's history without believing it is the only way to do things. Being able to keep in mind different ideas, and different *competing* ideas, is a rare and valuable skill. (There are very few "slam dunk" answers in real life; everything has trade-offs.) Importantly, being able to think for yourself is much more than merely *having opinions* that clash with others. And it is not at all the same thing as imagining that everyone else's ideas are lacking: lots of people are critical of the views of others (and many of these people spend a lot of time on social media explaining to others why they are wrong), but this is not evidence of critical-thinking skills. In fact, one of the most important critical-thinking skills is the ability to monitor your own thoughts and biases, to be wary of your own conclusions, to ask yourself, repeatedly and uncomfortably, "Why do I believe what I believe?" and "How might I be wrong?" (The physicist Richard Feynman once summed up this idea beautifully: "The first principle is that you must not fool yourself, and you are the easiest person to fool.")

Louis Newman's book is an essential guide for students who want to get the most out of their college years. It is based on his many decades of experience exploring why some students get a lot out of college, while others do not. If you read this book before you go to college and follow its precepts, you will undoubtedly get much more from your time in college than you would otherwise. But *Thinking Critically in College* is a book not just for college students and educators. It is a manifesto for a society where too many of us are overconfident about our opinions and under-curious about the views of those who disagree with us. It is a challenge for those of us who "know" which cable television channel tells the truth and which one trades in lies. It is a riposte to a world where many of us oscillate between a blind acceptance of some claims and an unthinking rejection of others.

This book is a strident call to take ideas seriously, but it is not a jeremiad. It will show you that the ability to think well is a skill, and it is a skill that can be learned. This is also a book that is written with experience, erudition and, yes, with love: it is an invitation to us all to sit down at the table of scholarship, to listen generously to others, but also to think carefully and skeptically, and then make our own contributions to the storehouses of human knowledge.

Shankar Vedantam
Host of *Hidden Brain*
2023

PREFACE AND ACKNOWLEDGMENTS

I have a distinct memory of the moment when the idea of writing this book first occurred to me.

I was sitting with a student reviewing a video recording of the oral presentation she had recently given in a seminar I was teaching. She was a senior and one of the most talented majors in my department that year. As we reviewed her presentation, I commented, "Rachel, this presentation was really substantive, and you made all your points very effectively. But it would have been that much better if you had just begun by spelling out for us the research questions you were addressing. That way, we would have understood exactly how all that great information answered those specific questions." She looked surprised but interested, so I continued. "It's always helpful to begin with the questions," I said. "Whatever you're talking about, you should set the stage by spelling out the questions to which this material is the answer. In fact, you can think about this when you're reading, too. Anytime you read something, you should be asking yourself, 'What questions were the authors asking, and why did they attempt to answer them this way?'" By now, Rachel was sitting up and really focused on taking in what I was saying, so I took it one step further. "In fact, when you get a course syllabus, you should be asking yourself, 'What are the questions this course is designed to address, and why has the professor chosen to organize the material in this particular way to explore them?' Learning is all about focusing on the questions, especially the unstated questions, that underlie whatever someone is telling us."

Rachel was now wide-eyed and clearly looked as if she had just discovered something extraordinary, though it seemed to me that all this was obvious.

Finally, in words that still echo in my ears nearly a decade later, she asked, "Why hasn't anyone ever told me this before?" Spoken with a mixture of sadness and frustration, that question registered with me as few students' questions have, either before or since. My first thought was, "How could a student as successful and smart as Rachel be hearing this for the first time late in her senior year?" But that question quickly gave way to another: "Why *don't* we tell students at the very beginning of their college careers that questions are the key to understanding, to research, and to analyzing pretty much everything they will encounter? How might their college education be enhanced if we spelled this out, along with the other keys to college-level thinking, and didn't just expect them to figure this out on their own?" As our meeting ended and I walked back to my office, my mind was spinning. Why had it taken me this long—by this point, I had been teaching undergraduates for nearly thirty years—to realize that they needed to be explicitly instructed on how to think critically in the ways my colleagues and I expected them to. And so, spurred by Rachel's penetrating question, I resolved to write a book.

▪ ▪ ▪

What intellectual skills and habits of mind do students need to succeed in college courses, and how can we most effectively introduce these at the very outset of their college careers? That question has animated this book. In the course of answering it, I have relied heavily on the work of educational psychologists, learning specialists, and advocates for critical thinking, as well as scholars in fields of study about which I claim no expertise. Along the way, I have also conferred with dozens of colleagues at diverse institutions to ensure that these lessons would be helpful in teaching first-year students in a variety of settings. I also shared drafts of chapters with students and held multiple focus groups to ensure that I was addressing the issues students actually faced as they adjusted to college-level learning.

In addition, I explored other "college success" books, of which there are dozens, to see what kind of guidance they provided. To my surprise, virtually none of them touched on the issues that students encounter in their courses. Typically, those books are full of valuable tactical advice about taking notes, going to professors' office hours, time management, study skills—even eating well, getting enough sleep, and getting along with roommates. But I looked in vain for anything that would have helped Rachel get any clearer about the intellectual challenges of college coursework.

But while my initial and primary motivation for writing this book was to orient students to college work, over time it became clear to me that there is far more at stake here than simply helping students tackle college assignments more effectively. The flip side of students' need to learn how to learn is higher education's commitment to prepare students for successful careers, engaged citizenship, and fulfilling lives.

It is widely recognized that colleges are failing to fulfill their own commitments to produce students who are critical thinkers, capable of asking penetrating questions about the information they are increasingly bombarded with (especially when they find it on the Internet). As faculty can attest, students are frequently incapable of distinguishing a well-supported argument from a sloppy one, much less articulating a reasoned and evidence-based critique of the latter. They need help making the transition from high school–level thinking, which frequently required only that they absorb and repeat what others had taught them, to college-level thinking, which requires them to analyze, synthesize, consider, and weigh alternative explanations of phenomena. Colleges purport to teach students critical thinking, to prepare them for "lifelong learning" and the responsibilities of citizenship; if you have any doubt, just look at the mission statement of just about every institution of higher education in this country. But if we look at the general-education requirements of most of those same institutions, we will find surprisingly few courses in which these intellectual skills are singled out and explicitly taught. It is my sincere hope that this book will help address this long-standing issue in higher education.

▪ ▪ ▪

While the impetus to write this book emerged after a single exchange with a gifted student, the ability to do so is the fruit of many years of teaching and many conversations with current and former students and faculty colleagues. It also involved a great deal of additional research as I delved into the literature on how students develop these critical-thinking skills. In that work, I was helped enormously by several very talented Stanford students—Jonah Glick-Unterman, Noah Howard, Ayesha Pasha, Rishabh Kapoor, Laura Tobar, Liv Jenks, Via Lamberti, Alex Li, Forrest Dollins, Alicia Purpur, and Ariana Davarpanah—all of whom served as research assistants at various points in the writing and editing of this volume. Collectively, they did more than just read the literature on a range of topics, digest it, and help organize this material in ways that enabled me to write this book. They were thought partners, helping me determine the sorts of features that would make this book more engaging and accessible to students. I am enormously grateful to all of them for their careful work, their creativity, and their dedication to this project. A number of former students were instrumental in shaping parts of this book, including Caleb Rakestraw-Morn, Josh Pitkovsky, Jesse Rothman, Jon Kagan-Kans, and Nadav Ziv.

Several colleagues have also contributed significantly to this book. Some have given me important advice about topics to include; others have graciously read drafts and made valuable editorial suggestions. These include Liz Ciner, Beth McKinsey, Chico Zimmerman, Fred Hagstrom, and Deborah Appleman, all former colleagues at Carleton College. I have also learned much from the feedback I received from faculty colleagues at Stanford who reviewed parts of the manuscript: Sam Wineburg, Tom Ehrlich, Jo Boaler, Dan Edelstein, Jim Campbell, Marvin Diogenes, and Tim Randazzo. Collectively, they helped me refine many points, improve my presentation, and make this book more user-friendly. I am indebted to Nicholas Santascoy, an academic coach in Stanford's Center for Teaching and Learning, who worked with me to craft some workshops based on the material in this book. In doing so, he helped me rethink the content and how best to present it.

I also consulted and received valuable input from many colleagues at other institutions: Elliot Dorff (American Jewish University), Andrew Flesher (Stony Brook University), Paul Lauritzen (John Carroll University), Joel Schlosser (Bryn Mawr College), Phyllis Brown (Santa Clara University), Jason Rivera and Kecia McBride (Ball State University), Darlene Guerrero (San Jose State University), Todd Silverstein (Willamette University), Geoff Clausen (Elon University), Max Mueller (University of Nebraska–Lincoln), Laza Razafimanjato (Philander Smith College), and Sara Adams (Madisonville Community College). I am also grateful to two friends, Robert Rees and Terri Elkin, lifelong public school teachers, who gave me valuable feedback on how to make this book useful to high school students.

I also received valuable feedback from students at the East Palo Alto Academy, which enrolls largely students of color hoping to become the first in their families to attend college. In addition, some students at Mount Tamalpais College, who are also incarcerated in San Quentin, graciously agreed to read some chapters and give me feedback. Finally, I convened several groups of Stanford students to talk with me about how they had learned to "think like college students" and to provide feedback on specific chapters. I am grateful to all of them for sharing their experiences and helping me refine innumerable points in the book.

I want to thank Carleton College for the generous support I received from its research fund for emeriti faculty and for giving me access to the archive of course assignments that are collected through its writing program. I could not have written this book without this assistance.

I am deeply grateful to Harry Elam, former vice provost for undergraduate education at Stanford, and to the current vice provost, Sarah Church, for their ongoing support. By allowing me to pursue my research and writing, even when it meant taking time away from my other responsibilities to Stanford, they enabled me to complete this book.

My agent, Peter Bernstein, gets much of the credit for seeing this book through to publication. His dedication and persistence have been a steady source of support through an extended process of locating the right publisher. I am enormously grateful for his belief in this project and his expert guidance. I also want to acknowledge Mark Fretz, my editor, Evan Phail, publishing coordinator, and the whole team at Radius Book Group. They have been a pleasure to work with at every step in the process of bringing this book into print.

My wife, Amy, is my most devoted champion and my most thoughtful critic. Her unwavering support of all my professional pursuits over more than twenty-five years has enabled me to overcome any number of obstacles and setbacks I experienced along the way. Her support is the unspoken subtext of every page in this book. Her love and devotion are an enormous source of blessing in my life.

I have dedicated this book to my teachers, colleagues, and students, which reflects my awareness that it is the fruit of a lifetime of learning and teaching. In writing it, I have attempted to speak directly to students much as I did in thousands of conversations with Carleton students, both in class and during my office hours. Over the years, they taught me how to teach more effectively by asking the sort of questions that enabled me to see when they were getting it and when they weren't (which invariably meant that I needed to do something different). In the intellectual dance that is teaching and learning, my students have been my best guides in crafting assignments that more effectively prompted the sorts of intellectual moves I wanted them to learn. In the process, I learned much about how to provide feedback on their work that enabled them to become better learners.

In similar ways, my colleagues have been invaluable guides for improving my teaching; many have served as significant role models whom I have sought to emulate. They have shaped my development as a teacher in more ways than I could possibly recount. In all, this book grows out of a lifetime of teaching and working alongside other dedicated teachers throughout my long and enormously rewarding career at Carleton College, including a stint as the director of the Pearlman Center for Learning and Teaching. I am grateful beyond words for the privilege of having been a member of the Carleton faculty for thirty-three years.

Since I began working on this book, I have been blessed with three grandchildren—Adin, Ezra, and Nava. They have graced our lives with more joy and delight than I could have imagined possible. Watching them has rekindled in me the sense of wonder at how, even at the earliest stages of our development, we as a species are programmed to explore and learn, to integrate new information in ever-widening frameworks of meaning, and then to apply this knowledge in new and unfamiliar circumstances. I have no way of knowing whether I will have the privilege of watching them someday begin their college journeys. But it is my hope that when they do, they will pick up this book and know that their Papa tried to ease their path just a little.

March 2023

A WORD TO TEACHERS

All of us who have the responsibility of teaching students, both college-bound high school students and first-year college students, know both the excitement of opening their minds to new ideas and the challenges of teaching them how to think critically. For many of us, trained in specific disciplines and tasked with making that content accessible to our students, we feel the responsibility to focus our efforts on content. There is so much our students need to learn—concepts and vocabulary, methods and theories. If we don't impart that knowledge in our courses, students will not be prepared for more advanced work in the discipline. There is no time to address more general issues—how to think analytically or quantitatively, much less how to study effectively or to cultivate metacognition.

And yet we know that many (likely, most) beginning college students are clueless about the sort of thinking we expect of them. They pick it up, if at all, by a process of trial and error. The result is mutual frustration—students frustrated that they are unclear what college-level thinking means and how to do it, and faculty frustrated that our students don't get it. In my view, there is only one way forward: to be explicit about what critical thinking is and how to do it and then to illustrate that in the way we teach, in the assignments we give, and in the feedback we provide them. It is my hope that this book will provide a concise and accessible framework for doing these things, without detracting significantly from the time needed to cover discipline-specific topics.

If you use this book as a text for one of your courses, I encourage you to do so in whatever ways best suit your needs and the needs of your students. The chapters do not need to be assigned in their entirety or in the order in which they appear here. Some may be more relevant to your purposes than others, and some may complement specific units in your course, which dictates when (or whether) you assign them. If you do use the book in its entirety, you will notice that some messages—such as seeking help and thinking critically to identify one's own biases—are reiterated at multiple points in the text.

It will be apparent that this book is written for an American audience. It assumes the context of American baccalaureate education, and the examples offered are typical of materials that students would encounter in American classrooms. In this regard, I am a product of my own education and of the educational institutions I have worked in. If you are teaching international students or in a non-American institution, you may need to supplement the reading selections with others that are more culturally familiar or be prepared to provide more context than I have here.

Similarly, the questions for reflection that appear at the conclusion of each chapter are meant to be suggestive. I wrote them with the intention that they could serve as brief written reflection assignments. But you may find that there are other prompts that will stimulate your students to practice what they have learned in these pages or to reflect on how they could apply those lessons to their academic work. The goals of these prompts are to help students review the main points covered in that chapter, to reflect on their own learning process, and to consider the ways in which they could apply what they have learned.

As I write this, our country appears to be coming out of a two-year period of grappling with the COVID-19 pandemic. Students have been profoundly affected by the altered learning environment they have endured during this period. While I do not believe that these disruptions have changed our goals to teach our students to think critically and creatively about the material we assign them, they have surely affected our students' readiness to do so. Things we assumed they had learned will likely need to be retaught. The lessons covered here may need to be scaffolded more carefully or introduced more slowly. All this may affect how you choose to use this book as you do the hard work of meeting students where they are. In all, it is my hope that the guide to college-level thinking presented here may be even more timely as students struggle to catch up on the fundamentals they need to succeed in college.

Finally, it is worth remembering that acquiring critical-thinking skills is the work of a lifetime. At best, we lay the foundations for that work—first by explaining that this is a long-term goal of higher education, and then by introducing some of the tools students need and demonstrating how to use them. It would be a disservice to students and to the cause of education to suggest that any single book could inculcate in them all the critical-thinking skills they will use throughout their lives. But we can—and must—show them how these skills are embedded in the work they are asked to do in college and how practicing these skills will serve them well, no matter what careers they choose. In that sense, the goals of this book are modest, even though I believe its purpose is of paramount importance for us as educators.

INTRODUCTION

Pack Your Bags: College as Intellectual Adventure Travel

The value of an education . . . is not the learning of many facts but the training of the mind.
—ALBERT EINSTEIN

Questions to Ask as You Begin This Journey

You are about to embark on a great adventure: your college education. As with any adventure, you are likely experiencing a mix of feelings—excitement and anxiety, anticipation and reticence. You may also have many questions, including some or all of the following:

- How well has high school prepared me for college?
- Will I make new friends? Will I enjoy being a college student?
- What classes should I take, and what should I major in?
- How can I balance my schoolwork with my other time commitments, like work, social life, student organizations, and recreation?

Depending on your particular circumstances, you may have additional questions:

- How can I continue to support my family—perhaps financially or emotionally—when I am no longer at home? How will they manage without me?

- Will I be accepted by all the talented people I will meet in college? Will I feel like I belong there?
- Will my family and community at home who haven't gone to college be able to relate to the experiences I'm having and the things I'm learning?
- Will my physical disabilities or learning differences affect my ability to succeed in college? What services will be available to support me?

College will be a new experience, no matter what your background is. So I suggest you think about college as the great adventure it is. When you head to any unfamiliar place, it's a good idea to prepare. You may want to learn some key phrases in the local dialect, read something about local history, or familiarize yourself with distinctive customs and attractions. Of course, you can travel somewhere new without doing these things, but if you prepare, the trip will likely go more smoothly, and you will probably get more out of the experience.

Here, then, is my first piece of advice: *prepare for college by asking yourself some basic questions.*

Question 1: What are my goals in going to college?

Give yourself some room to think about this question, and jot down your thoughts.

____

____

____

____

Your answer to this question will depend on several things, beginning with the college you've chosen, its programs and degrees. While this book is tailored to students attending four-year baccalaureate institutions, much of what's covered here will be relevant to students at all sorts of colleges. But first, be sure the college you've chosen is aligned with your goals and needs.

Approximately 75–80 percent of students indicate that they go to college to advance a career or to improve their earning potential, both worthy goals.[1] These students may realize that the percentage of jobs that require a college degree has risen in recent decades and is projected to continue rising.[2] They may also know that the lifetime earnings of college graduates are dramatically higher than those of high school graduates.[3] So if you complete your degree, college is a great long-term investment, even if you take on some loans to finance your education. (Of course, you should carefully consider your personal financial circumstances before deciding to take on significant debt, especially if you are concerned that you may not successfully complete your degree.)

But you may not realize that the relationship between college and career isn't as simple as these statistics suggest. The first job you get after graduation is probably just that—your first job. Eighteen- to twenty-four-year-olds change jobs five to seven times on average during this six-year period, so if you're thinking of college as a path to that job, you may be thinking too narrowly.[4] You really want to focus on how your college education—which you're going to spend a lot of time and money acquiring—will still be serving you in your second, third, or fourth job after you graduate.

In addition, when most of us think about what we want to do "when we grow up," our horizons tend to be limited by the jobs we've heard of (think about a typical first grader's response to that question). But the range of potential careers out there is far greater than all the jobs you and your classmates have been exposed to, combined! Keep in mind that new kinds of jobs are created every day, especially due to rapid technological change. Not so long ago, the idea that you could become a computer scientist or a software engineer was virtually unheard of; now, these jobs and the machines they support are vital to our everyday lives. So you want to consider how college will prepare you for jobs that don't even exist yet.

Finally, employers consistently say that they look to hire people who can think creatively, analyze complex problems, write and speak effectively, and work well in groups, among other generalizable skills; job-specific skills can be learned on the job.[5] Here is the good news: *those key abilities and habits of mind can be learned in any course of study you choose.* The specific thing you study in college can enable you to land that dream job, but it doesn't necessarily determine your career. In fact, most graduates will tell you that their college major has little connection to what they're doing now.

So yes, a college degree, especially from a four-year institution, is valuable in financial terms, but that value is less tied to the specific subject you study than you might imagine. A college degree in any subject will open lots of career opportunities. Which leads me to my second piece of advice: *use these years to learn things that will serve you well no matter where your career path takes you.* Study whatever excites and engages you, which will help you persist and complete your degree. Focus less on the information and more on the skills; the information may be outdated in ten years (or sooner), but the intellectual skills and habits of mind will last you a lifetime and help you succeed in every job you hold.

Question 2:
How prepared am I for the challenges of college?

College is demanding. At a minimum, it requires an enormous investment of time and money, and depending on the education you received in high school, it is also likely to be challenging academically. You will be required to read more complex material, to write longer papers, and to do more difficult computations, among other requirements. Your instructors may have higher grading standards, put more of the responsibility for learning on you, and enforce stricter deadlines.

As you work harder to meet the academic challenges of college, you may also be juggling other demands. Perhaps you're working to support yourself, to repay loans, or to care for family members. If you're moving to a residential campus, you may be adjusting to living away from home for the first time. Unlike high school, the people and structures that used to support you may be absent or less immediate, just as the lures of campus life—socializing and discovering new interests—compete for your attention. For many college students, time management is the greatest challenge of these years.

Finally, you are likely going through a formative time in your life, especially if you're enrolling just after high school.[6] Your values and identity may be changing. You may be exploring your sexuality and developing intimate relationships in a new way. You may find yourself living in a more diverse community, among people from other regions or countries who hold views different from yours and who lead you to question things you always took for granted. And your college studies themselves will open your mind to ideas and perspectives that may be unsettling or exciting—or both.

Given all these challenges, it is hardly surprising that college students report high levels of stress.[7] The COVID-19 pandemic and its ongoing effects have further contributed to mental-health issues among college students.[8] Other factors—economic pressures, family responsibilities, and marginalization—can exacerbate these challenges.

Considering all this, you will want to do everything you can to set yourself up for success. So my third piece of advice is this: *take the time to develop your support system at the outset of college, and expand and adjust it as you go.* Support systems will look different for each of you. For some, family, close friends, and roommates will be key sources of support. For others, that network will include academic advisors, job supervisors, residential staff, or faculty members. Every college has health services for students. Find out where these are and how to access them. In addition, you will want to find your community, the people who share your background, your interests, and/or your struggles. This can take time, so it is important to be patient with yourself. Developing this support network is especially important, as many studies have demonstrated that students who feel they belong, who have a strong sense of connection to others at their school, have higher rates of success.[9]

No matter how academically well-prepared you are for college, you will do better if you anticipate the kind of support you may need and know how to access it when you need it. Like all trips to unfamiliar places, this one might unfold differently than you imagine. Virtually all students find college challenging, no matter how confident they feel going in. So give yourself permission to be surprised, and embrace the twists and turns in the road ahead. If you go into this experience expecting the unexpected, you won't be thrown off balance when things don't work out exactly as planned.

With all this in mind, this would be a good time to make a list of all the sources of support you have that can help you as you begin this journey.

Once you have clarified your goals and identified the support you need to succeed, you are ready to ask yourself one final question:

Question 3: What academic skills will I need to develop to learn successfully in college?

Whatever else you hope to get out of college, one thing is certain: you are going to learn. College will require you to learn new things in new ways. Whatever your specific interests or long-range plans, you certainly wouldn't choose to devote this time and money to higher education if you weren't looking to become more educated. Obvious as that sounds, many students begin their college careers without reflecting on just what that means or what sort of trip they're about to take.

College is not an extension of high school. It is designed to make you think in more sophisticated ways and do things that you may or may not be prepared to do. For many, high school learning was largely about absorbing information directly from teachers or textbooks and then demonstrating your recall. Mostly, you did this by answering questions on tests or writing responses to simple, straightforward prompts. This is one part of what it means to learn, especially if what you're learning is well established, like the laws of thermodynamics or Spanish vocabulary. To be sure, you'll continue to use those skills in college, but your professors will assume you already know how to do this. Instead, college-level work requires you to master what are called higher-order or critical-thinking skills.

There are many such skills, and this book will not teach you how to handle every intellectual challenge you encounter. It will, however, cover the basic building blocks, the key critical-thinking skills you need to succeed in college. There is nothing particularly mysterious about these skills; many people have described them in books on critical thinking, research methods, and writing. (A few of these guides are listed among the resources at the end of this book.) All your professors have learned them and employ them in their work. Rarely, though, do they explicitly introduce these analytical skills, much less explain how to acquire, apply, and improve them.

In the chapters that follow, especially chapter 2, I walk you through these critical-thinking skills, showing you how to recognize such skills in the assignments you will receive in college. My goal is to teach you to think like a college student, to acquire the intellectual tools you will use repeatedly—and, over time, in more subtle and sophisticated ways—throughout college and beyond.

It might be helpful to think of these skills as tools in your toolbox. If you've ever tried fixing something around the house, you know that not every tool is needed for every job. You also know that it may take a while to become competent at using some of the tools in your toolkit. But as you encounter more tasks, you learn to identify more quickly what needs to be done and which tools will be most useful. The same is true for intellectual problem solving. Your professors will give you various kinds of questions to answer, and your ability to respond effectively or persuasively will depend on how many intellectual tools you have at your disposal, as well as how adept you are at using them.

If you have not already developed these skills, don't worry—for the most part, neither have your classmates. From my experience as a professor and an academic advisor, I have met many smart and talented college students who didn't know the sorts of tools they needed or have the skills to use them well. In fact, many could not consistently recognize what sort of task they were being asked to work on. Most of them learned these things eventually by trial and error. While this approach can work, it also typically results in more struggling and lower grades. Or, to use my original metaphor, it's like navigating unfamiliar terrain without planning and without GPS. You might eventually find your way around, but you'll probably spend a lot of time feeling lost.

This book is designed to provide that guide to the intellectual terrain of college. Of course, that doesn't mean this book will guarantee that you ace every assignment. Instead, it will help you get oriented and improve more quickly as you become familiar with the academic challenges of college and the skills you need to meet them. Remember, each assignment is an opportunity to practice those critical-thinking skills, a chance to improve them so you are ready to use them later in life. With enough practice, you will emerge able to think more subtly, to tackle more complex problems, and to engage with the world more broadly and creatively.

The Structure of the Book

This book is structured to guide you through the main skills and habits of mind that you'll need to succeed in college. Part I will introduce you to the basic skills you need to think in the ways your professors expect you to, to make sense of new subjects, and to tackle your assignments productively.

Chapter 1 focuses on what psychologists call "metacognition," that is, thinking about how we think. When you reflect on your learning process, you notice how your own learning happens, and you can think about how to become a more efficient, powerful learner.

Chapter 2 introduces the basic elements of critical thinking: exploring context, considering alternatives, weighing evidence, and identifying implications and new applications. These are the intellectual moves that college work routinely asks you to make, and having a good command of these skills will prepare you to understand everything more deeply and thoroughly.

Chapter 3 introduces you to academic disciplines. It explains how to orient yourself to a new subject so you can focus on what matters—the questions that scholars in this field ask, the methods they employ, the kind of evidence they appeal to, and the issues they still argue about.

Chapter 4 provides examples of actual college assignments and decodes them, making sure that you really understand what the professor is asking you to do. As you'll discover, the critical-thinking skills covered in chapter 2 are often embedded in the words of assignments, but not always in ways that are immediately obvious. You'll also discover that even though the assignments you get in history will look quite different from those in biology, the same basic critical-thinking skills are utilized across disciplines.

After covering these basics, part II of the book applies these critical-thinking skills to the work of reading (chapter 5), writing (chapter 6), and quantitative reasoning (chapter 7). It might seem odd to review such basic skills, but in college you will need to hone and apply these skills in more demanding contexts—to read and analyze more challenging material, to use writing as a means of fostering your critical thinking and then learning to convey your conclusions effectively, and to reason about data, especially in relation to experimental results and statistical analyses.

Chapter 8, finally, explains how to conduct research. At some point in your college career, you will need not only to understand the knowledge that others have created but to create new knowledge yourself. Conducting your own research will require that you practice the skills you have learned throughout the book—choosing a question to investigate, gathering the evidence you need to answer it, considering alternative ways of understanding that evidence, and spelling out the implications for others interested in your topic. Engaging in your own research can be among the most rewarding experiences you have in college.

Interspersed between the chapters are "Advice for the Road Ahead" mini-essays that highlight the key habits of mind you should cultivate throughout college. They are based on my own experience working with students for forty years. Getting the most from your college adventure depends not only on sharpening your intellectual skills but also on approaching your journey with an attitude of openness and curiosity.

In the conclusion, I invite you to consider the ways in which learning to think like a college student is a lifelong pursuit and to reflect on all the reasons why it is worth the effort. Apart from preparing you for a career, college will also give you the tools you need throughout your life to think about complex issues and work to resolve them.

While the structure of the book moves intentionally from introducing basic skills to their application, it is not necessary to read the chapters sequentially. The outlines at the beginning of each chapter enable you to quickly locate the specific skills you want to focus on. Feel free to allow your individual needs and interests to guide you to the parts of the book that are most relevant. Also, because many of the key ideas come up multiple times and are developed differently in different sections of the book, I have indicated when a particular skill mentioned in one place is discussed in greater detail elsewhere. At the end of the book, you'll find a list of additional resources for deeper dives into particular skills.

■ ■ ■

Here's the bottom line: *learning to think like a college student is all about learning how to learn even more effectively than you already do.* Top college students observe their own thinking and discover how to make their learning more efficient, more strategic, and more incisive. This means identifying the skills you need to acquire, to improve, and eventually, to master.

So I encourage you to keep this book close at hand as you set off on your intellectual journey and to let it be your guide in unfamiliar and sometimes challenging terrain. College will be daunting at times and exhilarating at others. The one thing it doesn't need to be is mystifying or frustrating. I hope that this book can be your academic GPS, enabling you to navigate college with greater confidence.

ADVICE FOR THE ROAD AHEAD

Ask for Help

Whatever else college is, it is sure to be challenging. The number of options available to you, academically and socially, is likely to be far greater than you have experienced before. The environment may be unfamiliar and a bit scary (especially if you're the first in your family to attend college). Your fellow students may be more diverse than your friend group in high school. The financial strain, especially if you're working to help support yourself, will be significant. And the work required in your courses will almost certainly be more intellectually demanding than what you're used to.

All this can be overwhelming at times, and almost all college students (if they're being honest) will tell you that they have struggled at least at some point during their college careers. But the good news is that your college is full of people prepared to help you overcome these challenges. *You just need to ask.*

Asking for help can be a challenge in itself. No one likes to look weak or needy. You may imagine that everyone else is doing just fine, which makes it even harder to identify yourself as someone who needs help. (In fact, everyone else is probably struggling in their own ways and feeling just as reluctant to admit it.) Perhaps you've never needed help before, and so asking now is a new experience. Perhaps your family or your culture encouraged self-reliance and discouraged seeking help from others. For some of you, help wasn't readily available, and so you've become accustomed to powering through on your own. Whatever your particular circumstances, asking for assistance may not come easily.

One of the most important things you can do to ensure your success in college is to give yourself permission to recognize when you need help and to seek it out. Typically, college orientation programs will introduce you to offices on campus that provide assistance of various types—health services, counseling services, financial aid, and academic support services. If you no longer remember what support services are available or where to find them, ask someone—perhaps an academic advisor, an RA in your residence hall, an instructor, or a work supervisor. The range of these services varies greatly from one campus to another, but if you're willing to seek help, you will very likely find someone whose job it is to support you in some (if not all) of the ways you need.

Many college success books emphasize the importance of going to your professors' office hours, the times they set aside specifically for student appointments. But most fail to acknowledge how intimidating it can be to begin a conversation with a professor who is an expert in the very thing you may be having trouble understanding. When you're working overtime at demonstrating that you're competent and successful, just about the last thing you want to do is admit you're struggling. At times like these, keep in mind that your faculty members are invested in helping you learn their subject. It's the reason they have chosen to teach college students. So swallow your pride, take a deep breath, and go talk to your professors. They can often be some of the best sources of support and encouragement.

Over my many years of working with students as a professor and advisor, I have lost count of the times students told me they wished they had asked for help sooner. When problems go unaddressed, they tend to get worse, whether that's a problem understanding something in class or dealing with a crisis in your personal life.

The bottom line is that while you will face challenges in college, you don't need to face them alone. The most successful college students, in my experience, aren't those who never need help; they're the ones who figured out early when they needed it and how to access it. If you take this lesson to heart, you will feel less isolated, lower your stress level, and be better positioned to overcome challenges when they arise. You will also be better prepared for life after college, when (big surprise!) you are sure to face other challenges and occasions when you can benefit from asking others for support.

PART I

The Basics

CHAPTER ONE

Learning How to Learn

An intellectual is someone whose mind watches itself.
—ALBERT CAMUS

Outline

In this chapter, you will learn how to maximize your learning by using study strategies that have been shown to be most effective. You will also learn some techniques for observing and monitoring your own learning process (metacognition), which will enhance your ability to learn, especially when you encounter obstacles or make mistakes.

- Becoming an Effective Learner: Honing Your Study Skills
  - Getting in Gear
- Making Your Brain Work Harder to Learn Better
  - Scientifically Proven Learning Strategies
  - Ways to Grasp Ideas More Quickly
- Becoming an Expert Learner: Practicing Metacognition
  - What Is Metacognition?
  - Self-Awareness—Pay Attention to What You're Doing
  - Self-Evaluation—Adjust Your Learning Strategies as You Go
  - Self-Reflection—Set Learning Goals and Track Your Progress
- Conclusion
- Questions for Reflection

▪ ▪ ▪

All of you have been learning your whole lives. Beginning at least in grade school, you have been learning academically—being introduced to new information, working to understand it, and then demonstrating that understanding through assignments from your teachers. In college, you will continue to do this, except that the material may be less familiar and harder to grasp, while the pace at which courses move may be faster. As a result, you may need to step up your game by adopting new study skills.

But college will present you with an additional, perhaps less familiar, challenge. The best college students aren't just learning material well; they are also (continuously) reflecting on the process of their own learning. They observe which learning strategies they are using, assess the effectiveness of those strategies, and make adjustments as necessary. This quality of self-reflectiveness is called **metacognition**—paying attention to your own cognitive processes and making it an explicit goal to improve them. In this sense, learning has two parts: learning content and learning how to learn. The unfortunate fact is that most beginning college students don't always do the first very effectively and don't do the second at all. In this chapter, I'll explain how you can improve your efficiency in both learning new material and becoming more self-aware, by focusing on learning how to learn better.

Becoming an Effective Learner: Honing Your Study Skills

Take a minute to think back to what you did the last time you sat down to tackle a new assignment, whether that was looking at a chapter of your chemistry textbook, reading a short story for your English class, or studying a new Spanish vocabulary list. How did you approach the learning challenge in front of you? Write your response below.

____

____

____

If you're like most students, you probably didn't do much to prepare at all; you just dove in. But the best college students take a moment to get ready before they begin learning something.

Getting in Gear

Here are some of the best ways to do that:

Establish your intention and goals. When you sit down to do your homework, try not to think of it as just a chore to complete and check off your to-do list. Take just a minute to get in gear by thinking about what you're about to do. Specifically, start by asking yourself one or more of these questions:

- What am I trying to learn here?
- What skills am I using to do this assignment?
- If I learn this well, how will this help me?

This takes just a minute of your time, but priming yourself in this way will put you in a better frame of mind to tackle whatever learning challenge you're facing.

Time and place matters. All of us are more alert and energetic at some times than at others. Perhaps you're a little sleepy after you eat and most energetic after you exercise. Pay attention to these rhythms and work with them. Try not to study when you're struggling to stay awake; if you do, you'll almost certainly be less efficient, waste precious time, and probably have a harder time remembering what you're studying.

Likewise, choose a setting that is conducive. Maybe you like to sit at a desk or to lounge in a comfortable chair. Maybe you do your best thinking in a completely quiet place or in a café with continuous background noise. You might need to be alone, or you may study better if you're sitting with others, even if you're not working together. Notice what works best for you, as well as when you need a change of venue to reenergize yourself. Successful students attend to their surroundings and put themselves in a place that signals to their body and brain: "I'm now in study gear."

Focus. Decide up front how much time you want to spend on each assignment and when you will take breaks. If you sit down to study for an indefinite period of time, you may feel a need to distract yourself to make it more tolerable. But knowing that you will focus for a specific period and then give your brain a rest (check your email, get a snack, call a friend) makes it more likely that you will focus and use this time productively.

Similarly, minimize distractions as much as possible during your study time. Turn off or silence any electronic devices that you're not actively using to do your schoolwork and put them out of sight and out of arm's reach. (Do this in class, too, since many professors will find it annoying and disrespectful if they see you checking your social media during their lectures.) You may believe that you can multitask effectively, but studies have demonstrated that you will retain less of what you're learning if your brain is simultaneously doing other things.[1] And even if that worked for doing your homework in high school, you may find that your college assignments demand more of your mental bandwidth.

Making Your Brain Work Harder to Learn Better

Scientifically Proven Learning Strategies

Everything you are assigned to study in college is part of a curriculum, a program of study designed to help you understand some subject. So at every point, you should be asking, *How is this information useful to me in the context of this course? How does it add to what I already know or clarify concepts I have already encountered?* Many college students let their minds shift into autopilot when they read textbooks and sit in lectures. Successful college students, by contrast, actively examine and interact with incoming information, questioning how and why it's useful. They are constantly assembling an intellectual jigsaw puzzle, asking how each piece fits within the larger picture. Doing this will help you sift through large volumes of information from which you are expected to extract what's most relevant. As a result, you'll process information more deliberately and effectively.

▪ ▪ ▪

All these steps are just preliminary—getting ready to study at a good time, in a good place, and with proper focus. But what happens during the time you're actually studying? What learning strategies are most effective for mastering new material and really retaining it? The good news is that we know a great deal from recent studies by cognitive scientists and educational researchers about how learning works and what you can do to minimize your chance of forgetting what you study.[2] The bad news, however, is that most students, and even many teachers, don't follow these recommendations. More than likely, you are accustomed to using strategies that have been shown to be ineffective.

What learning specialists have discovered is that our brains are wired to learn best in particular ways, especially with respect to retaining what we study. And when you think about it, that's the most basic measure of learning something: we are exposed to it, we memorize it, and then we retrieve it when we need to use it. The problem is that the most widely used strategies for retaining information—going over the same material repeatedly, or cramming—don't work long-term. You might remember something long enough to answer a question on a test, but after a week or two (much less a year or two), it's long gone. If all that matters is getting a passing grade on a test, that may be sufficient. But college is about more than just passing tests; it's about retaining and using what you learn. That's what makes your substantial investment of time and money really worthwhile.

To really learn something, you need to make your brain work hard. In more ways than you might imagine, your brain is like a muscle. Just as muscles get stronger only when you use them repeatedly and challenge them with increasingly difficult movements, you will get smarter only if you use your brain repeatedly and test it with new or more difficult material. In this way, the phrase *no pain, no gain* applies not only to muscles but also to brains. Research has shown that when we make our brains work harder, they learn better and retain information longer. Here are the key takeaways for how you should study for maximum effect.

Retrieve rather than review. Many research studies demonstrate that material is retained longer if you spend less time reviewing and more time retrieving. Going over the same information again and again feels like learning because you can quickly and easily call things to mind, but you learn better when you retrieve new information by quizzing yourself. This works even if you're able to recall only some, but not all, of what you just studied. Then, you should focus on the things you didn't recall, review those, and test yourself again to see what you can retrieve from memory. The constant self-testing and retrieval takes longer and is more effortful than just reviewing and re-reviewing, which is why it leads to better retention.

Try this the next time you have a list of terms you need to memorize. Give yourself thirty minutes to study the terms, then take a break for an hour. Then quiz yourself and see what you can and can't retrieve. Review it again, paying special attention to the things you had trouble with. Then try again in two hours. Then again after six hours, and again the next day, and so on. Increasing the intervals between retrieval efforts forces your brain to work gradually harder and harder to access what you first imprinted there.

Mix it up. There are other ways that experienced learners make their learning harder, and thus more effective. It helps to mix it up by interspersing one subject with another, a practice that scholars call "interleaving." If you have to study math, history, and chemistry on the same night, it is best to first devote half an hour to chemistry, then to math, and finally to history. Then go back to chemistry, which will force your brain to switch gears and recall what you had been working on. Since transitioning between distinct subjects is difficult, the more you mix things up, the harder you make your brain work. You'll not only avoid monotony and the zoning out that boredom produces, but you'll end up re-imprinting what you're learning in your brain each time you come back to that subject. Getting used to learning in shorter, more concentrated chunks of time will also allow you to make the most of your busy college lifestyle, in which you'll need to maximize shorter periods of time between classes, extracurriculars, work, and other responsibilities.

Stop cramming. Cramming—attempting to force a lot of material into your brain in a short period of time—is ineffective if you want to really learn something. Although it feels like an intensive mental workout, cramming requires less brain power than repeated retrieval over time (see retrieve rather than review, above). Cramming works in the short term, but what you absorb is just at the tip of your fingers, and it evaporates quickly. What you learn in a short period of time tends to stay with you for a short period of time; what you learn more slowly and repeatedly tends to be more durable.

All of these strategies come down to the principle that there are no real shortcuts to learning something and retaining it in your brain. Strain your muscles more, and they'll get stronger; strain your brain more, and it will learn better. But notice that whatever pain may be involved here is not a matter of how difficult the material is but rather how effortful the process of learning it is. There is no particular benefit in struggling to master the intricacies of quantum physics if you're just a beginning physics student, just as you wouldn't subject yourself to the training regimen of an Olympic athlete if you were a beginner in that sport. It would certainly be very painful, but it would probably not be very successful. In college, advanced courses are often restricted to students who have completed more basic courses, called prerequisites. This is a way of ensuring that you don't inadvertently end up in a course where you're in over your head. Sometimes, those institutional restrictions aren't enough, though, which is why you need to make sure that you have set reasonable educational goals for yourself.

Ways to Grasp Ideas More Quickly

Thus far, I have shown you strategies you can use to more effectively absorb new information. But learning is about more than just memorization and retention. It's about understanding concepts. In chapter 2, I'll suggest ways to think more deeply about everything you learn, to scrutinize it and understand it more fully. But for now, I want to emphasize just a few of the ways you can grasp ideas more quickly when you're first introduced to them.

Stay focused on the big picture. Many students approach each new assignment as if it were a discrete task, unrelated to others. But knowledge is interconnected; each new thing you learn is connected to things you already know. To really understand anything new, you want to assume that everything you're asked to learn fits within some larger structure of information. If you can see where this piece fits within a broader conceptual framework, you'll more quickly see how this information is meaningful. Instead of being just a random jigsaw puzzle piece, it will have a distinct place within a whole picture.

Sometimes, we can represent these connections using concept maps, diagrams that show the relationships among a cluster of ideas or terms. Putting concepts into visual structures (and there are many different commonly used designs) enables you to visualize the connections between causes and effects, evidence and conclusions, or general principles and concrete examples. Creating your own visualizations can be helpful in review or clarification.

Here is an example of a concept map that captures the process of respiration:[3]

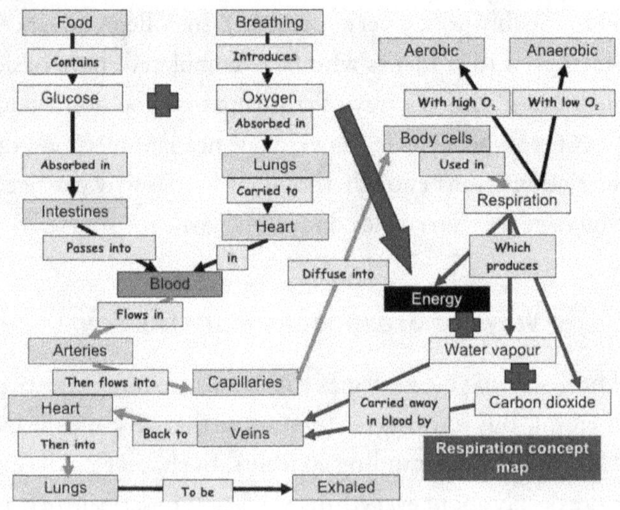

The process of respiration is complicated, so focusing on just one part of it, like how oxygen enters the blood, will make more sense if you can see this as part of a larger process.

Teach it to learn it. If you're feeling unsure about whether you really understand something, try explaining it to someone else, perhaps a friend or roommate. When that person asks questions about what isn't clear, you will be forced to explain it better. If you can, it will reinforce what you know; if you can't, it will help you see where your own understanding is fuzzy. Review anything you can't explain clearly and concisely until you grasp it well enough to teach it to someone else. "Knowing" something is an internal, mental activity, but for that knowledge to be utilized, we need to externalize it (usually into a visible or audible format). That's what tests are designed to do. Therefore, in trying to teach someone else, you can run a check on whether you have grasped something as fully as you believe you have.

This also explains why study groups can be valuable. In addition to the benefit of adding a social dimension to your study time, a good study group provides a supportive environment in which participants can learn from one another. If you understand something, you can teach it to others; if you're confused by something, others who understand it better can coach you through it. Everyone gains by putting their heads together and working collectively on complex material. Of course, if you're one of those people who can study effectively only by yourself or in a quiet environment, study groups may not work for you. It's also important to check with your professor about whether collaborative work on assignments is permitted.

Embrace your mistakes. Students often think of mistakes as failures. You may associate them with the red ink that your grade school teacher used to highlight the things you got wrong, which may have made you question your abilities. But the best students recognize mistakes as opportunities, because when you review the problems you got wrong, you can figure out exactly where you got off track and learn how to improve. Your mistakes—if you embrace them—can be the engines of deeper learning. So the next time you get a test or paper back from your instructor, instead of focusing only on the things you did well, pay special attention to the mistakes or places that were marked as needing improvement. The challenge is not to avoid mistakes altogether—all of us make them—but to learn from them how we can do better in the future. (For more on this, see the "Advice for the Road Ahead: Develop a Growth Mindset" piece that follows this chapter.)

When you are trying to learn something new, be sure to

- regularly test yourself on what you have grasped and what you haven't;
- mix things up, so that you practice learning different subjects or types of information in one session;
- gradually increase the time between your self-quizzes until you can readily recall what you've learned days or weeks later;
- focus on the connections among the seemingly discrete pieces of information that you're trying to learn, as well as on the ways in which all of those pieces are part of some larger whole;
- try to explain it to a friend or classmate. If you stumble when they ask you to clarify something, chances are good that you haven't fully learned it yet; and
- view the mistakes you will inevitably make not as hindrances to your progress but as the path toward improvement.

Becoming an Expert Learner: Practicing Metacognition

To become an expert learner, you need to do more than study effectively; *you need to observe your own mind as it's learning.* To begin, take this brief questionnaire on your learning habits. Don't worry; this isn't a test. Just answer honestly.

1. How often do you revisit old assignments or exams to see your mistakes?

   A. I never do that.
   B. Only rarely (most often when I've just received my results).

C. When I flunk an assignment/exam.
D. Frequently (with most assignments and exams).

2. What do you do when you get frustrated while working on a hard problem?

    A. Throw the book against the wall.
    B. Go to office hours to have the instructor explain it for me.
    C. Phone a friend for help and discuss it.
    D. Look at what I've done and see if there's something I missed.

3. What do you know about your own process of learning? Are there formats or modalities in which you learn more easily than others? Are there certain types of content you learn more easily than others? Why?

    ____

    ____

    ____

4. When did you last evaluate your progress in becoming a more effective, efficient learner?

    ____

    ____

    ____

What Is Metacognition?

The process of thinking about how we learn, and how we can learn better, is called *metacognition*. Simply put, metacognition is thinking about our thinking.[4] The best college students recognize that their goal is not just to learn new material, important as that is, but to become better, more confident learners. The question is how to do that.

It helps if we break metacognition down into three elements: self-awareness, self-evaluation, and self-reflection. As you will see, you can benefit from thinking about your learning process before, during, and after you try to learn something new.

Self-Awareness— Pay Attention to What You're Doing

The best way to begin enhancing your self-awareness is to practice the first of the strategies mentioned earlier—taking a minute as you begin studying to ask yourself what your goals are. Setting goals helps focus your attention; it primes you to use study time intentionally rather than with no specific aim, just hoping for the best.

You can also practice metacognition by reviewing the study strategies for effective learning mentioned above and asking yourself, "How often do I consciously employ these strategies? Am I practicing retrieval at increasing intervals? Am I shifting from one type of material to another?" It's one thing to know which study strategies work best; it's quite another to monitor yourself to see whether you're adopting these strategies. Metacognition begins with simply paying attention to what you're currently doing as you learn.

Here's another interesting way to enhance your self-awareness, which I learned from a faculty colleague many years ago. When she had a major piece of writing to do, she would keep a log of the time she had spent and what she had worked on in each session. When she first told me about this and showed me her log, I confess that this seemed like a lot of unnecessary extra work. Certainly, she knew what work she had done and didn't need to keep a record of it! But I came to appreciate that this made visible to her what she had been doing—how much time she had spent researching, outlining, drafting, revising, and so on. She could keep track of her own process and notice where she was bogged down or where she had had breakthroughs in her learning process. When she was feeling discouraged, it reminded her of her progress. Her log was a way of bringing greater awareness to her learning, especially when she was working on a large project over an extended period of time.

Whether you go to the trouble of keeping such a log or not, you can find your own ways to notice what you're doing and how long it's taking. Self-awareness is all about monitoring your own learning process.

Self-Evaluation—
Adjust Your Learning Strategies As You Go

Learning is hard work, and it doesn't always go smoothly. Part of metacognition is developing the practice of noticing when we hit roadblocks, evaluating what the obstacles are, and developing strategies for working through them. In addition to cultivating self-awareness, this step in metacognition involves self-critique, the ability to notice what we're not doing or what we're doing that isn't working.

Over the years, I have heard many students describe spending endless hours feeling stuck while trying to do their academic work, losing sleep, and getting increasingly frustrated. Their studying isn't productive, but they seem unable to diagnose the problem or to determine what to do about it. Often, of course, when you're struggling to understand something and feeling stymied, it can be difficult to take a step back to see what you might need to do differently. If it was easy, after all, you wouldn't be stuck in the first place. But these are precisely the moments when you most need to practice self-evaluation.

Here are some specific metacognitive strategies you can use to help you tackle the obstacles to your learning:

Go back to basics. All new knowledge is built on the foundation of older knowledge. When you're stuck trying to make sense of something new, it might be because there's something more fundamental that you've forgotten or never fully grasped in the first place. If you quit trying to solve your problem directly and review the more basic background knowledge, you may discover exactly the information you need to crack the case in front of you. When you do this, it's like giving yourself a running start; you have a better chance of clearing the (intellectual) hurdle in front of you if you don't begin by standing directly in front of it. Sometimes this is as simple as reviewing the earlier chapters in a textbook or lecture notes that you didn't realize were relevant to the problem you're now facing.

Zero in on exactly what the obstacle is. Sometimes, you can't successfully solve a problem because you haven't identified precisely where you're stuck. If you can laser-focus on exactly what you don't understand, the problem comes into focus, and with it, the answer (or at least where to look for it) also becomes clearer. So one valuable strategy is to begin by articulating—out loud to yourself or to someone else, or maybe in writing so you can see it clearly—exactly what isn't making sense to you. Maybe it's how a particular theory applies to some new set of data or that two things you've been asked to compare are so different there doesn't seem to be any basis for comparison. Once you can identify the problem with greater clarity, though, your chances of seeing the solution will increase substantially.

Check your assumptions. Sometimes you're stuck because you have made some incorrect assumptions about what the answer *should* look like. You expect that a problem fits the model of other problems you've solved in the past, but on closer examination, you realize that that assumption is incorrect. In a word, sometimes what you see is limited by what you think you're supposed to be looking for. If you can take a step back and notice what assumptions you're bringing to the problem in front of you, you can see where you've gone off track. We're all familiar with riddles that seem unsolvable only because we have made unwarranted assumptions about what the solution would look like.

For instance, some of you may be familiar with the following puzzle. Look at the nine dots arranged in a square on the following page and then connect all nine with just four straight lines without lifting your pen off the paper.

The puzzle seems unsolvable, because there is simply no way to draw just four lines that connect all nine dots. But the answer looks like this:

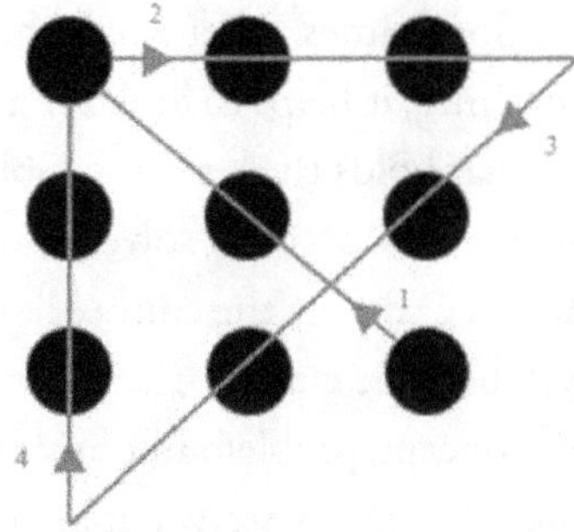

The solution isn't difficult, it only seemed unsolvable when you assumed that the lines needed to remain within the area defined by the dots—which is just the point. Many intellectual problems are likewise solvable when we become aware of the assumptions we're bringing to them, question those assumptions, and begin thinking outside the box.

Look for unstated implications. Sometimes we understand things because we unconsciously supply an implied crucial link that's not stated. Consider this exchange, which is an example of what linguists call "implicature":

Mary: How much longer will you be?

George: Grab a chair.

The exchange makes sense, even though George doesn't directly answer Mary's question. Saying "grab a chair" implies that however long he takes to get ready, it will be longer than Mary would want to keep standing. Sometimes, intellectual problems are like this, too. The connection between two pieces of information you have in front of you is implied but not explicit. If you look at them only superficially, they may seem unrelated. But if you look for the deeper relationship between them, you'll see how the pieces fit together. And if you train yourself to see these connections, each piece of information gains new meaning and the solution to your problem may become more apparent.

Look for an analogy. Sometimes, when you're having trouble understanding something, it helps to look for a problem that is analogous and see if that holds the key to the solution. In many cases, you'll discover that you have actually solved problems much like this one in the past, and once you see the connection, the solution to the problem at hand will become clearer. The central strategy here is to ask yourself, "Is this concept/problem like any other concept/problem that I have encountered in the past? What are the common features? What is there about this other concept/problem that might be applicable to the one I'm now trying to understand?"

Take a break and come back. When we're clueless about how to crack a problem, many times our tendency is simply to keep staring at it, believing that if we look at it long and hard enough, it will somehow all become clear. And sometimes, concentrating long and hard does lead to that breakthrough moment. But often, what is required is just the opposite. If you step back and focus for a while on something other than the problem, you may see it from another angle or in a new light when you return. This can be beneficial in several ways, as D. N. Perkins writes in *The Mind's Best Work*:

> There are many reasons why time away from a problem might help. For instance, you may return to a task physically

> refreshed and with a new will. You may forget the details of an approach or understanding or attitude concerning the problem and recover a kind of distance and openness to new possibilities. Even if a prior approach is remembered, the emotional commitment to it—the feeling of "I've invested so much time this way, I've got to make it work"—may have lessened, making other approaches emotionally acceptable. Finally, people often notice clues to the solution in supposedly irrelevant contexts while doing something else altogether.[5]

Self-Reflection— Set Learning Goals and Track Your Progress

Learning how to learn well happens over a long period of time. Beyond the metacognition you do before and during your study sessions, you want to cultivate self-reflection across your entire educational career. You can do this by imagining that in addition to the courses for which you are registered, there is a shadow course that doesn't appear on your transcript: Becoming a Better Learner. Whatever else you are studying, that course should always be part of your inner curriculum.

You can take this thought experiment a step further. If you were taking a course called Becoming a Better Learner, what would be on the syllabus? How would your grade be determined? Each of you might answer this question differently and would probably answer it differently as a junior or senior than as a first-year. But here are some general thoughts about a few of the elements that might be part of such an imaginary course:

1. Setting goals. Just as you set a goal when you sit down to study, set a goal for the semester and the year. Be specific. What are the individual steps you will take to grow as a learner? Then imagine your future self having achieved your learning goals. How does your future self *think*? How do you *behave*?

   ____

   ____

2. Assessing progress. What are you doing to advance toward those goals? Where are you experiencing success, and where have you struggled? What resources (e.g., writing center, faculty office hours, etc.) have you used to help you?

3. Application. Where are the opportunities to use your skills as a learner outside of your college classes? If you are learning to read more critically, analyze data more carefully, or write more persuasively, how can you apply what you've learned in your job, your volunteer work, or even just the challenges you face each day?

You won't get an actual grade in this imaginary course, but you can regularly assess your own development as a learner. This will keep you focused (at least partially) on the skills you're learning, in addition to the course content you're covering. There is evidence that college professors don't even expect you to remember their course content in twenty years but do hope you will leave their courses as engaged learners who can apply the skills you learned.[6] One of those skills is the practice of metacognition, because when you become more self-aware as a learner, you hold the key to learning everything more easily.

Conclusion

Slower, more effortful learning works better than pushing yourself to memorize new information quickly. Spending less time trying to learn new material and more time thinking about the process of your learning might help you learn that material better. Making mistakes in the process of learning can actually be helpful. When you're struggling to learn, the best option is sometimes to quit trying for a while, take a break, and come back later.

All of these conclusions may be counterintuitive, and following this advice may be difficult at first. But here are the two key principles: we learn best when we align our learning methods with the ways in which our brains naturally work and when we regularly stand back and observe our learning process so that we can improve it. To learn effectively, we need to become self-aware of who we are as learners, both in general (based on how the human mind works) and in particular (based on how your particular brain functions optimally).

The real value of metacognition is that it requires you to focus on the *process* of learning rather than just on the *content.* When your learning is content focused, you do master the material, which is certainly important, but that's where your learning ends. By contrast, when your learning is process focused, you're leveraging that act of learning to improve future learning. Each new thing you learn isn't just more material under your belt; it's also an opportunity to reflect on and refine the way you learn. By putting your own learning under the microscope, so to speak, you can see just how it's working and how it isn't. And that kind of self-reflection is what enables you to maximize your ability to learn in the future, no matter what the content may be. Learn to do this, and it will pay generous dividends throughout your life whenever you are challenged to learn something new.

Questions for Reflection

1. Have you ever engaged in metacognition? If not, can you think of a recent assignment you did where it would have been useful? If so, what did you notice when you did?
2. Getting better at metacognition is a lifelong goal of college-level thinking. Where does it make sense for you to begin? If you had only ten minutes a day to devote to this, what could you do to increase your own self-awareness about how your mind works or how you learn best?
3. Think of something that doesn't come easily to you. How might the practice of metacognition help make it easier? Try this with a subject you're currently studying.

ADVICE FOR THE ROAD AHEAD

Develop a Growth Mindset

Do you think your level of intelligence is set, or can you get smarter?

Research conducted by Carol Dweck, a Stanford professor of psychology, has demonstrated that your answer to this question can profoundly impact how well you do in school. She distinguishes between people with a "fixed mindset," who believe that their abilities are set and unchangeable, and those with a "growth mindset," who believe that their abilities can be improved and refined. It turns out that each attitude becomes a self-fulfilling prophecy.[7]

The two types of people differ in how they approach learning something new. Learning is sometimes difficult, even frustrating. If you have a fixed mindset, when you experience difficulty or failure, you are inclined to give up. After all, putting in extra effort is pointless if you believe your capacity to learn is limited. You feel certain you are incapable of succeeding.

If you have a growth mindset, on the other hand, you see challenges and setbacks as opportunities. Because you believe you can learn from your mistakes, you are prepared to put in the extra effort needed for mastery, even when it isn't easy (and college learning is often not easy!). For the same reason, you see critique from your professors as helpful, since it focuses you on where you need to improve. With a growth mindset, the only barrier to your success is your willingness to put in the work in order to achieve growth. By believing that you are capable of succeeding, you set yourself up for success.

That kind of belief in yourself is at the heart of resilience, the ability to face setbacks and yet muster the courage and confidence to push ahead. It involves trusting that the future will be different from the past, that making mistakes is not a reflection of you but only of your abilities at that time. Of course, believing in the possibility of improvement doesn't by itself guarantee that you will improve. But not believing in the possibility of improvement is almost certain to limit your chances before you start. In a very real sense, a growth mindset is the power of positive thinking at work; believing you can learn from past mistakes helps you do so.

Another benefit of focusing on growth is that you put less emphasis on grades. When you think about it, a grade is a judgment about the quality of a particular piece of work—an assignment, a problem set, or a paper. It tells you very little about how much you learned in the process of working on it. Think of all the high-tech entrepreneurs who started companies that failed. Each of those failures would have earned an F. But in the process of failing, even spectacularly, they may have learned exactly the lessons that enabled them to be successful in their next venture. Think about your education the same way. If you are focused on your progress and recognize that falling short is an inevitable part of the process, you will make the process of learning the focal point of your education. Of course, grades matter, especially if you are counting on a high GPA to get a particular scholarship or to get into a graduate program. But to the extent that you can see yourself as moving gradually along a trajectory of learning, you will put less significance on those letter grades and more significance on how you're growing as a student.

Sometimes, of course, you may hit a limit on your ability to learn something, and when you do, it's important to be able to recognize that and know when it's time to refocus on another subject or switch majors. Often, a good advisor or mentor can help you decide when it's time to let go of a course of study that isn't working for you and move on. But students more often give up too soon because they haven't cultivated enough resilience to drive past the rough places on the road. If you've ever watched toddlers learning to walk or anyone learning to ride a bike, you've seen this attitude at work. No matter how many times they stumble and fall, they just keep getting back up. And eventually, they learn to master this new skill, because they are determined and believe they can do it.

Encountering setbacks and disappointments in college is beyond your control. But you can control how you respond to them. If you build resilience by recalling how you have overcome previous obstacles and believing in the possibility of improving, you will greatly increase your odds of succeeding in college.

CHAPTER TWO

Critical Thinking 101

Information doesn't become knowledge
until we think critically about it.
—JOHN CHAFFEE

Outline

In this chapter, you will learn the four key elements of critical thinking, which are the tools you need to do the work you will be assigned in college. Knowing what questions to ask—about context, alternatives, evidence, and implications—enables you to learn everything more deeply; it also gives you the tools you need to analyze and evaluate the information you will encounter throughout your life.

- Learning to Ask Questions
- Four Essential Elements of Critical Thinking
  - Where Does This Come From: Exploring Context
  - The Road Not Taken: Considering Alternatives
  - Making Sure You've Got the Goods: Weighing Evidence
  - What Can You Do with What You Know: Finding Implications and New Applications
- Conclusion
- Questions for Reflection

▪ ▪ ▪

Learning to Ask Questions

Throughout college your professors will give you assignments that ask you to "explain," "analyze," "interpret," and "critique." Unfortunately, they rarely explain how to do these things. This whole book is devoted to doing just that, helping you understand what types of thinking your professors will expect you to do and how to develop those critical-thinking skills. But the first thing you need to know is that it's all about questions. *The key to your academic work is learning to ask questions.*

Why are questions the key to critical thinking? When you ask a new question or an old question in a new context, you discover or uncover something that has been there but that you didn't see before. You see not only what was said but why it's important, unusual, or controversial. You move from seeing things just as they are to seeing why they are that way and why that matters. *Develop the habit of asking questions and focusing on the questions that others have asked, and you will understand things more completely and subtly.*

Of course, there will be times when all you need to do is memorize some information—the names of amino acids or dates of key events leading up to the American Revolution, for example. But by far the harder part of college—both because it requires more intellectual work and because you are less likely to have experience doing it—involves interrogating the material you're given. In essence, your college education is designed to help you think more deeply and critically about everything you encounter by asking probing questions.

But you may be wondering, What questions should I ask? How do I know if the questions I'm asking are worthwhile or helpful? The short answer is that at first, you probably won't. *Part of the challenge of college is gradually, with repeated practice, becoming more adept at asking increasingly interesting and useful questions.* Sometimes, you will think of those questions on your own. Sometimes, professors include some sample questions in the assignments they give you. But even when some questions are provided, you shouldn't limit yourself just to those. Let those questions prompt you to develop more questions, and then try to answer the most relevant and consequential ones.

Generally, numerous questions could be asked about the same information. For example, if you are given a large data set of average monthly temperatures in twenty North American cities over several years, you could try to use these data to answer any number of pertinent questions: What causes temperatures to vary from month to month? What causes temperatures to vary from one place to another? What trends, if any, are there in these variations, and what factors would account for these trends? Unlike the classic game show Jeopardy, in which there is generally one clear question behind the information presented to the contestants, college material usually prompts many questions. Sometimes it will be especially fruitful to look at the same information in light of several questions simultaneously. As you will discover, some of the most interesting debates you will encounter (or participate in) boil down to disagreements about which questions are most interesting or helpful rather than about the facts themselves.

Four Essential Elements of Critical Thinking

Becoming a successful college student begins with understanding that your learning is all about asking questions. But it doesn't end there. You'll need to understand the specific skills that comprise critical thinking, and then you'll need to practice those skills repeatedly and in different contexts. This chapter is devoted to the first of these tasks, while the remainder of the book will help you practice these skills in the context of work you will do in college.

While scholars differ on exactly how to define critical thinking, there are four key elements that encompass most of what your professors will expect you to do:[1]

- explore context;
- consider alternative answers and explanations;
- weigh evidence; and
- find implications and new applications.

Developing these skills involves asking particular kinds of questions. Let's examine each of these key skills in turn.

I. Where Does This Come From: Exploring Context

For me context is the key—
from that comes the understanding of everything.
—KENNETH NOLAND[2]

Students sometimes act as if the material given to them appeared out of nowhere. As a result, they approach that material—an essay, a data set, or a piece of music—as an isolated phenomenon, entirely without context. Successful college students, by contrast, are always looking for the context, including the intellectual context, that surrounds what they read.

Questions about context can take various forms depending on the sort of thing you're studying, but here are three basic questions about context that you can almost always ask.

What Historical Circumstances Influenced This Phenomenon?

Everything we encounter is a product of some time and place. You have probably already been asked to consider how an author's biography or historical circumstances influenced her writing (like how Zora Neale Hurston's study of anthropology influenced her novels) or how social circumstances influenced a movement (like how World War II and its aftermath set the stage for feminism and the civil rights movement in the 1960s). But the same can be said for scientific investigations. A new reliance on observation and testing hypotheses in the 1600s stemmed from challenges to religious authority and tradition, like the Protestant Reformation a century earlier. You always need to ask, "*What were the historical conditions—events, prevalent ideas, social and economic circumstances—that gave rise to what I'm looking at (or reading)?*" Knowing the answers to that question may not tell you everything you need to know, but placing things in historical context gives you important clues about their origins and significance.

What Question(s) Is This Author Trying to Answer?

Just as college is teaching you to ask questions, you should approach everything you encounter with a realization that *the creator of that material was also responding to some question (sometimes more than one).* Behind every thesis lies a question; work backward from the statements to the question(s) that generated it. Always ask yourself, "What questions were the authors attempting to answer when they produced this, and what made those questions seem important?" Frequently, these questions will be implicit rather than explicit. To figure out what prompted the creator of this information, you will have to look for the problem, issue, or question that was on that person's mind. When you begin to investigate this, you will often discover why something that seems obvious actually isn't or why something that seems unimportant is actually quite meaningful. For example, when Jane Goodall first began to study chimpanzees in Tanzania during the 1960s, many people—even fellow scientists—thought she was completely out of her mind. Once they learned that her research aimed to answer the question "What can we learn about human behavior by studying the behavior of a closely related species," however, many of those doubters became supporters.

What Assumptions Is the Author Making?

Every argument, intellectual position, or method relies on some set of assumptions. Often, those assumptions won't be stated explicitly, because the author or researcher is writing for an audience of other experts who share critical background knowledge. But as a college student, you may not possess that knowledge, so you'll need to uncover this background information to understand what this is about. Be sure to ask, *"What is the author or creator of this material assuming to be true?"*

Pinpointing unstated assumptions helps you evaluate, not just understand, what you're reading. Often, what is useful or sensible in one context is less so in another, but you won't notice this limitation if you haven't identified the background assumptions at work. Sometimes, assumptions that seemed obvious in an earlier period (e.g., that you could determine people's intelligence by examining the size of their head), have long since been refuted. Get in the habit of asking about the assumptions behind everything you encounter, and you'll be better positioned to understand it and recognize its limitations. (A good portion of chapter 5 will be devoted to reading critically by attending to multiple contexts.)

Exercise. Consider this passage from Lincoln's famous Gettysburg Address:

> Four score and seven years ago our fathers brought forth, on this continent, a new nation, conceived in Liberty, and dedicated to the proposition that all men are created equal. Now we are engaged in a great civil war, testing whether that nation, or any nation so conceived and so dedicated, can long endure. We are met on a great battle-field of that war. We have come to dedicate a portion of that field, as a final resting place for those who here gave their lives that that nation might live. It is altogether fitting and proper that we should do this.

Now answer these three basic questions in relation to the text above:

What historical circumstances influenced this author?

____

____

____

What question(s) was this author trying to answer?

____

____

____

What assumptions was the author making?

____

____

____

II. The Road Not Taken: Considering Alternatives

It does take great maturity to understand that the opinion we are arguing for is merely the hypothesis we favor, necessarily imperfect, probably transitory, which only very limited minds can declare to be a certainty or a truth.

—MILAN KUNDERA[3]

Many discussions you have in college involve addressing unresolved questions. That's why we're still discussing them! Of course, in some classes, you'll be learning material that is settled knowledge, especially in math and the natural sciences. But in most courses, and even in advanced STEM classes, you'll be stepping into controversial territory, exploring issues about which scholars disagree. You will constantly evaluate which viewpoints are more persuasive and more consequential, which in turn helps you justify your own viewpoints. Which interpretation makes more sense? Are the conclusions drawn by the author really strongly supported? Rendering an opinion and defending it requires you to consider alternatives and to weigh the strengths and weaknesses of each.

Whenever you're looking at information or presenting information in support of your conclusions, always ask yourself:

- Have I examined a range of views on this topic from diverse sources to ensure I have considered all potentially relevant perspectives?
- Have I read and deeply thought about the views on this topic that I might not agree with?
- Have I not only looked at the views I found on this topic but also taken the time to think about alternative positions that these authors might not have considered?
- Have I tried to determine what factors led these authors to adopt the views they did rather than any of the alternatives?

Developing a habit of considering alternatives to everything you encounter in college will have several important consequences. It will help you avoid accepting any claim or argument at face value, for there may be more there than meets the eye. It will also make you more aware of your own biases, which sometimes lead you to be less critical of positions with which you already agree, or help you uncover assumptions, which I talked about in the previous section. And it will help you evaluate the strength of a claim because you will see it against the background of other claims (real or imagined) that are also options to consider. It's worth addressing each of these points separately.

Exploring Alternatives Is Important in Contextualizing Information and Making Sure You're Well Informed

Broadly speaking, there are two possible outcomes of considering alternatives. You may find alternative viewpoints that bring up valid counterarguments to your conclusion. In that case, you can use those alternative perspectives to your advantage, incorporating them into your argument to make your argument stronger. Or you may find that the alternatives are weak and unconvincing. This, too, is positive because it will only give you more confidence in the conclusion you originally endorsed. This is why it is so important to ask yourself whenever you read something or listen to others making a case for their point of view, "What alternatives might there be to this conclusion, method, interpretation, or perspective?"

Assessing alternatives is essential any time you are constructing an argument (e.g., when you're performing a lab to test a hypothesis or when you're writing your reaction to an assigned course reading). Before you reach any conclusion—whether it's adopting a particular point of view or presenting an argument in a piece of writing—make sure you've explored alternatives to reach as robust, well-informed, and comprehensive a position as possible. When you do encounter plausible alternatives to your view, it is the hallmark of sophisticated critical thinking to account for that counterargument in your analysis and allow it to further refine your argument.

Exploring Alternatives Helps You Recognize and Confront Your Own Biases

All of us sometimes have long-held or passionate beliefs that we are reluctant to revise or abandon. In fact, researchers have demonstrated that we automatically discount or overlook information that challenges our preconceived ideas and are drawn to information that confirms them (this is known as confirmation bias).[4] Our minds are programmed to preserve and cling to established beliefs, given how disruptive or even upsetting it can be to constantly reconsider them. One of the key values of critical thinking, then, is that it challenges this tendency.

When we're confronted with alternatives that challenge our views, our first reaction is frequently to engage in a process of rationalization; that is, we invent reasons to continue holding those views even though they no longer stand up to critical scrutiny. We're all familiar with rationalizations we use to defend ourselves against feeling disappointed ("I didn't get that job, but I didn't really want it anyway"). In intellectual contexts, the defense mechanism works the same way, but the goal is not to protect us from feeling bad; it is to protect us from having to admit we were wrong. For example, if we oppose an increase in the minimum wage because we believe it will result in higher levels of unemployment, we will resist learning that many economists who have studied the issue have reached the opposite conclusion.[5] One of the challenges of becoming a critical thinker in college is to recognize when you yourself are rationalizing and not only when others are doing so (which is almost always easier).

This readiness, even eagerness, to challenge your established views requires a kind of intellectual courage. No one wants to discover that something they have long believed is actually mistaken. It may feel embarrassing or isolating, especially if changing your views means that you no longer fit within groups to which you belong. Many of you will likely face these sorts of challenges to your political or religious views, both through the things you study in college and through interactions with peers who don't share those views. Suffice it to say, you will be challenged to reexamine views you have long held, which may cause you to change them, or to reaffirm them, but now in a more grounded, sophisticated way.

Understanding Alternatives to Establish (or Challenge) Significance

Looking for alternatives helps you determine whether a particular assertion or interpretation is truly significant. No one is impressed if you make a strong case for a proposition that no one disagrees with in the first place. When you read something, you want to ask whether there is widespread consensus about this interpretation being the only possible one. If so, why? If there are alternatives, what are they, and why has this author chosen to advocate for this view over the other options?

Many assignments you get in college will require you to do just this sort of thinking, like this history assignment:

> To what extent did the accession of the National Party, with its platform of apartheid, mark a watershed in South African political history—a moment of genuine change—and to what extent was apartheid continuous with prior policy? How would you balance change and continuity in your account?

Here, the essay prompt is asking you to argue for the significance of one interpretation of historical events—that the imposition of apartheid was a "moment of genuine change" in South African politics—against an alternative interpretation—that it was the culmination of the National Party's long-standing political objectives and not a departure from past policies. This sort of assignment requires you to weigh alternative understandings of a single set of facts and developments. The underlying assumption is that you can't really know whether the first interpretation is warranted until you have considered an alternative.

It's important, too, not to assume that there are only two options. Sometimes an author will attempt to convince you of their position by making it seem as if there is only one alternative and that it is unacceptable (maybe lacking in evidence or contrary to common sense). If you investigate further, you may well discover additional options that are preferable to those the author has offered for your consideration. This is the power of always looking for alternatives.

You will sometimes find this invitation to consider alternatives in the conclusions of an article you read. While researchers will put forth their interpretation of their results, they will generally leave room for, or even explicitly mention, other potential interpretations. This is often what stimulates further research. Here is a brief section from a psychological study that concluded that people were less satisfied with a choice they made when they were initially given more options to choose from. This conclusion goes against our general assumption that people will be happier when given more choices. Researchers Iyengar and Lepper realized that more questions can be asked about this.

> How can there be so much dissatisfaction in the face of so much opportunity? More than providing a conclusive answer to this question, the present findings raise a number of questions of both theoretical and practical relevance that are worth considering in future research. Perhaps it is not that people are made unhappy by the decisions they make in the face of abundant options but that they are instead unsure—that they are burdened by the responsibility of distinguishing good from bad decisions.[6]

The authors of this study are still weighing alternative explanations for the results they found, and in the process, they are inviting others to do the same.

Exploring alternatives to establish significance is certainly necessary when evaluating the strength of the views you encounter, but it will be particularly important when it comes to evaluating your own views. At every stage in your thinking, you'll want to consider the alternatives to establish the significance of an idea, proposal, argument, or interpretation.

Exercise. Here's a chance for you to practice considering alternatives. Think of a controversial issue about which you have firmly held beliefs (e.g., your stance on vaccination, abortion, climate change, the military, etc.).

Now answer these questions:

What factors led me to hold this belief in the first place?

What reasons do I have today for continuing to hold this belief?

What are some of the common reasons that people from the opposing side of the issue give for holding their beliefs?

What rationality can I see in those reasons? (Take this opportunity to flex your empathy muscles. *Really* try to see the issue from the opposition's point of view.)

III. Making Sure You've Got the Goods: Weighing Evidence

I believe in evidence. I believe in observation, measurement, and reasoning, confirmed by independent observers. I'll believe anything, no matter how wild and ridiculous, if there is evidence for it. The wilder and more ridiculous something is, however, the firmer and more solid the evidence will have to be.

—ISAAC ASIMOV[7]

Academic debates or arguments are all about reason, which is all about evidence. You must be able to provide reasons to support the views you hold, and those reasons always take the form of some *evidence* or *data* you offer, together with an explanation of how that evidence is relevant to your conclusion. A position you put forward is only as strong as the evidence you provide on its behalf. In college, you will likely have the experience of a professor responding to your work with words to this effect: "Your conclusion is sound, but you didn't provide the right kind of evidence to support it." *Arguments often fail to be persuasive because the supporting evidence is inadequate or the connection between the evidence and the conclusion is questionable.* In many respects, weighing the strength and applicability of evidence is the key component in critical thinking.

Here are the questions you should ask yourself whenever you're examining evidence, either to support a conclusion you're presenting or to evaluate the validity of conclusions that others have offered:

Is this evidence factually true and persuasive? Is it closely connected to the conclusions that have been drawn from it?

One of the greatest challenges for beginning college students is getting a handle on how to evaluate the strength of evidence, especially since in high school you probably weren't required to carefully scrutinize the information you learned. What counts as evidence, and where you will find it, varies significantly from one discipline to the next. In many courses, your assignments will invite you to use the material you have been provided as evidence for or against some position. In other cases, you will be required to go searching through databases, archives, or other sources to find the information you need to build an argument. In those cases, the challenge will be to quickly identify the best places to find the kinds of information that will serve as strong evidence for the sort of argument you want to make.

The more connections you can draw between the evidence and your conclusions and the clearer those connections are, the more convincing your work will be. But that will likely still leave some space for others to challenge your work—by citing evidence you didn't consider, interpreting your evidence differently, or suggesting that it isn't as reliable as you assumed. The goal of much college learning is just this: *to train you in evaluating evidence carefully so that the conclusions you draw are really supported by the evidence you have.*

Many students assume that they need to prove something absolutely, leading them to make more definitive claims than they can support. As a result, they effectively overplay their hand, which makes their arguments *less* persuasive than if they had acknowledged the potential limitations of their claims. Actually, your job is to make a case that your conclusions are plausible, and you do this by choosing and weighing your evidence carefully. In this sense, college encourages you to resist black-and-white thinking and all-or-nothing claims. College will train you to become a more sophisticated thinker who can assess and create arguments with more nuance.[8]

Does the supporting information come from a credible source—qualified and unbiased?

In doing your work, you will often come across a source that agrees with the point you're trying to defend. But that is no different than finding a friend who agrees with you. It doesn't guarantee that you (or your friend) are right. The next challenge, then, is determining that the information is accurate and reliable, which requires examining the source of that information and assessing if it is trustworthy.

Students often assume that if they find a quote from a scholar who teaches at a college or university and that quote supports their position, they're done. But the best students will take it a step further. What is that scholar's reputation? How was that scholar's work reviewed or received by their peers? Has it been discredited by subsequent scholars? Was that scholar's work supported by an organization that had an agenda (e.g., did the sugar industry pay for the study that concluded that sugar isn't so bad for us?).[9] Is this scholar even an expert in the specific subject about which they offered an opinion?

In college, you will be expected to do your own investigative reporting, which is another way of saying that you are being trained not to take things at face value. Often this requires you to follow footnotes that lead you to the original source of the information you have found. It may involve looking at the reputation of the journal in which an article appeared or examining the credentials of the people whose work you are citing. If you're relying on scientific data, you'll want to know how the experiments were conducted that yielded those data, the reputation of the peer-reviewed journal that published the paper, and whether the results have been replicated by others. As you'll discover, even scientific studies, presumably based on strong evidence, are sometimes overturned, even years later, when it emerges that there were flaws in the ways the evidence was gathered or interpreted.[10] Asking these and similar questions will help you establish that the evidence you have is credible and reliable.

Has the author resorted to rhetorical strategies to make up for a lack of factual support?

There are many kinds of appeals to "evidence" that are essentially empty. In many cases, these appeals seem reasonable, but on further reflection, they don't actually establish the truth of what they assert; they are fallacies. You're likely familiar with these from advertising campaigns, political rhetoric, and even ordinary conversation. Here are a few of the most common fallacies that you will want to avoid in college work:

- Appeal to popularity—where the "evidence" supporting a claim is simply that many people support it (e.g., "Thousands of people use product X, so it must be effective."). Notice that there is actually no evidence provided to demonstrate that the product works.
- Appeal to authority—where someone's status, rather than relevant evidence, is used to endorse an argument (e.g., "Tom Brady drinks this sports drink, so it must help with energy during workouts."). Of course, we do often defer to subject-matter experts when we don't know much about a subject. But it's still important to be cautious about how much credence we give any authority, given that experts frequently disagree, and often express opinions about subjects in which they are not experts.
- The slippery-slope fallacy—where one argues that one shouldn't believe or support a claim because it would lead to accepting other unfavorable outcomes that don't necessarily follow (e.g., "If we allow students to avoid this requirement, soon they will ask to be released from more and more requirements, and eventually we won't be able to enforce requirements at all, and they will all

become meaningless."). The validity of this conclusion rests on a whole series of events happening, which is based here on speculation, not specific evidence.

- Hasty generalization—where one or very few observations or experiences are used to support a sweeping conclusion without regard for whether they are representative of a general rule or universal experience (e.g., "I didn't eat gluten for a day, and I felt really sick, so a gluten-free diet must be unhealthy"; or conversely, "I didn't eat gluten for a day and I felt much better, so a gluten-free diet must be healthy."). A single experience doesn't provide evidence for a general rule.
- Straw man—where the opposing viewpoint is intentionally mischaracterized in a way that makes it appear less persuasive than it is and thus easy to refute (e.g., "Candidate X's proposal to raise income taxes on millionaires will encourage the government to waste our hard-earned tax dollars on unnecessary projects."). Notice that the question of whether the government engages in wasteful spending is separable from the question of whether there's a reason to raise taxes on millionaires, such as whether it would rectify inequities in the tax code.
- You, too (known by the Latin name, *tu quoque*)—where someone responds to a claim by accusing the speaker of hypocrisy, essentially, that they are guilty of the same offense that they have accused someone else of committing (e.g., "You claim that this policy is flawed, but you yourself endorsed it last year."). Note that even if this were true, it doesn't address the question of whether the policy is actually flawed.

In these and similar kinds of rhetorical moves, you'll notice that there is some assumption being made, but not explicitly expressed, that purportedly connects the "evidence" to the conclusion—that any product used by thousands of people must be effective, or what we allow students to do about this requirement will lead to wholesale disregard for others. Because of this, you need to be wary of empty reasoning posing as evidence.

Have you overlooked other evidence that would challenge your perspective? How could you incorporate that evidence into your argument?

One of the most important ways in which you can ensure that your arguments are well founded is to bring a healthy skepticism to your own thinking. It's relatively easy to find evidence that supports your conclusion and stop there. It's also easy to get so focused on making your case as convincingly as you can that you overlook anything standing in your way, whether intentionally or just subconsciously. But it is precisely by amassing a lot of evidence and looking especially for evidence that leads in a different direction that you can make your case stronger. Perhaps it will force you to completely change what you thought, or possibly just to adjust that conclusion somewhat. Either way, it will result in a conclusion that takes account of all the evidence available to you, which is precisely what will make it more persuasive.

In some academic studies, especially those that may have implications for human life or health, such as medical studies, we will not declare a treatment to be safe and effective until we have demonstrated this beyond a reasonable doubt. But in academic debates, there is frequently more gray area than that. The goal is not necessarily to present an open-and-shut case. Generally, it is sufficient to present a highly plausible case, one that is persuasive though not necessarily airtight.

In short, college thinking will involve training yourself to be a kind of impartial skeptic, someone who does not just assume that anything published must be true, that information considered true upon publication must still be true, or that information that is in fact still true necessarily supports a particular conclusion (when there is other information that might contradict it). This kind of healthy skepticism will serve you well in everyday life, which will give you endless opportunities to practice this skill of interrogating the validity, reliability, and applicability of the evidence you encounter, as well as the claims that are made based on that evidence.

Exercise. See if you can identify the sort of fallacy represented by each of the following statements:

"I've met three computer science majors who want to work for Google solely for the large paychecks. That means that computer science majors are in it for the money."

"One in twenty Americans vapes every day, so it can't be *that* harmful."

"Candidate X proposes that we cut funding to the National Endowment for the Humanities, which will result in a nation without significant museums, individual artists, or preservation programs."

IV. What Can You Do with What You Know?: Finding Implications and New Applications

Education is the acquisition of the art of the utilization of knowledge. This is an art very difficult to impart.

—ALFRED NORTH WHITEHEAD[11]

In college, you will be expected to demonstrate more than just superficial knowledge of the material you study. You will be asked to show that you have grasped *how this knowledge is useful, how it can be applied* (in familiar and unfamiliar contexts), *and what its implications are.* You can think of this as the difference between knowing something in a flat, unidimensional way and comprehending it in a robust, three-dimensional way. To acquire that deeper knowledge, you will have to explore all the things that you can do with what you know. This is, as Whitehead said in the quote above, "An art very difficult to impart." Fortunately, there are some specific strategies you will be encouraged to develop in college that will help you learn this art.

Here are a few questions you should always ask to help you flesh out the import and application of anything you study:

What implications does this information have? Where does it lead?

All ideas have implications; all conclusions have consequences. To know something fully is to know where it leads. Looking down the road from a particular idea, argument, or conclusion can tell you something about its significance (or lack thereof). To take one classic example, the Declaration of Independence proclaims that "all men are created equal, endowed by their Creator with unalienable rights." At the time he penned those words, Thomas Jefferson certainly didn't think they referred to the rights of people who were enslaved or to women, immigrants, people with disabilities, and other marginalized groups. Yet those words have had implications, especially for social reformers and activists throughout American history who have fought for more universal rights by appealing to that ideal embedded in the Declaration of Independence. Those implications, even if they weren't evident in the eighteenth century, are part of what makes that idea so powerful and enduring.

You, too, will be called on to evaluate ideas and arguments based on where they lead. If you offer an argument but haven't noticed that taking it to its logical conclusion yields unacceptable results, you haven't thought about it carefully enough. Sometimes, this is a matter of checking whether a claim (e.g., that all falling objects behave in a certain way) is applicable under all circumstances. At other times, it's a matter of asking yourself, "If this hypothesis is right, what else would we expect to be true?"

Why does this information matter, and to whom? Who has a stake in this particular result, and why?

As I explained above, critical thinking is driven by the questions we ask. But whether a particular question is worth asking, or perhaps even worth devoting a great deal of time to pursuing, depends in large part on what its implications might be. Some questions are more consequential than others. As we'll discuss in chapter 8, setting a research agenda always involves being able to answer the "So what?" question. What difference will it make—in practical terms or in terms of our understanding of some larger issue—if you can provide a persuasive answer to this research question? You don't really understand what you're asking if you don't know why it matters. This is why most research papers conclude with a set of questions for further investigation that suggests ways by which this set of results could be the springboard for other studies. By speculating on the importance of an idea or finding, we can advance the scholarly conversation in a particular direction, which brings other questions more clearly into view or suggests that certain policies should be reexamined.

Here's an example of a study that concludes by pointing to its implications:

> In summary, we found that this dose regimen of intravenous Remdesivir was adequately tolerated but did not provide significant clinical or antiviral effects in seriously ill patients with COVID-19. However, we could not exclude clinically meaningful differences and saw numerical reductions in some clinical parameters. Ongoing studies with larger sample sizes will continue to inform our understanding of the effect of Remdesivir on COVID-19. Furthermore, strategies to enhance the antiviral potency of Remdesivir (e.g., higher-dose regimens, combination with other antivirals, or SARS-CoV-2 neutralising antibodies) and to mitigate immunopathological host responses contributing to COVID-19 severity (e.g., inhibitors of IL-6, IL-1, or TNFα) require rigorous study in patients with severe COVID-19.[12]

This study concluded that the drug Remdesivir did "not provide significant clinical or antiviral effects in seriously ill patients," while pointing to its small study size as a potential limitation. Acknowledging the implication of this possible impediment, the study authors recommend that further research, specifically studies with larger sample sizes of patients with severe COVID-19, be conducted. Their specific recommendation, that the efficacy of Remdesivir be further investigated in conjunction with other therapeutics, requires an application and interpretation of their own study findings.

How can I apply what I've learned in some new context or to some new data?

Much of your work in college will require you not just to recall what you've learned but to apply it in new ways or in unfamiliar contexts. For example, you may be given a problem on an exam that is different from anything you have encountered before. The expectation is that you understand the course concepts deeply enough that you can apply them in novel contexts. This is one of the most significant ways in which the thinking expected of you in college is more advanced than what you were probably expected to do in high school. It is also one of the key ways in which college thinking prepares you for careers in which you won't have a textbook or exams but where you will be expected to creatively apply what you know to new problems. In college, you will be given many assignments that require you to use what you have learned in new ways and to demonstrate your understanding of an abstract theory by applying it to some specific material. Often, this requires a kind of analogical thinking, that is, finding the similarities between something you know and something you are being asked to work on. When you can see what is analogous, you have the key to seeing how to transfer that knowledge from a familiar context to an unfamiliar one.

Exercise. Here's a chance to practice thinking about implications.

> The second law of thermodynamics states that in an isolated system, entropy (the amount of energy in the system that is not available to do work) cannot decrease; it can only remain constant or increase. This has important implications for many real-world situations and/or problems. Can you think of a few?

____

____

____

____

> In *How Democracies Die*, coauthors Steven Levitsky and Daniel Ziblatt argue that when certain key democratic norms are violated, democracies falter. Two of these are "mutual toleration," which means accepting the legitimacy of one's political opponents, as long as they win in free and fair elections, and "institutional forbearance," which means that political actors agree not to weaponize their control of institutions to marginalize their opponents.[13] What implications would you draw from these conclusions?

____

____

____

____

Bottom line—when you're assessing the value or implication of something you're studying, always ask yourself:

- Why is this argument important beyond this author's text?
- If I accept this assertion, what are the consequences (for my beliefs, for future research, for further analysis)?
- How can I apply this information to analyze a different situation?

Conclusion

Learning to become a critical thinker isn't like a simple math formula that you can immediately learn and apply. It is more like learning a language, where you gradually move along a spectrum from beginner to someone who is fluent, more articulate, and skilled in your powers of expression. In the process of learning a language, there are many elements—vocabulary, rules of grammar, syntax, and idioms—that must be mastered before you can really communicate effectively. Critical thinking, too, has its elements, which I have introduced in this chapter—exploring context, considering alternatives, weighing evidence, and finding implications and new applications. Although each element has a unique function, it would be a mistake to imagine that you will encounter them in isolation from one another. Most academic assignments will require you to use two, three, or all four of these components in combination. And just as speakers of a foreign language still encounter phrases they don't understand even after years of practice, you are likely to come across academic challenges that baffle you even after you think you have mastered these skills. When that happens, keep in mind that it happens to your professors, too. It is not uncommon for a scholar who employs critical thinking superbly in their own field to fail to do so when thinking about something unfamiliar.

Some of you will likely find this academic language foreign and even somewhat alienating. This may especially be the case if you have not grown up surrounded by people fluent in this academic language, people who themselves went to college and so are relatively comfortable raising the kinds of critical questions discussed in this chapter. In effect, when you go to college, whatever your background, you are being invited to join a community of scholars, of people who think, question, analyze, speak, and write in particular ways. If these are new to you, it may feel as though you need to code switch in order to blend into this academic community. That may be uncomfortable at first, especially if you find yourself switching back and forth between the academic language you speak at school and a more informal way of thinking and talking with your family or friends back home. If you find yourself in this situation, I encourage you to seek support from those who understand this challenge, especially faculty members who themselves were first-generation college students. Hopefully, in time you will begin to feel more at home in this new environment and more comfortable thinking and speaking in the more formal and rigorous ways that college demands.

The basic building blocks of critical thinking are worth studying because they apply across all disciplines. *Fundamentally, all knowledge is discovered and refined through exploring context, considering alternatives, weighing evidence, and finding implications and new applications.* So as you continue honing these skills—each of which has many dimensions, as we have seen—you will be better prepared to do the academic work college professors will ask of you. With practice, these domains of critical thinking will become more familiar and easier to call upon, no matter what you're studying. At some point, you will notice that you're employing these skills without having to think about them, just as speakers of a second language cross a threshold of fluency and begin instinctively thinking in their new language.

But this, perhaps, is where this metaphor ends, because the language of critical thinking is not really separable from your native language. You don't completely switch back and forth between critical and non-critical thinking as you might between English and French. Rather, your fluency in thinking critically will become a part of the way you think *all the time*, no matter what natural language you're speaking, both inside and outside of the classroom. That is ultimately the power of learning to think like a college student. It trains your mind to question *everything you encounter*. College doesn't just make you smarter, in the sense that you know more things; it makes you more intellectually discerning, better able to distinguish what is sensible from what is nonsense, what is significant from what is trivial, what is plausible from what isn't. And those abilities, once learned, will stay with you long after you have forgotten most of the actual content of the courses you take.

Questions for Reflection

1. This chapter identifies the key components of critical thinking—exploring context, considering alternatives, weighing evidence, and finding implications and new applications. Which of these intellectual skills have you employed in the past? Where? How did this help you delve more deeply into something than you had before?
2. Over the course of the coming week, when you're reading or listening to a lecture, make a point of noting when the author or speaker employs one of these critical-thinking skills. Pay attention to how often they come up. How do they contribute to the academic argument being presented? Are these elements of critical thinking explicitly identified, or are they just implicit in the text or lecture?
3. The next time you have a reading assignment, keep these four critical-thinking skills on a card on your desk. Stop briefly at the end of every section of the reading and look at the list. Consider which of these skills you could draw on to analyze or critique the reading. Make your own list of questions you would want to raise about the reading and bring it to class with you to see if your professor raises those same questions or others. If the opportunity presents itself, raise one of the questions from your list with your professor or classmates.

ADVICE FOR THE ROAD AHEAD

What to Pay Attention To in Class

You've come to college to learn from professors who are experts in their fields. Even when they're teaching a course for the first time or teaching something outside their area of expertise, you can safely assume that they know more than you do about the subject matter. Often, students assume that you learn by absorbing the material the professors talk about in class and then demonstrating that you know it. Sometimes, this is the case. But often, what your professors are really there to teach you is a new way of thinking, and there's no better way to learn it than to pay close attention to how *they* think. So rather than taking notes only on the information they convey, tune in to the questions they ask. As you write down your professors' questions, you should be asking some of your own:

- If this isn't a question you had thought to ask, why not? Or better, which specific aspect of the material led your professor to ask that question?
- Was the professor's question articulated in a way that helped you see something you've been learning in a different light? How was it helpful?
- When the professor asks a series of questions that seem to frame the whole class session, pay particular attention to that sequence. How did each question build on the one(s) before it? How were

they guiding you through a set of issues that enabled you to delve more deeply into the material?

- When your professor demonstrates how to solve a problem, pay close attention to the steps they took and the order in which they took them. If you don't understand any step in the process, be sure to ask!
- When your professor responds to a student's comment or question, pay attention. If the response indicated the student's comment was off-base in some way, what had they overlooked or misunderstood? Professors often do their most important teaching through the ways in which they respond to students in class. It's best to assume that, even when they're not talking directly to you, they're telling you something important!

When you pay close attention to your faculty members' questions and responses, you are really tracking the way their minds work, at least with respect to the subject matter at hand. (And if you are puzzled by the questions your professor is asking, it's a pretty good sign that you're probably not grasping something important, which would make it a good time to go to office hours and ask them to explain the questions.)

Sometimes, professors provide information in class without explaining how it answers some question(s) they're thinking about but not stating explicitly. When this happens, you will often have the feeling of being a bit lost; you may understand the information but not why it's important. This is a good time to raise your hand and ask, "What question or problem are we working on right now?" This is also a good time to refer back to the four basic critical-thinking skills discussed in the previous chapter. You will likely discover that they will at least help you to home in on the intellectual problem the professor is addressing.

The good news is that as you get more adept at zeroing in on your professors' questions, it gets easier. Pretty soon, you might find that you're able to anticipate them, maybe even before you've set foot in class. And once you are on the same intellectual wavelength as your professor, you will discover that learning the material is not only easier; it's more fun.

Faculty have gotten where they are by learning how to think in a highly sophisticated way; observe and learn to reproduce the way they think rather than just the information they convey, and you will be on your way to becoming an expert learner in that subject.

CHAPTER THREE

What Am I Doing in This Class, Anyway? An Introduction to Disciplinary Thinking

No matter what the discipline, all areas of academic study are constructed on assumptions regarding what scholars in those disciplines regard as legitimate knowledge.

—STEPHEN D. BROOKFIELD

Outline

In this chapter, you will learn what academic disciplines are and how they differ from one another. For each discipline, knowing how to focus on the questions scholars in that field ask, the methods they employ to answer them, and the issues they argue about will help you get oriented to every subject you encounter in college.

- What Are Disciplines, and Why Do They Matter?
- Natural Sciences
  - Questions Scientists Ask
  - Methods in the Natural Sciences
  - Debates and Challenges in Science
- Social Sciences
  - Questions Social Scientists Ask

▪ ▪ ▪

What Are Disciplines, and Why Do They Matter?

Imagine that you walk into a large room full of people engaged in lively intellectual conversation. As you make your way around the room, you eavesdrop on the various exchanges that are happening simultaneously, sometimes among small groups, sometimes just between two individuals. You begin to notice that all the conversations seem to focus on a fairly small number of topics and that pieces of the discussion happening in different parts of the room seem to relate to one another. It's as if all of these mini-conversations intersect, so that as you move between them, you hear echoes of what others have said in other small circles. Sometimes these conversations are very congenial; other times people are engaged in heated arguments with one another.

As you spend more time there, you discover that people sometimes refer to conversation partners who left the room, perhaps many years ago, but whose comments and questions continue to be discussed by those who remain. Sometimes new people enter the room and join in, repeating points that others have made before, adding or taking issue with what their predecessors have said, explaining why this or that piece of conversation matters to them (or doesn't). You stay in the room for many weeks, trying to make sense of who has talked with whom, who agrees with whom, and which topics are debated. Gradually, you come to feel that you have a pretty good grasp of what this intellectual conversation is all about, though there may still be fine points that elude you.

When you've heard enough of this conversation, you may leave and walk down the hall to another large room, where another extended, interconnected set of conversations are happening—except this time, the topics are all different. The people in this room have a different vocabulary, focus on different ideas, and argue about different issues. But in every other respect, this conversation mirrors the one taking place just down the hall. Each of these larger "conversation halls" is a collection of people with similar interests but with diverse ways of thinking and talking about those topics.

▪ ▪ ▪

Each of these conversation halls is a **discipline**, and in college, you'll be walking between rooms like this all the time. Think of a discipline as a field of study defined by the subject matter under investigation but also by the questions being asked and the ways in which those questions are explored. In college, learning isn't only about being introduced to established knowledge—the things about which scholars largely agree. It is also about *entering the messy conversations about what is true and how we know it.* In those conversations, scholars exchange ideas about what new evidence is significant and why, what theories best explain the phenomena they study and when they need to be revised, and even what words to use to describe their subject matter.

Thinking of your college education in this way will enable you to do a number of things:

- You will appreciate that every course is an opportunity to think about how a certain field of knowledge is constructed.
- You will be focused not only on the *content* of the course but on the different *questions* that generated this material, as well as on the different *theories* represented by different readings on the syllabus.
- You will ask yourself where your professors stand within the debates that have defined this discipline, which side they have taken, and why (you might even ask them directly!).

- You will begin to see how disciplines differ from one another, not only in the subjects they focus on but also in the *methods* they use to study those subjects.

In short, you will be able to orient yourself more quickly to the new disciplines you will be exposed to in college.

As you encounter each new subject area, ask yourself:

- What are the *questions* that scholars in this field ask?
- What *methods* do they employ to answer those questions?
- What are the *live debates*, the unanswered questions, within this field?

Asking these questions will give you a broad framework for joining a new disciplinary conversation more quickly and help you focus your attention on the things that matter most in this course.

▪ ▪ ▪

In this chapter, it certainly isn't possible to summarize all the different disciplines that you will encounter in college, but I will introduce you to three broad categories of disciplines: natural sciences, social sciences, and humanities. Despite clear differences among the disciplines within these categories—between physics and biology, or between history and philosophy, for example—there are some broad similarities that will help orient you to the distinctive thinking that occurs in those disciplinary categories.

Natural Sciences

Throughout human history, we have been fascinated by the world around us.[1] Though scientists study a vast array of phenomena using a great many different methods, the natural sciences share a focus on understanding, and sometimes manipulating, the natural world. There are four major divisions in science:

- Physics is concerned with the nature of matter and energy and the interactions between them.
- Chemistry is concerned with the structure and transformations of atoms and molecules.
- Biology is concerned with the structure, function, origins, and interactions of living things.
- Geology and the earth sciences are concerned with the forces that created our planet and continue to shape its evolution.

Note that the boundaries between these disciplines are less clearly defined than you might imagine. For example, if you think about the ways in which medicines, which are chemical compounds, affect your body, which is comprised of complex biological systems, you can appreciate that different scientific disciplines interact and overlap in important ways.

Within each area of science, there is a distinction between theoretical and experimental research. Theoretical research aims to understand the natural world's mechanisms, components, and history using theoretical and mathematical models. Experimental research deals with observing the real world, describing phenomena, and noting the impacts of our manipulations of natural processes. For example, theoretical physicists may use computers to model and make predictions about natural phenomena, while experimental physicists may use instruments in a laboratory to test the results of exposing materials to large amounts of radiation.

It is worth noting that many scientists apply the findings of scientific research to solve real-world problems, and you will likely encounter courses that do this in college. Examples include many fields of engineering (civil, aeronautical, mechanical, biomedical), medicine, computer science, agricultural sciences, and product design, among others.

Questions Scientists Ask

There are a number of basic types of questions that scientists ask. Although you have undoubtedly taken science courses in high school, you may never have considered how scientists generally think and what they think about. You will understand your science courses better if you focus on what scientific inquiry is really all about.

1. How can we precisely and accurately describe phenomena in the natural world?

Since the beginning of recorded time, human beings have observed the world around them and tried to make sense of these observations. Even in ancient times, figures like Archimedes (third century BCE) were making discoveries about physics, mechanics, mathematics, and other fields that are still accepted today. Over time, scientists have developed increasingly specific and sophisticated systems for describing the natural world, including specialized vocabulary and conventions of notation and classification. This technical, scientific language enables researchers to share and cross-check their results. To nonexperts, however, this same specialized language can be something of an obstacle, since understanding the work of virtually any scientist will require becoming familiar with that technical dialect. As an example, we may all have our intuitions about the motion of objects, but physicists will describe theirs in terms of quantitative variables that are precisely defined by mathematical relationships or equations about the object's position, velocity, and acceleration. Here's a specific example:

Let X_1 represent an object's position at time t_1 and X_2 represent an object's position at t_2. The object's average velocity is given as:

$$\bar{v} = \frac{x_2 - x_1}{t_2 - t_1}$$

2. How and why do certain natural phenomena occur?

Of course, scientists don't just want to describe the natural world; they want to understand it, which requires asking questions about the origins and causes of phenomena. In a sense, scientists are always asking how and why the world came to be this way and how it functions. Given the enormous complexity of our universe at every level—from the behavior of subatomic particles to the nature of black holes—there's certainly no shortage of phenomena to investigate. And in every case, scientists will be drawn to find the general principles or natural laws that explain what they observe or that can be deduced from what they observe. Consider these examples:

Physics: Why do a feather and a brick, when simultaneously dropped in a vacuum, hit the ground at the same time?

Answer: In a vacuum, the only force acting on objects is gravity. Acceleration due to gravity is constant, irrespective of mass, near the earth's surface.

Biology: What causes us to shiver when we are cold?

Answer: Sensors in the hypothalamus detect a drop in temperature and send signals causing our muscles to contract.

In each of these cases, scientists provide an explanation of how a particular phenomenon works. But notice that these "explanations" are of somewhat different types. In this physics example, we are satisfied with our answer to a question if we can connect a phenomenon to basic principles—in this instance, we can describe and explain how the force of gravity affects objects in a vacuum. Once we have done that, we understand the phenomenon in question (the way feathers and bricks fall in a vacuum). But in the biology example, understanding that the sensors in our brains respond to temperature changes and send signals to our muscles explains only the mechanism that causes us to shiver when we're cold; it doesn't explain *why* our bodies are designed this way. Because biologists study living beings rather than inanimate objects and forces, there is always the option of exploring the *purpose* of a particular biological phenomenon. We can ask why biological traits evolved in terms of their benefit to the organism in question. In the case above, the answer is that shivering helps an animal maintain its body temperature in a cold environment. This is one example of the many subtle differences in the types of questions that scientists of differing disciplines may ask. However, the sciences are united in their pursuit of causal explanations for natural phenomena.

3. Can we make predictions about how natural systems will behave? Once scientists have understood the network of causal relationships underlying some phenomenon, they can apply this understanding to predict how a system will behave under certain conditions. Consider the classic introductory physics problem: What happens to the brightness of a bulb in a series circuit if we add a second bulb? To predict the effect of adding a bulb, we must first understand what causes bulbs to glow: current moving through the filament of the bulb. Then, we should ask what the effect of adding a bulb is on the current flowing through the first bulb. A relation called Ohm's law allows us to predict that this should decrease current flow by increasing resistance in the circuit.[2] Thus, by applying our theoretical understanding of what causes bulbs to glow and how resistance is related to current, we arrive at the prediction that adding a bulb in a series circuit will decrease the brightness of the remaining bulb.

Methods in the Natural Sciences

Your goal in high school science classes may have been to try to absorb and correctly explain various scientific facts, concepts, and systems and to use basic math equations to predict behavior. Your goal in college science classes includes those things, but more fundamentally, it is *to learn how to think like a scientist.* All that information that fills your science textbooks is the result of many individuals who have struggled over many centuries to make sense of the natural world in the ways explained above. The question is, how have they gone about doing it? What are the characteristic ways in which scientists analyze the information they collect and then draw conclusions from it that enable them to produce such detailed, highly technical theories about how the world works? The answer is that they do this through concept organization, a multistep approach to problem solving, and a combination of inductive and deductive reasoning. Let's look at each of these in more detail.

Concept Organization. In science courses, you will encounter a great many concepts, so many that you will likely have trouble remembering and making sense of them all. Trying to memorize definitions and formulas is unlikely to help you much, however, if you don't have a deep understanding of them. One of the keys to success, then, is to understand *the relationships among these concepts, the ways in which they are organized into larger frameworks that help scientists answer the questions outlined above.*

Often, scientific concepts are organized hierarchically, in which case, you will want to focus on the broader concepts and the subconcepts that fit under them. Focusing only on the subconcepts is like noticing the individual pieces of a jigsaw puzzle but ignoring the larger picture those pieces create; the point is to look for the relationship of each piece to the larger whole. Sometimes, those relationships between broader concepts and subconcepts will be complex, so you need to be attuned to the ways in which a single concept might be connected to several others. For example, in chemistry and physics, the ideal gas law describes the quantities of volume, pressure and temperature. Although volume appears in the ideal gas law, it is also used to calculate density. These relationships might be combined to calculate the density of an ideal gas from temperature and pressure.

In addition to looking at the interconnections among concepts and systems, scientists are also constantly connecting facts to general principles. General principles can be useful in explaining a wide and diverse set of facts. So learning that placing one's hands on a Van de Graaff generator causes one's hair to stand on end is an isolated fact; it is best explained as an application of static electricity and the principle that like charges repel.

Source: Van de Graaff at American Museum of Science and Energy, Oak Ridge, TN

■ ■ ■

Recognizing that scientific concepts are organized hierarchically and that general principles are used to explain discrete facts, you can appreciate that *much scientific thinking is about finding the connections between one set of facts or concepts and others that are either more or less complex.* So some scientific explanations involve reducing complex systems into their component parts. This reductionist way of thinking is analogous to explaining how an internal combustion engine works by taking it apart and analyzing the contribution of the pistons, spark plugs, valves, and so on. On the other hand, sometimes a scientific explanation points in the opposite direction, constructing an understanding of a larger whole by a study of the interactions of the parts. For example, climate scientists must integrate knowledge of the dynamics of the atmosphere, ocean, and polar ice sheets to predict how warming temperatures might affect weather patterns around the world.

To conclude this section on concept organization, let's consider two common roadblocks to conceptual mastery in science. The first challenge might occur when you understand a concept in one context but don't see its applicability elsewhere. For example, you may easily identify a chemical reaction when it occurs between two separate molecules but fail to recognize a similar reaction within two parts of the same molecule. You learned the reaction in the context of two separate molecules and overlooked the possibility that the same factors that drive this reaction forward also occur within a single molecule. The best way to appreciate the full range of a principle's applicability is to practice applying it in a variety of contexts, many of which superficially appear dissimilar (e.g., a reaction involving one versus two molecules) but share a deeper conceptual similarity.[3]

A different issue arises when you can't recognize the conditions under which a concept does not apply. Science is full of concepts that appear virtually identical to novices but, in fact, are fundamentally distinct because they apply in different situations. For example, failure to distinguish between related concepts might occur in a physics class in which you are permitted to bring equation sheets to exams. But you select the wrong equation for a given problem because you fail to connect the problem at hand and the constraints of the selected equation. The best way to learn the limits of a concept's applicability is to pay attention to examples that appear superficially similar but differ in their deep conceptual structure. When solving physics questions, for example, pay attention not only to the equation that gets you the right answer but also to the reasons why an alternative, seemingly similar, approach might or might not have given you the same result (e.g., why is this a force problem and not a work problem?).[4]

When you find yourself overwhelmed by scientific principles, concepts, or facts, always ask yourself:

- How are these concepts related to one another? Which concepts are higher or lower, broader or narrower, than others?
- How does this scientific concept or principle explain particular observations or phenomena?

- Is this an example of explaining a complex system by looking at its component parts or an example of examining the parts to develop a fuller understanding of a more complex system?
- Where does this concept apply? Where doesn't it? Why?

Problem Solving. A key feature of the way scientists think involves the orderly, step-by-step approach they use to answer questions or solve problems. Here again, the challenges of college science classes may be new to you if you have mostly been asked just to memorize equations and plug data or quantities into those formulae to generate answers. The goal now will be to understand why those particular equations are necessary to solve those particular types of problems. And this requires a deeper understanding of problem-solving methods. Quantitative problems in a range of disciplines—from physics to chemistry to population biology—are often approached using some variation of the following five-step process:

Step 1: Represent the problem. Scientists generally represent the specific phenomenon they're studying in more abstract, symbolic ways. So if physicists are studying how stones fall under certain circumstances, they will abstract from the fact that this is a stone and not some other object. Since there are no physics equations or principles that are unique to stones, the researcher will refer to more general equations describing the influence of gravity on objects. The problem of the falling stone, then, will be represented in a diagram using a point (to represent the object) together with a downward arrow (to represent the force of gravity). This is often called a free body diagram.

Translating a problem statement into a visual representation guides our thinking toward the general principles at play (e.g., gravity) and also enables us to convey our understanding of the phenomenon in question in precise, easily communicable forms.

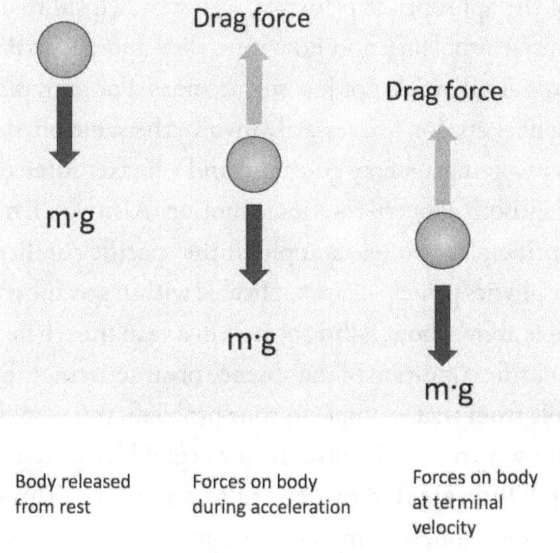

Free Body Diagram

Step 2: Identify knowns, unknowns, and assumptions. Focus on what is known about the natural phenomenon you're studying and what remains unknown. What is the desired quantity you are trying to solve for? Notice particularly if you can ignore elements that are not relevant to the solution you're seeking. That is, can this problem be simplified by assuming that certain elements are not factors you need to consider in solving the problem?

Step 3: Select the appropriate principles or equations to solve this problem. Consider which general scientific rules or principles would apply to this particular problem. You know you have identified the right principle or equation when you see that it directly relates the known and unknown elements. Sometimes, however, there is no obvious principle or equation that enables you to solve the problem. In that case, you will want to see if you can deconstruct the problem into a series of subproblems that are solvable using principles and equations that you know. Deconstructing a problem in this way requires some careful planning; you need to determine what steps you will take, and in what order, to get you from what you know to what you're trying to answer. You will also need to determine which principles or equations will be needed at each step in the process.

In selecting the appropriate principle, it's often helpful to ask, "Where have I seen similar problems, and how were they approached?" Search for deep, conceptual similarities, not just surface ones. For example, two problems involving buckets don't necessarily involve the same physics principle, but a problem involving a merry-go-round and a bucket rotated on a string might, since they both concern rotational motion. Also, you'll need to make sure that the principles you select apply to the specific conditions of your problem. Most physics principles are applicable within specific conditions, as with the example above about falling objects in a vacuum, where the vacuum indicates the specific condition of the absence of air resistance. Before applying the principle from that example to your problem, you would need to assume that your own problem involves no (or negligible) air resistance.

Step 4: Apply the selected principles or equations. This typically requires computations and, in complex cases, may require a computer.

Step 5: Assess your answer. Multistep problems have multiple opportunities for error, both mechanical (algebraic/arithmetic errors) and conceptual (choice of appropriate model/equation). It is therefore essential to do a reality check after obtaining an answer. Here are some easy ways to check your answer:

- Compare your answer to an established reference or baseline quantity. For example, the speed of light (3×10^8 meters/second) is the "cosmological speed limit." If the answer you obtained is a speed greater than this, either this particular situation is not possible, or (more likely) you made a mistake somewhere in your calculation.
- Perform the calculation in a different but equally valid way. For example, select a different sequence of equations, and check to ensure that you arrive at the same answer.
- Ensure that the units of your final answer are consistent with the units of the desired quantity. For example, if the problem asks you to determine a volume (cubic meters), and your final answer is in kilograms (a unit of mass), you made an error somewhere along the way.

Eventually, once you become knowledgeable about a certain group of problems, your intuition can help you determine reasonableness. Of course, this only comes with practice and review.

If your answer does not pass this reality check, practice your metacognition: Where might I have made a mistake? Did I represent the problem inaccurately? Did I use the wrong principle or equation for this problem? Did I make a computational error?

Exercise. A particle weighing 1.0 kilogram is placed in an electric field and experiences a constant force of 2.0 Newtons to the right. If the particle is initially at rest, what is its velocity after 10 seconds?

Step 1: *Represent the problem.*

Step 2: *Identify knowns, unknowns, and assumptions.*

Step 3: *Select the appropriate principles or equations to solve this problem.*

Step 4: *Apply the selected principles and/or equations.*

Step 5: *Assess your answer.*

Using Deductive and Inductive Logic. Scientific reasoning makes use of two distinct forms of thinking—induction and deduction.[5] Inductive reasoning involves drawing a general conclusion from a series of observations. For example, when you observe repeatedly that letting go of an object will cause it to fall to the ground, you predict that each time you do this in the future, the same thing will happen. Deductive reasoning works in precisely the opposite direction, moving not from specific observations to general principles but from general principles to specific conclusions. Deduction in scientific disciplines is generally used to make predictions based on general principles about how the world operates. For example, we may start from Newton's law of gravitation, which predicts an attractive force between any two bodies with mass, and conclude that a dropped object (with mass) will fall to the surface of the Earth. Much of theoretical math, physics, and chemistry is concerned with deriving increasingly specific equations from the mathematical manipulation of more fundamental laws. Most equations in introductory physics are manipulations of Newton's laws.

What we call the "scientific method" involves combining inductive and deductive reasoning to answer the kinds of questions raised by the types of scientific observations described above.[6] Throughout this section, I will illustrate the steps of the scientific method with the account of a famous experiment by seventeenth-century scientist Francesco Redi that disproved the theory of spontaneous generation, which held that life could be generated from inanimate matter.[7]

Like all good scientists, Redi began with an observation that led to a research question and then to some conclusions about how the world works with respect to that phenomenon. Redi observed that, left exposed, pieces of meat became infested with maggots and flies. At first, only a few flies appeared, and then the number exponentially increased. At the time, it was commonly assumed that this could be explained by the "spontaneous generation" of new flies from the meat. But Redi wondered, "Do new flies on meat appear from elsewhere and then reproduce?" This led him to formulate a testable, falsifiable hypothesis: if new flies always appear from elsewhere, meat sealed inside a jar will not become infested with flies. This is an application of deductive logic—Redi made a specific claim (about sealed meat) from a general principle.[8] In this case, if meat inside the sealed jar became infested with flies, then the flies could not have come from elsewhere and must have spontaneously generated within the meat. For this reason, Redi's hypothesis was falsifiable.

Redi then tested his hypothesis. He observed that while meat left exposed to the environment quickly became fly infested, sealed meat remained free of flies. This supported his original hypothesis, and Redi claimed that all flies come from other flies. Using inductive reasoning, he generalized this hypothesis to all living things, claiming that "all life comes from life." One objection to Redi's experiment was that by sealing the meat off, he had blocked the access of flies but in doing so had also prevented an influx of new air from reaching the meat. An alternative explanation of the results was that flies do spontaneously appear but that this spontaneous generation requires air circulation. To address this objection, Redi repeated the experiment, this time with small slits in the jar that were big enough to permit air but not flies to enter. He found once again that even when the meat was exposed to new air, no flies were generated inside the jar, which confirmed his original hypothesis. Even then, some other scientists might have disputed Redi's general principle that "life is necessary to produce life," agreeing with the claim that all flies come from other flies but questioning whether all fungi come from other fungi, moths from other moths, and so on.

Debates and Challenges in Science

As the last example illustrates, scientists often question the conclusions of their peers by raising objections to the choice of research methods or the interpretation of the results. Differing research methods often yield differing results, and even a single result is often open to multiple interpretations. This is why scientific research is always subject to a rigorous process of peer review before publication, a process in which other, impartial scientists review the methods used and the data collected to determine whether the conclusions reached are sound.

Scientific debate may arise for a multitude of reasons. Sometimes a debate stems from incomplete evidence. In 2003, scientists in Indonesia discovered the skeleton of a small-bodied archaic human, nicknamed "hobbit."[9] Intense debate followed as to whether the skeleton represented a new species of human (distinct from our species, *Homo sapiens*) or whether it was merely the remains of a modern human with a skeletal abnormality. These alternative interpretations reflected the incomplete nature of archaeological evidence; it's impossible to go back in time to observe the hobbit. Both hypotheses were consistent with the observation of a single small-bodied skeleton. Over time, the discovery of nine more skeletons like the hobbit, together with an analysis that these fossils predated the arrival of *Homo sapiens* by at least ten thousand years, settled the issue for most archeologists. These findings are more consistent with the presence of a different species of small-bodied archaic humans, called *Homo floresiensis*. This controversy illustrates the incremental and dynamic nature of scientific research. Scientists must draw the most rational conclusion from the evidence currently available, but the most rational conclusion must also evolve to keep pace with new discoveries of more exhaustive evidence.

Incomplete evidence isn't the only cause of scientific disagreements. Sometimes the dispute stems from differing disciplinary perspectives and assumptions.[10] We find a key example of this in modern physics, which is defined by two major theories: Einstein's theory of relativity, which describes the behavior of large-scale objects like planets and black holes, and quantum mechanics, which explains the world of subatomic particles. Although the two theories are remarkably successful in explaining their respective domains, they draw on fundamentally incompatible assumptions. Relativity assumes that the universe is made up of a combination of space and time that physically warps around massive bodies, while quantum mechanics assumes that time and space are invariant. In a discipline marked by logical consistency, such a disagreement in the fundamental assumptions of two core theories is deeply unsettling to scholars. Physicists since Einstein have been searching relentlessly—and so far unsuccessfully—for a unified theory that can reconcile the conflicting assumptions of quantum mechanics and relativity.

Social Sciences

Humans are social creatures. We live in groups, and even those who choose to live in relative isolation from others cannot help but think of themselves as part of a larger entity, namely, the human family. The social sciences are a cluster of disciplines that examine the nature of societies and the behavior of individuals within those societies. When social scientists study individual experiences and behaviors—for example, your preferences for certain foods or your career choices—they tend to consider them as part of larger patterns of behavior and experience that exist among groups of individuals. Those experiences and behaviors, after all, were not created by you alone but rather in relation to others. Social scientists help us understand how and why society functions as it does, how we interact with each other, and how we adapt to every aspect of our environment.

Questions Social Scientists Ask

The social sciences include sociology, economics, psychology, anthropology, linguistics, political science, international relations, management and business, education, social work, geography, criminology, and law. There are obviously an enormous range of questions that scholars in these fields ask, among them:

- How is authority established and maintained in social groups?
- What facilitates economic growth?
- What motivates voting behavior?
- How does growing up in a single-parent household affect childhood development?
- How do we effectively market a new product?
- What factors most influence human happiness?
- How does the structure of one's native language influence one's thoughts and perceptions?
- What are the most effective methods of teaching, and what can we do to influence the ability of students to learn?

In addressing these and many other questions, social scientists conduct research, often with large groups of participants over an extended period, that allows them to find patterns of behavior, to search for causes and effects of social phenomena, and to offer general principles that explain human behavior. Frequently, the stated purpose of this research is to improve human experience or to influence public policy, but even when that is not its purpose, it can be its practical effect.

Because of their focus on observation and experimentation, the social sciences share certain features with the natural sciences. Many social scientists develop hypotheses and test them in a variety of laboratory conditions or real-world settings. But the goal is to discover some general principles that can explain a particular aspect of human experience or behavior with respect to large groups of people. Of course, social scientists are aware that they are similar to and often interacting with the people they are studying, which gives rise to a host of challenges.

Methods in the Social Sciences

While not all social sciences are strictly empirical, proceeding through observation and experimentation, virtually all are grounded in data that was obtained in these ways. Beyond that, however, social scientists employ an array of methods for gathering and analyzing data, including surveys, focus groups, analyzing statistical data gathered by governments or others, administering performance tests, observing physiological responses, and gathering and analyzing first-person accounts, among others. Overall, these methods can be divided into **quantitative** and **qualitative** approaches, though it is important to note that these categories exist on a spectrum. Many scholars use a combination of these approaches.

Quantitative research is most akin to research in the natural sciences. It is hypothesis driven, generates numerical data, and seeks to identify conclusions that are applicable to a whole population (or another defined scope of study). In general, it relies on selecting research subjects randomly or, at least, striving to eliminate any factors that might introduce bias. When pollsters conduct surveys to determine voting preferences or when educators study the learning outcomes of students engaged in online learning, they are attempting to obtain results that are as objective and scientific as possible. The goal is to predict the behavior of the voters or learners who were not studied but who can be assumed to exhibit the same traits as those who were. This use of quantitative reasoning will be explored further in chapter 7.

Qualitative research is more concerned with capturing aspects of human experience and behavior that cannot be reduced to or easily explained with numerical data. Using interviews, case studies, observation, and written/oral accounts of personal experiences, qualitative researchers attempt to understand the texture and depth of their subjects' lives. Such research relies more on individual cases, since it emphasizes that some elements of human experience, like the way we experience familial relationships, may not be fully understood through experimentation or data collection alone.

The approach of individual scholars depends in part on the sorts of questions they ask, as well as on the conventions of the discipline. If a sociologist is studying the relationship between growing up in a single-parent household and the likelihood of having a long-term marriage as an adult, it makes sense to use a quantitative approach, such as building a statistical model from thousands of such individuals. On the other hand, if an anthropologist was interested in the nature of the relationships between those individuals and their single parents, qualitative methods would likely be more helpful. A quantitative approach may be more objective and more useful in making predictions, but it may miss important dimensions of the lives of its subjects and their individual situations. A qualitative approach may capture a social phenomenon more fully and in a more nuanced way, but it is more susceptible to being affected by the specific individuals studied and by the biases (conscious or not) of the researcher conducting the study.

Since both qualitative and quantitative methods have benefits and limitations, many social scientists employ mixed methods. For example, a scholar studying the impact of a training for physicians designed to improve medical outcomes for their patients might examine medical records of patients to determine how they responded to treatment (quantitative) but also conduct interviews with some patients to determine how they experienced their interaction with their physicians (qualitative). Because physicians and patients have relationships with one another, the medical data alone might not tell the whole story of how patients felt about the care they received, which in turn could affect their outcomes.

Whenever social scientists interact with the people they are studying, they can bias their questions or their interpretation of the results. Even more fundamentally, the interactions between the researcher and subject(s) could affect behavior, since when people know they are being studied, they might behave differently than they would otherwise. Anthropologists have long recognized these risks when they spend time studying a foreign culture, insofar as they try both to remain outsiders with an objective perspective and to become the insiders who understand a culture as it is experienced by those within it. In trying to walk that line, they may compromise their objectivity, alter the behavior of the people they're studying, or both.

Moreover, like all of us, social scientists are human beings whose experiences have shaped the way they think, what they believe, and how they view other people. As a result, they themselves may have biases, conscious or unconscious, that color how they conduct their research or interpret their results. There is no iron-clad way to know just from examining a research study whether some prejudices skewed the work. This is one of the reasons researchers care whether the results of any study are replicable, whether other scholars studying the same material have reached similar conclusions.

Social scientists also face the challenge that their subjects may not be honest in their responses, a problem that natural scientists don't have when studying inanimate objects. This issue can arise especially when the issue under study is controversial or taboo, like studies of racist attitudes or relationships with authority figures. Researchers must be careful not to accept personal narratives at face value, because people don't necessarily offer reliable accounts of what happened or valid explanations of behavior, either their own or that of others.

Many social scientific studies rely on the use of case studies, which are detailed examinations of one setting, a single subject, a single depository of documents, or one particular event. Looking closely at a single example can often illuminate a wide range of similar phenomena in other contexts. Here, too, of course, there are some caveats: the case selected may not be representative, or the presentation of it may omit important information. But the rationale behind case studies is that looking closely at this particular case gives us a window into a broader range of phenomena.

Finally, surveys or questionnaires are among the most common tools of social scientists. Often, surveys involve both quantitative questions ("Rate this customer service experience on a scale from 1 to 5") as well as qualitative questions ("Tell us how you felt about your travel experience"). What you may not realize is that how these questions are phrased can result in very different responses. "Tell us how you felt about your travel experience" will probably prompt different reactions than "Tell us what you liked best (or least) about your travel experience." Survey methods are employed in a wide range of contexts, from companies that want to evaluate their customer service to the gathering of demographic data every ten years through the United States census.

In every survey, there are risks of error, including the chance that the people who answer the survey (or don't) will be skewed in favor of certain characteristics. For example, people who want to complain about their customer service may be more likely to complete a survey than those who were satisfied. Social scientists have developed sophisticated statistical methods to attempt to correct these potential errors, but they can never be eliminated, which is why the results of such surveys regularly report a "margin of error." You will want to be aware of these issues if you ever design a survey, but it also helps when you are trying to interpret them (or to assess if a given interpretation is plausible).

Exercise. Below are some examples of research goals that a social scientist might want to accomplish. For each, indicate whether you think the research question lends itself more to a quantitative or a qualitative approach (or both).

- An economist wants to see how the United States' Gini coefficient (a measure of economic inequality) has changed over the past century and use that data to predict changes in the next twenty years.
- A psychologist wants to ask patients with schizophrenia what it feels like to experience an auditory hallucination.
- An economist wants to ask a low-income family what the process of filing for unemployment was like for them.
- A psychologist wants to examine the level of neural activation in the hippocampus during a memory exercise.
- A sociologist wants to see how the percentage of African Americans who claim to experience racism on a daily basis has changed over time.

Debates and Challenges in the Social Sciences

All social science research raises profound ethical issues. Studying other human beings has an impact on them, so it is always possible that researchers will harm those they study. Over the course of the twentieth century, several general principles have been developed and widely accepted by social scientists. Here are four of the most prominent:

- It is essential to get informed consent from research subjects. This means that subjects need to understand the nature and questions of the study and to agree to participate. They also have a right to know that any private information about them will not be identifiable and/or that it will not be released without their consent.
- When work is done on vulnerable populations, extra precautions need to be taken to protect them from being exploited. This includes work with children, people with cognitive or other

disabilities, marginalized groups such as racial minorities, or prisoners.

- Research subjects need to know that they can withdraw from a research study at any time and without repercussions, and they need to know whom they can contact if they have concerns.
- Finally, all academic social science research must be reviewed by an independent body, known as an institutional review board, that is set up for the purpose of reviewing research proposals before the work begins and is responsible for ensuring that this work will be conducted according to accepted ethical standards.

These ethical safeguards were developed because past researchers sometimes conducted experiments with deception or manipulation that resulted in trauma or physical harm.

But other kinds of issues arise for social scientists, even within the bounds of ethical research. Suppose we wanted to test the hypothesis "Women are better at multitasking than men." To answer this, we would select a representative sample of women and men, determine what kind of multitasking would be used to test the hypothesis, set a period of time for observation, and, finally, define and measure "successful multitasking." Then the results of this experiment would be analyzed for statistical significance to see how likely it was that any differences discovered were the results of random chance.

But even that doesn't entirely resolve the question. Suppose that our study determined that women did, indeed, score better at multitasking than men did. Did we really find a true, consistent difference in behavior between the genders? Are men really worse at multitasking, or would they improve significantly after practice or training? Does our definition of multitasking hold up to scrutiny? Would the results hold up if we extended the period of observation? Does the age of the subjects matter? Or their racial/ethnic background? Would the results hold up if we chose a different kind of multitasking for this experiment? And of course, getting this particular result will tell us a fact about human behavior, but it won't explain why that difference exists or how it might be connected to other differences between men and women.

The point of this example is to underscore that *scientific studies of human behavior are invariably complex and involve a great many factors of study design and data analysis.* As a result, work in the social sciences, even more than in the natural sciences, tends to be provisional, always capable of being revised or overturned by future studies with the same question but different methods that yield different results. Moreover, unlike scientists doing lab experiments, social scientists can't generally manipulate the conditions of their subjects and run the same experiment multiple times. (Imagine having parents refuse to talk with their children for long periods of time to determine how this affects their language acquisition!). This sort of limitation often constrains the sorts of claims that social scientists can make about human behavior.

On a more abstract level, many larger questions animate the social sciences. Since the goal is to explain how human beings behave and evolve, both individually and collectively, there are deep philosophical questions at the heart of these academic fields:

- To what extent are human beings determined by their environments, and to what extent are their traits biologically determined? How do these two factors interact?
- How accurately can we predict human behavior? How can we improve the accuracy of our predictions?
- To what extent is our behavior motivated by the pursuit of self-interest, and to what extent are we genuinely altruistic?
- Are certain social structures (e.g., the family) natural, and if not, what accounts for the prevalence of these structures across cultures?
- Are certain types of behavior dysfunctional, and what makes them so?
- How objective can social science be, given that researchers are shaped by the same forces that have shaped the subjects of their study?
- What methods and criteria should we use to understand human behavior?

These are just a few of the questions that engage social scientists across many different disciplines. But even this brief list should give you an indication of how significant this work can be for our understanding of human experience.

You will encounter the work of social scientists in many areas of life well beyond your work in college. Businesses interested in developing and marketing new products will be interested in knowing something about people's interests and needs, as well as which strategies are most effective in reaching new customers. Governments are interested in knowing which policies are most effective in achieving particular goals. And of course, people in all walks of life are interested in understanding how our society works, how individuals think and behave, how different groups of people interact, and how languages shape our thinking, among many other issues. In all these ways, social scientists are often at the forefront of work that helps us make sense of ourselves.

Humanities

Humans are creative creatures. From the earliest records of human history to the present, humans have expressed themselves through stories and artistic creations. They have also reflected on their own existence—on their dreams and aspirations, on the inevitability of suffering and death, on childhood and family, work and leisure. And they have created cultural artifacts that help them represent and make sense of human experience, through language and literature, philosophy and religion, music and drama.

All this is at the heart of what we call the humanities—fields that address the purpose, scope, and meaning of human experience as captured in the many different forms of human expression. In college, these issues will be addressed in such departments and programs as languages, literature, history, philosophy, the arts, religious studies, classics, area studies (e.g., Middle Eastern studies), and archeology, as well as subdivisions of these fields.

It is difficult to generalize across such a wide range of disciplines and to define the questions and methods applicable in all humanities classes. But to the extent that there is a common factor, it is that they use human artifacts—such as written documents, pieces of art, buildings, cultural practices—to understand the experiences of those who created them and their meaning and value for others. They also study the history of human communities—the events that have shaped them, the ways in which societies, cultures, and peoples have interacted, and how events in the past continue to influence people long afterward. In short, the goal of the humanities is to better grasp the complexity of human existence by understanding the vast array of things that humans have created and done throughout history.

Questions Humanists Ask

In general, humanities scholars ask questions such as, What is the meaning and significance of this human artifact or historical event? What aspects of human experience does it reflect? How has its meaning changed over time? What role does this artifact or event play in larger contexts, such as within a particular culture, in a specific political struggle, or within a tradition of literature or art?

But because the humanities attend to so many different dimensions of human experience, the way these questions show up in different disciplines can vary widely. Here are just a few characteristic examples.

English literature: What is narrative? What is distinctive about the styles of specific authors, and how have some authors influenced others? What was the historical context from which specific literary works, or forms, emerged? In what ways are the literary form and meaning of a specific work connected?

History: What were the causes of specific historical events or movements, and how did they, in turn, lead to others? How do interpretations of the past shape the present and future? How is political, social, and economic power established, maintained, and challenged?

Art: What counts as art? What is excluded from that category, and what are the implications of how we answer that question? What is the purpose of art? Does it make sense to talk about the meaning of a work of art, and if so, in what terms? How do works of art enable us to see the world and engage with it differently than other mediums allow? How does art affect audiences, evoking deep feelings and unconscious reactions?

Classics: How do the works of ancient civilizations (for Western universities, the focus is generally on Greece and Rome but often includes other civilizations, too) give us insights into their citizens' beliefs, values, and culture? How have these works (of literature, architecture, or art) influenced subsequent civilizations?

Philosophy: How do we know what we know? How do we understand the nature of the good and of our obligation to pursue it? What is real or true? What is the nature of the self? What is causation?

Religious studies: What are the origins of religion? How have specific religious traditions evolved? What are the components of a religion and how are they interconnected? What is the relationship between religion, society, and culture?

Even this brief survey reveals how complex and varied the study of humanity is. Clearly, studying human history and forms of creative expression does not lend itself to the sort of systematic, experimental methods that scientists employ in studying the natural world. But then, how do humanists answer the sorts of questions sketched above? What are their tools? And how can their results be tested or verified?

Methods in the Humanities

Most scholars in the humanities would agree that the questions they ask aren't susceptible to definitive answers in the way that most physics or chemistry questions are. After all, human experience is multifaceted, dynamic, and interactive and therefore subject to many layers of interpretation.

But the fact that there aren't once-and-for-all answers to these sorts of questions hardly means that any old opinion is valid. Scholars in each field have developed their own practices and standards for making sense of the materials they study, which constitute their **hermeneutics**, or methods of interpretation. So their disagreements are often as much about the methods they use as about the conclusions they reach.

When you study the humanities, then, you will want to focus especially on the theories that are used to justify the ways in which things are interpreted. For example, in a history course, your reading assignments or lectures might employ a Marxist theory about class struggle or a feminist theory about gender inequalities to explain particular social movements. Sometimes, too, the theories in play may be implied rather than explicit. So in a literature or art history course, your professor might interpret specific works in terms of the biography of the author/artist, in terms of the historical context in which these works were created, or in terms of the responses that they evoke in readers/viewers. Each of these approaches relies on a different way of understanding the meaning or significance of the material being studied. Most likely, within the same course, you'll be exposed to many approaches to understanding the subject matter.

But what all these approaches have in common is that they rely less on quantitative than on qualitative information. You might take many humanities courses without ever encountering a graph, chart, or equation. The information you're trying to understand, after all, is human creativity, which can't generally be captured in quantitative terms.

That said, in recent years, some humanists have employed methods from computing, statistics, and information science to expedite or deepen their humanities research. This new and growing field is often referred to as "digital humanities," and much exciting work is being done using these techniques. For example, a computer program could comb through a database of titles of British novels to determine that such titles grew shorter in the nineteenth century, perhaps due to serialization and the pressures of an evolving publishing industry.[11] Databases that enable word searching can be harnessed to support research questions by analyzing a greater volume of material than ever before. In addition, many digital humanities projects involve computerizing photographs, maps, oral histories, and other archival materials, which makes them available for digital analysis.

In very broad terms, there are two different approaches to interpretation that humanities scholars employ—**extrinsic (or contextual)** and **intrinsic**. An extrinsic framework holds that we can't properly understand the meaning of something without paying attention to the circumstances in which it arose or the people who created it. Intrinsic interpretations focus on the relationships among the different elements that constitute a piece and seek to explain its value or meaning in terms of the thing itself, without reference to its context. Each of these general approaches to interpretation in the humanities includes a number of more specific methods.

Contextualists will sometimes look at the biographical or psychological dimensions of an author or artist's life in an effort to connect the meaning of their experience and the things they created. A contextualist interested in these dimensions might ask,

> How did Van Gogh's battle with mental illness affect his paintings? How are his struggles revealed—or perhaps concealed—through his style and aesthetic?

Sometimes, the focus is not on the individual creator but on the institutions or social conditions that gave rise to this specific piece of work. This approach is often used in gender and sexuality studies as well as race and ethnicity studies because of its focus on the prevailing power structures within a society at a given time. A humanist concerned with the impact of institutional and social constructs might contemplate,

> What social forces motivated the abolitionist movement of the nineteenth century, and how did these same forces contribute to the women's suffrage movement?

Some of these institutional or social interpreters focus specifically on economic conditions, on the theory that all attitudes, values, and expressions in human societies are linked to the economic conditions of daily life. For example,

> How did industrialization in the eighteenth century impact the extent and use of leisure time, and how did this change in lifestyle contribute to the popularity of the novel?

Some humanists are less interested in the social or economic context of a work than in its place within a history of ideas. Intellectual historians, as they are sometimes called, focus on the ways in which ideas have a force and dynamism all their own. From their perspective, understanding a specific human creation requires us to locate it within the evolution of these ideas, which could be philosophical, religious, scientific, or social. Here is one example:

> How did the seventeenth-century thinker John Locke's ideas about social contract influence the political philosophy of figures such as Alexander Hamilton, Thomas Jefferson, and James Madison?

Finally, some scholars in the humanities focus on the history and evolution of artistic forms or genres. According to them, uncovering the meaning of a piece requires that we attend to the specifics of the form in which it is expressed. In the history of poetry, for example, there are conventions that dictate the form and rhyme scheme of sonnets. Attending to the way those forms have changed over time is important for appreciating the aesthetic value and meaning of a work. Humanists interested in forms and genres might research questions such as,

> How did the modernist writers James Joyce, Virginia Woolf, and Ezra Pound transform or challenge long-accepted conventions in writing?

> How did Beethoven's Symphony No. 3 depart from earlier forms of symphonic composition?

Intrinsic approaches to the humanities were championed by many scholars in the twentieth century, partly in reaction to a long history of interpretation that overlooked the inherent elements of a work in favor of these external contexts. They emphasize treating works as independent and autonomous modes of expression and communication that stand on their own, often through attempts to understand a creative work by looking solely at the formal elements that comprise it. For literature, that might be character development, plot, and narrative voice; for paintings, it might be color and tonality, perspective, and composition. For example,

> How does Robert Frost use nature imagery in his poem "Stopping by Woods on a Snowy Evening" to evoke elements of human experience?

This might also include special attention to the relationships among elements within a work, where they fit within a structure. For example,

> How have the creators of this political TV ad combined pictures of the American flag, newsreel clips, voiceovers of the candidate, and written endorsements scrolling across the screen to create an appealing image of the candidate in contrast to her opponent?

Exercise. Below are some examples of questions that humanists might ask about a human artifact. For each, indicate whether the approach is more extrinsic or intrinsic.

- What aspect of Kurt Vonnegut's personal experience prompted him to write *Slaughterhouse Five*? How are those experiences conveyed in the narrative?
- How do camera angle, sound, and editing combine to create suspense in Alfred Hitchcock's *Psycho*?
- How has the popularity of rap music in the United States since the 1980s influenced the identity formation of young adults in the African American and Latinx communities?
- How do religious myths function to articulate and resolve basic dichotomies of human experience, for example, life/death, nature/culture, male/female?
- What were the political conditions that prompted Picasso to create *Guernica*? Why was cubism an appropriate style for this work?

- How did the notion of individualism influence the concept of a social contract in the works of Hobbes, Locke, and Rousseau?

Debates and Challenges in the Humanities

The humanities are messy. In contrast to the natural sciences, where there is broad agreement on the proper methods for answering most questions, in the humanities, there is considerable disagreement about how to approach the subject matter. Human beings, after all, are capable of independent thought and are also shaped by the times and cultures in which they live. They interact with one another and with their environments in enormously complex and varied ways; they have unconscious minds, so that there is much they are not aware of; they are capable of deception (both of others and even of themselves); they express things indirectly, through symbols and metaphors, and also directly, in many different genres and media; and they are aware of their own mortality and strive to transcend the limits of their finitude. For these and many other reasons, understanding anything that humans do or create is a potentially limitless endeavor, without a clear starting point or a definitive end.

When you step into a humanities classroom, then, you will find yourself facing debates in which we are often lacking an established and unanimously endorsed set of facts, a generally accepted method for addressing the facts in question, or both. Here are just a few examples from a range of disciplines:

- Do we have free will? (Philosophy)
- What were the causes of the Algerian Revolution? (History)
- Did Shakespeare write all the plays attributed to him, and if not, who did? (English)

For humanists, the messiness and indeterminacy of these subjects is not a drawback; it is part of their appeal. Delving into the richness and complexity of human experience can give us a window into people who lived in times and places far removed from our own and simultaneously give us insight into our own lives. Discovering new interpretations of previously explored subjects, then, can be a way of uncovering new dimensions of the human experience that have been there all along but are only now becoming salient.

Interdisciplinary Studies

To return to the opening metaphor of this chapter, sometimes the scholars in those conversation halls move between rooms, taking with them questions, methods, or ideas. The result is a conversation that blurs the boundaries between those groups, creating a new hybrid, interdisciplinary conversation. In addition, scholars with interests in the same subject but who generally move within different disciplinary rooms sometimes leave and begin a new conversation in a separate room—and a new field of study is created.

Some of the most innovative academic work occurs at the intersection between traditional disciplines, in fields like biomedical engineering (biology, medicine, and engineering), genomics (computer science and genetics), ethnomusicology (ethnic studies and music history), and psycholinguistics (psychology and linguistics). Many of these involve intentionally bringing together scholars from a number of established disciplines to study a particular subject from multiple perspectives simultaneously. This is the case for fields such as American studies or Middle Eastern studies, where historians, sociologists, literary scholars, and others collectively attempt to understand the cultures and societies of a particular segment of humanity. It is worth noting, too, that certain scholars who have embraced interdisciplinary approaches to their subjects have believed that the usual boundaries of disciplines are either artificial or confining; in a sense, they are counter-disciplinary, as much as interdisciplinary. The important point here is for you to realize that *the number and range of departments and programs in a university is not fixed but rather evolves in response to social changes, as well as the interests of faculty*. By way of illustration, I'll briefly introduce just one of these, environmental science.

Environmental science sits at the intersection of the natural sciences (biology, geology, chemistry) and the social sciences (economics, public policy, public health, and political science). It is a prime example of an academic field that has arisen in response to changing social circumstances. Beginning in the late 1960s and '70s, prompted in part by rising awareness of environmental hazards and the establishment in 1970 of the Environmental Protection Agency, universities began to create programs in environmental studies. Their goal was to address the many threats to our environmental and human health from human behavior, to study those changes scientifically, to raise public awareness of those threats, and ultimately to affect public policy. As the urgency of global warming increases, the topics addressed by environmental scientists have moved beyond just air and water to issues of food security, climate science, energy systems, global biodiversity, and sustainable development.

Conclusion

When you step into a classroom, you're entering an academic conversation. In this conversation, you face certain challenges, including understanding the questions scholars in this field ask and the ways they attempt to answer them. Each class, each academic discipline, invites you to join that conversation, even if you are only observing and have no intention of contributing to the debates.

But why is this eavesdropping valuable? What do you gain from moving among these conversations and becoming even modestly conversant in the particular discourses you discover in college? Each disciplinary or interdisciplinary conversation you engage with gives you a new set of lenses through which to understand the world. It expands the vocabulary at your disposal for understanding a whole range of issues—from the structure of the natural world to the development of human societies, from the perspectives of humans long gone to insights into human experience today. It doesn't matter that you may never master this new language or contribute to this field. You will still have a richer understanding of the world outside of that classroom, which, after all, is the world you'll live in for the rest of your life.

Students frequently assume that their primary course goal is to understand the material on the syllabus. In fact, it is to understand the distinctive ways of questioning, thinking, and understanding represented by that material. The essence of being educated is to have the ability to see the world from a wide range of perspectives. It's why colleges have general-education requirements and why employers in every industry are attracted to college graduates. When you can move readily between perspectives, you develop creativity, flexibility, and open-mindedness.[12] This will enable you both to get more out of any course you take and to take the perspectives you gain there out of the classroom and into the world. The world will never look the same again.

Questions for Reflection

1. The next time you're sitting in a new class listening to the instructor, or when you're reviewing your notes after class, make a list of the questions that this course addresses and the methods being used to answer them. Review this list periodically and add to it or revise it in light of how the course has unfolded. Do this often enough that it becomes a habit.
2. When you read something, whether for a course or for some other purpose, try to imagine a conversation about that topic from a range of perspectives. If the topic is educational reform, imagine how a parent, a teacher, a school superintendent, and a legislator (at the city or state level) might think about it. What assumptions would they make? What factors would they weigh to make decisions about reforms that are needed (or not)?
3. Interview a few college graduates who majored in different fields. Ask them what they remember about their college education. What aspects of what they learned remain useful to them, and how? What habits of mind or perspectives did their major instill in them? How have these expanded their outlook or restricted it?

ADVICE FOR THE ROAD AHEAD

Join a Team

At some point during college, you're very likely to be in a class that requires group work. Collaborating with classmates in producing a joint product is often challenging, but it can also foster greater creativity as you work together to refine one another's ideas and strategies. But in class, even when you're not explicitly working with other students, your learning is still intertwined with theirs. Learning is a group activity.

Each time you walk into class and take your seat, look around you and take in who is on this journey with you. In most cases, you won't know them, but given that you are classmates, you have an opportunity to contribute to their learning, and they to yours. When you listen carefully to a classmate's question or comment in class, think of it as an opportunity.

- Perhaps they understand something better than you do, and you can gain some insight from their comments.
- Maybe they have misconstrued something in the assigned reading or homework, and their questions enable you to see more clearly what this material is really about.
- Maybe they raise a question that gets you thinking in a new way about something you thought you already understood.

In all these ways, paying attention to what your classmates say can contribute to your learning, even when their comment turns out to be mistaken.

This is most obvious in small, seminar-type classes, where discussion and engaging with others is explicitly part of the coursework (and sometimes part of the grade for the course). But even in large lecture courses, where students generally sit and absorb the material separately, the truth is that the other anonymous students can teach you a lot, if only you see them as engaged in a common enterprise.

This is why students often choose to study in groups, because they know instinctively that several minds working together are almost always better than one working alone. The give and take of conversation as you help one another understand the material is stimulating—things you found tedious may become less so when you see how they excite someone else, things you found puzzling may make more sense as you talk them through with others. Reviewing what you're learning with someone else reinforces it, especially when you have to explain it to someone less familiar with the material. Their questions enable you to see aspects of the material you hadn't noticed, force you to verbalize what you know, and help you identify the points you're still trying to understand.

Sitting in a classroom with lots of students may seem a lot like sitting on a plane or bus with lots of strangers, but it isn't. Public transportation will get you where you're going whether or not you collaborate with those seated beside you. But in a classroom, the things you say and the way you listen to what others say can actually help you get to your destination sooner. They may even help you to arrive at a far better destination.

CHAPTER FOUR

How Am I Supposed to Do This Assignment?

Learning is not attained by chance, it must be sought
for with ardour and attended to with diligence.
—ABIGAIL ADAMS

Outline

In this chapter, you will learn how to successfully tackle your college work by identifying the common components in all assignments and focusing on the critical-thinking challenges that they present. Approached in this way, each assignment you do can help you with every other one.

- Some Practical Suggestions for Completing Your College Work
  - Know What You're Required to Do
  - Ask for Help
  - Review before You Submit
  - Turn Your Work in on Time
- The Three Essential Components of All College Assignments
  - Product
  - Scope and Assumptions
  - Action Items
- Sample Assignments
  - Engineering

    - Math
    - Political science
    - Psychology
    - History
    - English
- Conclusion
- Questions for Reflection

▪ ▪ ▪

Most of the work you do in college, apart from exams, will be completing assignments—papers, problem sets, or projects. Many students approach assignments as an unpleasant but necessary chore; finish all the required assignments for all the required courses, and you cross the finish line and get your degree. But while not all assignments will contribute equally to your learning—and certainly not all of them are equally interesting—they all provide you with opportunities to hone your skills. By completing those assignments, you exercise your critical-thinking skills and demonstrate your mastery of a discipline's key concepts and methods. When you look at them this way, they may even turn out to be more interesting and worthwhile than you thought.

It will help if you don't view each assignment in isolation. If you see the relationship between assignments, you will find that they are easier to do. First, because in most courses assignments build on one another, you can't do later, more complex assignments until you have become proficient at doing the earlier, simpler ones. Moreover, beneath all the specific details in each assignment is the expectation that you will exercise the critical-thinking abilities discussed in chapter 2—exploring context, considering alternatives, weighing evidence, and finding implications and new applications. In this sense, each assignment is potentially a continuation of work you have already done, even if it was completed in another course. When you focus on these connections, any assignment can help you hone skills needed for future assignments. It takes some work to recognize these critical-thinking skills embedded in your assignments, but I'll walk you through a couple of examples, using assignments from actual college courses.

Some Practical Suggestions for Completing Your College Work

Know what you're required to do. Pay attention to all the instructions, as well as to the resources listed, the assumptions made, and the expected final product. Sometimes these will include guidelines about formatting, citations, or length. I'll highlight these elements in the example assignments below. Every professor has had students who have turned in a well-done assignment but received a poor grade because they didn't do what the assignment asked.

Ask for help. If at any point you still aren't completely sure what is being asked of you, talk to your professor or TA. It may be easier or more comfortable to guess and hope for the best, but understanding the intentions of your grader will often save you lots of time spent going off in the wrong direction. It may also give you more ideas (and more confidence) to address the assignment successfully.

Review before you submit. You are likely to make mistakes, especially when you're rushing or working late at night. You are more likely to catch these mistakes if you give yourself time to review your work before submission. Proofread, check for completeness, and double-check your calculations. It takes extra time, of course, but you will catch errors you didn't see and improve your metacognition.

Turn your work in on time. Every assignment has a deadline. Observe it. Plan to give yourself the time you need, and then add some extra time to account for delays and revision. If you have a genuine emergency and need an extension, ask for it respectfully. Don't assume you can turn work in late and explain it after the fact. And if it's late, be prepared to get marked down for being late, depending on your professor's policies. Practicing punctuality will serve you not just now but for the rest of your career.

The Three Essential Components of All College Assignments

Here are some assignments that illustrate the kinds of intellectual work you will do in college. In each case, the critical-thinking skills you must employ to complete the assignment will be *italicized*. Before you can begin to do this critical-thinking work, however, you'll need to break down an assignment into its components, so you can see exactly what it entails and what steps you'll need to take to complete it. You'll notice that for many of them, I have identified the elements you need to pay attention to by highlighting them as follows:

> **Product** = What are you being asked to produce—a final project, paper, report, presentation, or something else?
>
> Scope and assumptions = What questions do you need to address to complete this assignment? What assumptions should you make, and what parameters should you work within?
>
> Action items = What steps do you need to take to generate that final product? What specific methods should you use to complete this assignment?

Throughout this chapter, the actual assignments (which have sometimes been abbreviated for the sake of this analysis) are boxed. After each assignment, you'll find a set of questions that prompt you to think about how you will tackle it, followed by some guidance that I provide.

Sample Assignments

Assignment 1: Civil Engineering (Energy Planning)

This **report** involves quantifying the current end-use energy consumed in all energy sectors in a country, territory, province, state, city, town, or community then coming up with a plan to replace the current energy with entirely clean, renewable energy produced by wind, water, and solar (WWS) power. Current energy includes coal, oil, natural gas, biofuels/biomass, nuclear, renewable heat, and/or renewable electricity. All-purpose energy includes electricity, transportation, building heating/cooling, and industry and any other energy not included in one of these categories. Assume that the conversion can occur today, so there is no need to project energy use to a future year.

The next step is to convert each current fuel to WWS electricity or heat using the method described in class.

Then, come up with the percent of end-use demand met by each WWS technology. Translate that end-use load for each technology (total end-use load multiplied by fraction supplied by each technology) to the number of devices needed for each technology. For example, for onshore and offshore wind, find data typical of mean wind speeds at hub height and then calculate the capacity of a typical wind turbine at each location. Then use that information to estimate the number of onshore and offshore wind turbines needed to meet wind's share of end-use demand. Similarly, for other technologies, estimate capacity factors at a location where each technology might be installed and back-calculate the number of devices needed.

Use typical spacing and footprint areas to estimate the areas needed for each technology. Check that the areas needed do not exceed the area available. In the case of cities and smaller, assume energy devices can be placed out of the city, except for rooftop Photovoltaics.

The report should **include some graphs and/or figures**. Additional pages of graphs and figures are permitted beyond the page limits. All data used should be cited with a reference. A few volunteer students may give a presentation of their results at the end of the quarter.

For every assignment you encounter, ask yourself

1. How would I approach this prompt?

2. What is and isn't clear to me? What would I ask for help on?

3. What steps would I take to start and complete the assignment?

4. What critical-thinking skills am I practicing here?

This assignment is complex, so let's begin by breaking down the goals and steps involved before explaining the critical-thinking skills required (this is something you'll want to do whenever you have an assignment with multiple components or several sets of assumptions embedded within it). The overall goal is to provide a comparison of our current energy production and use to our new energy production and use from solely renewable sources. The rest of the prompt outlines the steps needed to accomplish this within the particular parameters that the professor has defined. Try to come up with an outline of the steps yourself before reviewing the main steps below. Here is my constructed to-do list:

- Define the scope of study—a country, a city, a company, and so on.
- Quantify current end-use energy by sector (e.g., residential, commercial).
- Replace current energy production with renewable energy by
    - finding the end-use energy after replacement (the paper assumes that such a conversion will change the energy end-use); and
    - finding the new mix of renewable energy to meet the end-use demand.
- Estimate the area needed for the new energy supply.
- Estimate the capacity factor, or the efficiency, of the energy supply.
- From that, find the number of devices needed.
- From that, estimate the area needed, given a rate of area/device.

There are a couple of additional, implicit steps, not spelled out in the prompt, that will help you connect the given steps together:

- Quantify the present-day sources of energy. This will help you understand what renewable energy sources are already being utilized, so you won't need to recalculate these sources in the final energy supply projection.
- Find the renewable energy resources in your area of study. Knowing this will help you understand what mix of renewable

energy is available to be used and figure out the capacity factor, which is dependent on the quality of renewable resources.

To make such a complex assignment more manageable, the professor has established some assumptions and parameters. Pay close attention to these, since they limit the extent of the research you need to do. Keep in mind that you may need to make other assumptions beyond those specified in the prompt as you work through this assignment. If you do, you'll need to include these in your report, of course.

- The professor has given you the definition of end-use energy as "electricity, transportation, building heating/cooling, and industry and any other energy not included in one of these categories."
- You should assume that the conversion occurs today, so you don't need to calculate the increased demand in energy due to population growth or the time it takes to construct power plants, for example.
- You are told to use the "method described in class," so you will want to review that and make sure you know how to apply that method to this sort of problem.
- You have one example—how to calculate the capacity of a typical wind turbine—that you can use as a model for how you will calculate other sorts of renewable energy sources, for example solar and hydroelectric.
- Finally, if you choose to focus on a city, you can assume that energy devices (e.g., wind turbines, solar panels, etc.) can be placed outside the urban boundaries.

Once you understand the goal of the assignment, the questions you need to answer, the parameters within which you will work, and the elements you need to include in the final report, you are ready to outline the specific steps required to complete the assignment successfully. This will be slightly different from the outline provided by the professor because you need to create an outline that will work for you. Think about what you already know, what further research you need to do, and what questions you need answered by the professor. From there, what specific concrete steps do you need to take? These should be manageable pieces, ones that would allow you to finish any particular step by itself.

- Choose the study area (for purposes of illustration, we'll choose the state of Utah).
- Find data on end-use energy in Utah, including electricity, transportation, heating, and so on.
- Find data on energy sources in Utah, including fossil fuels, renewables, nuclear, and so on.
- Find the potential of renewable energy sources in Utah.
- Organize and understand these data.
- Calculate the final energy portfolio.
- Find the final end-use energy using the methods introduced in class from the end-use energy you researched.
- Find the new mix of renewable energy based on this final end-use energy and the various potentials of renewable energy in Utah.
- Find the average capacity factor based on the potential of renewable energy in Utah.
- Based on this mixture of renewables and the capacity factor, figure out the number of devices and then the required land area, making sure this area is less than the state of Utah (or your study area).

The critical-thinking skills involved in doing these things will now be clearer. You will need to *gather evidence* about current energy use and the capacity of renewable energy sources in Utah, and *evaluate the strength and reliability of the evidence you find*. You will need to *compare evidence* (data) *regarding alternative* energy sources. You will need to *explore the implications of various choices* for future energy use. And finally, you will need to *apply knowledge you learned in the course* (the method introduced in the course for converting current fuel into sustainable energy) *to a new set of data.*

Assignment 2: Math Problem Set (Precalculus)

(Note that problem sets sometimes include reading from a book, which often gives context to the problem set or the following lectures.)

1. **Construct a mathematical model of the world**. The monthly cost of driving a car depends on the number of miles driven. Lynn found that in May it cost her $380 to drive 480 miles, and in June it cost her $460 to drive 800 miles.
   (a) Express the monthly cost C as a function of the variable distance driven d, assuming that a linear relationship gives a suitable model.
   (b) Use part (a) to predict the cost of driving 1500 miles per month.
   (c) Draw the graph of the linear function. What does the slope represent?
   (d) What does the C-intercept represent?
   (e) Why does a linear function give a suitable model in this situation?

2. Recall functions and their types.
   (a) If f and g are both even functions, is f + g even? Justify or give a counterexample.
   (b) If f and g are both odd functions, is f + g odd? Justify or give a counterexample.

3. Know the properties of functions. Consider the function given by the rule $f(x) = \ln(x + 3)$
   (a) What is the domain of f? Give your answer in interval notation.
   (b) Give the function f^{-1}.

4. Use geometry and trigonometry to simplify the problem. Let θ be angle such that $\sin \theta = x/2$
   (a) Write down an expression for $\tan \theta$ in terms of x. Hint: draw a picture.
   (b) Write down an expression for 4–x2/x2 in terms of θ.

5. Manipulate the expression. Give the partial fraction decomposition of the following rational functions.
   (a) (x3−2x2+3x)/(x2−2x+1)
   (b) (2x2+x−5)/(x3−2x2+x-2)

Problem sets—colloquially called "p-sets"—are among the most common types of assignment in college, especially in STEM courses. Like your traditional homework assignments in high school, a p-set is a set of questions you have to answer, often due at the next class. Most problem sets are just a way for you to practice the material and wrestle with the concepts covered in class. They are designed to test whether you understand the concepts and whether you can apply them to new situations. You will also need to be able to explain how you arrived at your answer.

Problem sets offer you opportunities to practice your metacognitive skills. When you approach them, ask yourself:

- Am I frustrated when doing this problem set, and if so, why? Is it because I keep getting wrong answers? Is it because I don't understand what it's asking me to do? Is it because I'm completely lost?
- How long am I spending to complete the problems? Is it taking me more or less time than I expected? Are there other methods of doing the problems I haven't considered? Can I seek out support from professors, teaching assistants, or peers if I am struggling to complete the problems?
- How well did I do on the last problem set? If it didn't go well, what didn't I understand? (Most courses are cumulative, so if you're not understanding something early on, you will want to seek help before you are so lost that it's hard to recover.)

Working on p-sets gives you many opportunities to practice your critical-thinking skills. Here are just some of the skills that will come into play:

- *Exploring alternatives*: What are different ways to approach this problem?
- *Weighing evidence:* Have I utilized all the relevant data and connected them to the mathematical formula correctly?
- *Implications and applications*: What are other ways in which this material could be applied? What other problems could be solved with thought processes similar to the one I used to solve this problem?

Assignment 3: Political Science

In this assignment, you will have an opportunity to develop your own hypothesis about income inequality and test it against the data.

Your dependent variable will be a measure of inequality for a commuting zone (CZ) in the US. You will select ONE independent variable from racial segregation, high school dropout rate, migration outflow rate, percent divorced, percent religious, fraction working in manufacturing, violent crime rate, and percent single mother households.

Develop a hypothesis that you could test with the data set we will provide to you. Identify ONE independent variable, hypothesis, and causal logic. Remember: it's ok to be wrong! Next, see whether the data support or challenge your prediction. Your **final essay** should be a carefully crafted and succinct evaluation of your hypothesis in light of the data. **Your paper should include an introduction, a hypothesis, interpretation of the data, and a conclusion.**

Developing and testing a hypothesis is a fundamental skill in social science disciplines. It involves *evaluating the source and strength of evidence, exploring alternative ways of understanding that evidence* in relationship to a claim (hypothesis), *considering evidence that challenges your conclusions,* and finally, *considering the plausibility of your claim.* Notice in particular that you are being asked to "see whether the data support or challenge your prediction." Remember that you are asked to make a case that is plausible, not to prove that you're absolutely right. This last element is specifically called out in the prompt: "It's ok to be wrong!" Remember that even when the evidence suggests your hypothesis is wrong, this is also a significant finding. After all, you couldn't have known that until you evaluated the claim "in light of the data," which means you've done exactly what the prompt asked of you. Drawing causal connections between any two elements of human experience or behavior—in this case, between any of the independent variables listed in the prompt and income inequality in a particular area—is always somewhat speculative. The point of this assignment is to offer a hypothesis grounded in evidence and provide a reasoned argument in support of that hypothesis.

Completing this assignment: You'll need to decide which of the independent variables you believe is most likely to be correlated with income inequality, or at least which of them you are most interested in exploring. Before you examine the data set that is provided, you'll want to consider what the data would look like if your hypothesis were correct (or incorrect). Note that you might bump into evidence that challenges your biases about the sources of income inequality, so you'll want to be attentive to this possibility.

Though the prompt doesn't explicitly require you to use other information you learned in the course, it is always prudent to keep this in mind. Every assignment is designed to test or deepen your understanding of material you've learned in the course. So you'll want to ask yourself whether any of the topics or methods covered has a bearing on the specific issue of income inequality or other similar social or economic phenomena. In the present example, this may be most relevant to the question of the logic that connects the data to the hypothesis you've chosen. As you analyze the data, you'll want to keep in mind that this final product will have four parts: introduction, hypothesis, analysis of the data, and conclusion. You'll want to make sure you have thought about what belongs in each section of your paper and how to make the best possible case for your interpretation of the data.

Assignment 4: Psychology

One goal of this course is to enhance your ability to both understand and evaluate developmental research. To that effect, you will write a **paper** that critically discusses a debate in developmental psychology. Your paper should:

Present a topic and explain why it is theoretically interesting and important.

Present a debate in the field related to this topic.

Present a research study that was designed to address this debate and discuss which side the findings support and why.

Present one counter argument the other side used (or would/could use) to address the findings.

Conclusion (which should include your own opinion).

Review the prompt for this assignment, and then answer these questions:

1. What are you being asked to produce—a final project, paper, report, presentation, or something else?

____

____

____

____

2. What questions do you need to address to complete this assignment? What assumptions should you make, and what parameters should you work within?

____

____

____

____

3. What steps do you need to take to generate that final product? What specific methods should you use to complete this assignment?

____

____

____

____

4. What critical-thinking skills are you practicing here?

____

____

____

____

This assignment focuses on evaluating debates in the field of developmental psychology. The course presumably has introduced you to a number of those debates, such as the relative importance of nature versus nurture in human development, how malleable human behavior is, and the identifiable stages in human development. Scholars in this field have argued about these and similar issues for many decades; your assignment is to join that conversation and take a stand on one of those debates. This will involve looking at the positions of scholars and asking, *What assumptions are these scholars making? What alternative explanations could be offered to explain this phenomenon? How plausible is this author's position? Is there evidence that would challenge this theory? What are the implications of competing theories, even if their authors haven't articulated them?* Completing this assignment requires thinking like a psychologist, which involves evaluating the strengths and weaknesses of theories that attempt to explain the complexities of human experience. Once again, your goal isn't to produce a definitive answer to these questions—after all, the scholars who have devoted their lives to these questions haven't yet!—but only to take a side and defend the plausibility of the position you choose.

Completing this assignment: Since you've been given the option of choosing which debate to write about, you'll want to make sure you've selected one in which there is genuine disagreement among scholars. If everyone seems to agree that childhood trauma has a lasting impact on well-being later in life, you will want to focus on something about which scholars disagree, perhaps how deep or pervasive that effect is or whether it is different depending on some other factors (e.g., when or how frequently the trauma occurred). Because the focus is on debates, you'll probably want to begin by identifying the issues within a topic that are disputed. It might help to begin thinking in pros and cons, perhaps even organizing your notes on each theory or position you review in this format. Next, you'll want to look for a research study that you can clearly relate to the debate you've chosen, which may require some research into your topic beyond what was covered in class. As you look at potential research studies to use, you will want to imagine how someone would challenge the implications of that study and to make notes about that, too.

This prompt spells out very clearly what the component parts of this paper should be, and you'll want to make sure your paper includes each component in the proper order. Remember: even though the prompt gives concise descriptions of each portion of the essay, that doesn't mean that each part should take up the same amount of space.

Here, the instructions tell you you're being tested on your skills of understanding and evaluating developmental research through a critical discussion of a debate in the field. Presenting the debate, the research essay, and the counterargument, then, should form the bulk of your essay.

Assignment 5: History

One of the greatest skills for any historian is the ability to find and analyze a range of primary sources. Available sources on surveillance are numerous, but they can also be tricky. Government officials, spies, and dissidents often wrote ambiguously. In this sense, surveillance sources provide a productive place to practice how to infer and analyze vague sources.

A wealth of primary sources about surveillance are available through government agencies and other institutions, waiting to be researched. The main assignment for this course, therefore, will be uncovering primary sources about surveillance from these databases and then **writing a source analysis (five hundred to a thousand words) about them**. These analyses are not long, so take time to choose an interesting or provocative source, and then write a **focused report** on what the document is really saying and how a historian might use it.

It's easy to write five hundred words, but it's hard to say why something really matters in five hundred words, so give it some thought and some time.

Each primary source analysis should begin with the basic information about the document (author, subject, date, country of origin, archival location, etc.). Next, write a brief summary of the primary source so that someone who has not read the document can understand its content. Finally, the main body of the text should be reserved for analysis.

An appropriate topic for analysis will differ based on the exact primary source, but analyses might include situating the source in its historical context, identifying inferences that we can make from the text, pointing out silences of what the text is not discussing, examining particularly puzzling aspects of the source, or identifying additional research questions that the document poses.

As you consider this assignment, ask

1. How should you approach this prompt?

2. What is and isn't clear to you? What should you ask for help on?

3. What steps should you take to start and complete the assignment?

4. What critical-thinking skills are you practicing here?

The essence of this assignment is to find and analyze primary sources related to surveillance. Remember that "analyzing" is an instruction that always requires you to ask questions. In this case, the prompt already identifies what some of those questions might be—How does this source reflect a particular historical context? What is the significance of the silences within the text? But notice, too, that the prompt invites you to consider implications—inferences you could draw from this text, as well as potential further research questions you might pursue based on this text.

The larger goal of the assignment is to get you to think like a historian, which is presumably what the course has modeled for you all along. That's what the prompt means by asking that your reports determine "what each document is really saying and how a historian might use it." To do this, you'll need to ask yourself, What kinds of questions interest historians? How do they go about answering them?

Completing this assignment: Your first step will be to find interesting sources about surveillance. You'll want to find documents with historical and political implications that have plenty of substance to analyze and unpack. You may want to begin with sources (archives, databases, or other repositories of documents) you've been introduced to in the course and then see if they lead you to others. And because the prompt requires you to do a few things for each source—provide basic information, a summary, and an analysis—you will want to be sure that you structure each five hundred–word source report in exactly that order.

Assignment 6: English (Gothic Literature)

In this **paper**, you will compare, in some focused and well-defined way, two works we have read this term. Your goal is not merely to identify interesting, specific similarities and differences between these two works but rather to generate a meaningful argument about the relationship between the two texts—that is, an argument about the significance of the similarities and differences you find. (Note that because the two texts are inherently different, your thesis will in all likelihood make a claim about the significance of the difference between them). In developing your thesis, you might consider what your comparison reveals about these two authors, these two novels, gothic as a genre, the development of this genre, or the challenges inherent to this form.

The phrase *compare and contrast* appears so often in college assignments that it has become a cliché. But as this prompt makes explicit, just noting similarities and differences is not very meaningful, though you will need to do this before you can do the real work of critical analysis. And that happens when you ask a question about those similarities and differences. What underlying features of the authors or books do they reveal? Do they tell us something about the authors' goals, audiences, or styles that is important? Does this comparison illuminate something about the larger category to which both works belong (e.g., the gothic genre)? You want to develop an argument about those contrasts, and that requires asking *what implications these similarities or dissimilarities have for other issues*. In effect, you want to ask yourself, "Having noticed that these two works of literature are similar in these ways, but different in those ways, what conclusion does that insight point to, and why does it matter?"

This prompt makes explicit something that is often implicit in other assignments of this type—that you always want to *look for the implications of the things you're studying*, to see how they are instances or reflections of larger themes and issues that have been introduced in the course. The assignment's focus on implications explains why the professor has left the choice of which course materials to compare entirely to you. Fundamentally, it doesn't matter what you choose to analyze, so long as you can make some important point through that comparative analysis. But the value placed on a thorough, discerning analysis tells you something else important, namely, that you want to choose those works for comparison with care. Which works have enough in common that a comparison is possible but differ in enough interesting ways that a comparison is worthwhile? In fact, your decision about which works you want to compare should be driven by your sense of how that comparison will serve your argument.

Completing this assignment: Writing comparative papers always requires you to figure out how you will structure your discussion. Do you begin by discussing all the features of work 1, then all the features of work 2, and then proceed to the comparative analysis? Or is it better to organize your discussion around the points of comparison, moving back and forth between works 1 and 2 to highlight the contrasts? The answer is that it doesn't really matter. What does matter is that you have chosen works that enable you to "generate a meaningful argument about the relationship between the two texts" and that you put that argument front and center so that your reader understands the point of this comparison. Of course, you also need to make sure you have understood each of them well enough on its own terms and that you are not overlooking important aspects of the texts.

While this assignment makes these critical-thinking goals explicit, other assignments that ask you to compare—two methods, or works of art, or procedures for solving a problem—may be less clear. But remember: whether the prompt tells you this or not, the comparison is almost never an end in itself; rather, it is a means of making a larger point about some issue that transcends the specifics of what you're comparing. Stay focused on that, and the job of comparing will be both easier and more meaningful.

Conclusion

While the assignments you will encounter in college come in many shapes and sizes, what they all have in common are the critical-thinking skills you need to use to complete them successfully. Sometimes, those critical-thinking skills will be named explicitly, which makes your job a bit easier. At other times, you will need to read between the lines to determine the kind of thinking your instructor is asking you to do. But either way, you should assume that the assignments you receive in college are designed either to reinforce higher-level thinking skills in the course or to invite you to apply those skills beyond the examples in class. Even if an assignment feels like busywork, try to approach it in a way that helps you explore your interests, solidify your understanding, or challenge your abilities.

Focusing on the common critical-thinking skills that underlie the many different assignments you get throughout college is key to becoming a more sophisticated learner and a more successful student. Even when the task in front of you appears to be completely unlike anything you've seen before, remember that you have very likely already practiced some of the required critical-thinking skills. Use each assignment as leverage to help you tackle others. The skills used in various parts of your education are applicable across assignments and disciplines, just as the skills from one sport—agility, balance, or teamwork—are applicable to another, even if the rules of that sport are entirely different. At the end of the day, becoming the best critical thinker you can be requires that your past learning informs your current learning. When you get into the habit of doing this, you'll discover that your education adds up to more than just the sum of all the assignments you've successfully completed; it is a set of skills that you have internalized and can apply to any problem you may encounter.

Questions for Reflection

1. Think back over assignments you did in high school. Which were hardest? Which were most interesting or engaging? What made them so? From which of them do you feel you learned the most?
2. A famous philosophy professor at Harvard used to give the same question on the final exam of every course he taught: "Ask a question and answer it." (Think about how a strong answer to such a question would require you to employ the key critical-thinking skills discussed in chapter 2!). As you reach the end of each course, ask yourself, "What questions do I have that would be interesting to tackle, and how would I do that?"
3. Before you sit down to work on an assignment, try asking yourself, "What are the learning challenges embedded in this assignment? What is the professor trying to get me to learn, practice, or apply? How can I complete the assignment in a way that will demonstrate I have mastered this material?"

ADVICE FOR THE ROAD AHEAD

Get Off the Sidelines

At sporting events, there are two types of people: observers and players. Observers stand apart from the action, cheering on the athletes or criticizing them from a distance. Observers have the luxury of being disengaged, distracted, or even bored. Players, on the other hand, have skin in the game. Whether they're amateurs or professionals, winning or losing, they have no choice but to be engaged. They make the best moves they can, take risks, and sometimes get bruised in the process.

To be a player, of course, you have to believe in your ability to play the game. You have to trust that you have something to contribute to the team, that the skills that got you this far—you did get into college, after all!—will serve you well. There may be days when you have your doubts about this, especially if you don't have the support system at home or at school to prop you up when you encounter challenges. But even on the days when being a successful student feels like an uphill climb, try to remind yourself that it's worth suiting up, getting out on the field, and giving it your best shot. You might be surprised to discover you have more to offer the team than you imagined.

College learning requires being invested in the work you're doing. It can't be done at arm's length. And that means taking some risks. When you speak up and offer an opinion about how to solve that math problem or interpret that poem, you may be challenged. Your answers may not withstand the scrutiny of your professors and your peers. When this happens, your intellectual ego may get bruised, or you may feel embarrassed.

But there is no learning without some failures. No athlete has ever scored every shot or won every race. The goal is to give it your best effort, see what results you get, assess what you can do to improve, and then get back out and try again. All of this takes resilience and determination, of course. But first and foremost, it takes a willingness to be part of the action. As Wayne Gretzky, the famous hockey player, is reported to have said, “You miss 100 percent of the shots you don’t take.” Learning is hard work, but it’s also captivating and fulfilling. On our best days, it’s even exhilarating.

PART II

Critical Thinking in Practice

CHAPTER FIVE

Reading 2.0: How to Read the Words That Aren't on the Page and Really Understand the Ones That Are

In a good book, the best is between the lines.
—SWEDISH PROVERB

Reading is an active, imaginative act; it takes work.
—KHALED HOSSEINI

Outline

In this chapter, you will learn some techniques for reading difficult material and some questions to ask that will enable you to read everything more deeply and critically. You will also be introduced to the challenges of reading visual images and of assessing the trustworthiness of online information.

- Strategies for Active, Engaged Reading
  - Pre-read
  - Cross-Reference
  - Reread
  - Outline and Find Key Terms

■ ■ ■

We all know how to read and have been doing it since we were in grade school. Mostly, reading the words on the page is easy. But college-level reading may be more challenging than high school–level reading was—in two ways. First, the texts themselves may be harder—more technical, denser, more puzzling. Reading difficult material requires more mental energy and more focused attention; you need to work harder just to make sense of what the author is saying. In addition, college reading will demand more of you because your professors will expect that you do more than just comprehend the surface meaning. You will be expected to read critically, to think about the context of this material, to notice what's implied but not stated, and to raise questions about what the author says, among other things. In this chapter, I'll give you some pointers for reading more sophisticated material in a more penetrating way.

Strategies for Active, Engaged Reading

Many of the readings you are assigned in college will be hard to make sense of. They may include technical terms you're not familiar with. They may be dense, containing lots of information in a relatively compressed form, which makes it difficult to absorb the main ideas. Or the logic and structure of the reading may be obscure, so that you have a hard time following the author's argument from one paragraph to the next. Some readings will be challenging in all these ways at once.

When you're faced with reading something complex, here are some strategies that experienced readers use:

1. **Pre-read.** Begin by getting an overview of the material. Scan the reading quickly to get a sense of the components and structure of this text before delving into the details. Once you have the gist of this reading, it will be easier to make sense of the details. It will often also be easier to determine which sections are most important and require the most attention.

2. **Cross-reference.** Most students think you need to read every sentence sequentially. But sophisticated readers will occasionally flip back to retrace the line of argument or jump ahead to see if something introduced here is developed more later. By moving back and forth in the text, you will be able to see more quickly how all the pieces fit together.

3. **Reread.** Some things will be intelligible on the first read; many others won't. For those more complex readings, it will be necessary to go back over especially dense or confusing passages. Sometimes, even individual sentences need to be taken apart or parsed, digested phrase by phrase, and then reassembled. All this requires reading more slowly and deliberately; you can't skim difficult material and expect to get much out of it.

4. **Outline and find key terms.** Be sure to attend to titles, headings, and words that are highlighted, underlined, or italicized. Authors use these features to structure their writing and highlight key points (just as I have done in this book). If you pay attention to these signposts, you will track the author's ideas more easily.
5. **Underline and make notes.** Not every sentence is equally important. If you highlight the main points, it will be easier to find what you need when you review the reading or want to quote it in something you're writing.
6. **Look it up.** College reading assignments often include unfamiliar words and concepts. If you feel that you are understanding most of it, that may be okay. But if you're feeling lost, it's time to identify the unfamiliar key words and concepts and to look them up in an appropriate reference.
7. **Read self-reflectively.** Deep readers are constantly questioning how well they're understanding things as they read. Some of the questions might include:
   A. What don't I understand about this? What exactly makes it confusing or unclear?
   B. Is this similar to anything I've read or heard about in the past?
   C. Does this reading contribute to my understanding of anything else I've been learning, either in this course or somewhere else?

Some readers even ask themselves these questions aloud (probably not a good strategy if you're in a library, though).

These strategies will be helpful in all kinds of reading but can be especially useful with textbooks. In college, as in high school, you'll find that many courses have a required textbook. These books by their nature tend to be fairly dense—the whole goal is to pack a lot of information into a relatively small number of pages. Absorbing all that material is difficult; it helps if you do some pre-reading to get the overview of a chapter, pay attention to the headings, summaries, and underlined words, and move back and forth in the text when some passage isn't clear.

Questions for Critical Reading

Apart from these general strategies, college-level reading will require you to *ask questions about the author, the text itself, and the larger world reflected in this particular piece of writing (context).* This is what it means to move from a superficial understanding to a deeper and more critical grasp of your reading. Here are the key questions you'll want to ask about virtually everything you read:

Who is this author? The words on the page don't come out of nowhere, belonging to no one in particular. They constitute some particular person's voice. So the first thing you need to ask about every piece of writing is, "*Who's talking to me through this text? What do we know about this author?*"[1] Information can include professional affiliation, credentials, personal experiences, and the period in which the author lived.

Sometimes, what you learn about authors will color the way you read their words. Consider how you would approach "A Frank Statement to Cigarette Smokers" in a 1954 newspaper by the Tobacco Industry Research Committee and "Systematic Effects of Smoking" in *Chest*, a peer-reviewed medical journal by the American College of Chest Physicians.[2] Both are about the effects of smoking on human health, but they make widely different claims, presumably because these articles were produced by two different groups with very different agendas.[3] Savvy readers know to ask themselves, "What relationship does this author have to this subject?" Here's a sample text to consider:

Nelson Mandela, *Conversations with Myself* (2010)

There are stages when one in a position of authority has to go . . . public to commit the organisation. If you want to take an action and you are convinced that this is a correct action, you do so and confront that situation. You have to *carefully* choose the opportunity and make sure that history would be on your side. . . . We discussed it [the decision to form MK, the armed wing of the African National Congress] because when Comrade Walter was going overseas, in 1953, I then said to him, "When you reach the People's Republic of China, you must tell them, ask them, that we want to start an armed struggle and get arms." . . . I made a speech in Sophiatown. I was pulled up for this but I remained convinced that this was the correct strategy for us. And then when I was underground I then discussed the matter with Comrade Walter and we decided to *raise* it at a meeting of the Working Committee. We raised the matter but . . . I was dismissed very cheaply, because . . . the secretary of the Party . . . [argued that] the time had not come for that.[4]

To understand this selection, it helps to know that Nelson Mandela was a leader of the African National Congress (ANC), which spearheaded the struggle for the rights of Black people in South Africa during the era of apartheid. It also helps to know that Mandela and the ANC began with a commitment to nonviolence but chose to support violent resistance in response to the actions of the white South African government. This selection is taken from Mandela's memoir, in which he recounts his own leadership in this movement and how he came to change his views about the best strategy for effecting political change. Notice that you don't need to know all of Mandela's biography to make sense of this text. You only need to know certain key aspects of his life that are pertinent to the particular issues discussed in this selection. If this were a selection about his personal life, the relevant biographical fact about him might be that he married three times and divorced twice.

Whenever you read anything, ask yourself:

- Who is the author? What elements of his or her life are pertinent to the subject of this text?
- What is this person's relationship to the subject they are writing about?
- What might have motivated this person to write this text?

- How might this author's personal history have influenced the perspective or argument advanced by this text?

What are the features of this text? Sophisticated readers pay attention to the characteristics of each piece of writing they read. You have all done this, though maybe unconsciously. Think about how your reading changes between a newspaper editorial, a textbook, a poem, and a checklist. But critical readers go a step further and ask themselves, "*What do the specific features of this text tell me about what it means, what its purpose is, and how I should read it*?" The techniques speakers and writers use to inform, persuade, or motivate others is called "rhetoric," and the forms of rhetoric have been studied since ancient times. When we attend to the rhetorical features of a text, we notice how those elements support the author's message.

There is no way to include here all the rhetorical strategies you will encounter in college readings, but here is an example that will help you focus on how the form of a text contains clues that help you interpret it. Sometimes the form of a document signals something about the purpose for which it was written, like this excerpt:

Seneca Falls Women's Rights Convention, Resolutions (1848)

Resolved, That woman has too long rested satisfied in the circumscribed limits which corrupt customs and a perverted application of the Scriptures have marked out for her, and that it is time she should move in the enlarged sphere which her great Creator has assigned her.

Resolved, That it is the duty of the women of this country to secure to themselves their sacred right to the elective franchise.

Resolved, That the equality of human rights results necessarily from the fact of the identity of the race in capabilities and responsibilities.

Resolved, therefore, That, being invested by the Creator with the same capabilities, and the same consciousness of responsibility for their exercise, it is demonstrably the right and duty of woman, equally with man, to promote every righteous cause, by every righteous means; and especially in regard to the great subjects of morals and religion, it

> is self-evidently her right to participate with her brother in teaching them, both in private and in public, by writing and by speaking, by any instrumentalities proper to be used, and in any assemblies proper to be held; and this being a self-evident truth, growing out of the divinely implanted principles of human nature, any custom or authority adverse to it, whether modern or wearing the hoary sanction of antiquity, is to be regarded as self-evident falsehood, and at war with the interests of mankind.[5]

The repetition of the word *resolved* at the beginning of each statement signals that this is a declaration of principles, a manifesto. Its authors (a group of women and men) intend to make a case and to persuade a hesitant audience, and so this declaration is cast in a form that emphasizes a series of key assertions. Since people don't generally write declarations if they think people already agree, we can infer that these declarations are controversial, at least that they were at the time this was written. Of course, it would be helpful to know more about the individual authors and the convention context, but there is already much that you can infer just from the form of the text.

Here is another example to consider:

Fran Landesman, "Come with Me"

Come with me, go with me, burn with me, glow with me,
Write me a sonnet or two
Sleep with me, wake with me, give with me, take with me
Love me the way I love you.

Let me get high with you, laugh with you, cry with you,
Be with you when I am blue
Rest with you, fight with you, day with you, night with you,
Love me whatever I do.

Work with me, play with me, run with me, stay with me
Make me your partner in crime
Handle me, fondle me, cradle me tenderly
Say I'm your reason and rhyme

Pray with me, sin with me, lose with me, win with me
Love me with all of my scars
Rise with me, fall with me, hide from it all with me,
Nothing is mine now, it's ours.[6]

When a piece of writing makes use of repeated formal features, such as repeated words or phrases, parallelism, metaphor, alliteration, or grammatical structures, always ask yourself:

- What is the author drawing our attention to through these formal structures?
- How might this particular form of writing be a clue to the author's purpose?
- How does the style in which this is written help convey the author's message?

Is specialized language being used? Another challenge of college-level reading involves specialized language. All of us sometimes encounter words we don't know. In college, this will be a regular occurrence, but you will also come across familiar words that have gained a new, more technical or specific meaning. Those words will have an ordinary use and then a very particular definition that won't be immediately obvious. Sometimes, these new definitions will be the whole point of the reading. When you come across specialized language of this sort, you'll need to consult a dictionary or find other articles by the same author to see if that word is explained there.

Here is an example from the world of economics:

Congressional Testimony on the Costs of Rapidly Growing Government Debt

Yesterday (November 20, 2019) I testified at the Committee on the Budget of the House of Representatives. John Yarmuth chaired, and Steve Womack was the ranking member. The Committee titled the hearing "Reexamining the Economic Costs of Debt." I reported that a fiscal consolidation plan which reduced debt to GDP would lead to an immediate and permanent increase in real GDP.

This reexamination implies the need for a credible fiscal consolidation strategy. Under such a strategy spending would still grow, but at a slower rate than GDP, thereby reducing debt as a share of GDP compared with current projections. Such a fiscal strategy would greatly benefit the American economy. It would also reduce the risk of the debt spiraling up. This conclusion is robust.

In the 1970s the United States imposed wage and price controls and the Fed helped finance the federal deficit by creating money. The result was a terrible economy with unemployment and inflation both rising. This ended when money growth was reduced in the late 1970s and early 1980s. It is an example where poor economic reasoning led to poor economic policy and poor economic performance. It was reversed when good economics again prevailed, and policy changed.[7]

Notice that this passage contains a lot of words you're likely familiar with, such as *fiscal*, *consolidation*, and *plan*, but here these are combined into a technical concept in economics that you would need to investigate if you wanted to understand the author's point. Similarly, *wage and price controls*, *GDP*, and even *inflation* may mean something quite specific to economists that wouldn't be immediately obvious to the general reader.

When you come across words that you've never seen before or that seem to mean something different from what you'd expect, always ask yourself:

- Which words or phrases are obscure to me, and where can I look to find out what they mean in this context?
- Once I have looked up the words I don't know, can I paraphrase the passage in a way that makes sense to me?

What is the historical context? Knowing something about the historical context in which something was written is almost always relevant to understanding the purpose or meaning of the writing. This is obviously the case with texts that were created in response to a specific historical event, for example Lenin's letter to American workers during the Bolshevik Revolution.[8] But it is no less true when you read something like "Little Boxes," a song written by Malvina Reynolds in 1962 and made famous by the folk singer Pete Seeger:

Little Boxes
Little boxes on the hillside,
Little boxes made of ticky tacky,
Little boxes on the hillside,
Little boxes all the same;
There's a green one and a pink one
And a blue one and a yellow one
And they're all made out of ticky tacky
And they all look just the same.
And the people in the houses
All went to the university,
Where they were put in boxes
And they came out all the same,
And there's doctors and there's lawyers
And business executives,
And they're all made out of ticky tacky
And they all look just the same.[9]

The words of the song are entirely understandable on their own. But the true, underlying purpose of this piece is to satirize the rapid growth of suburbia in the 1950s and '60s. Such growth was possible because of prefabricated housing, which was easy to construct and cost-effective but resulted in neighborhoods filled with houses that looked virtually identical. The idea that houses were made of "ticky-tacky" is a reference to the cheap, second-rate building materials that were used. Reynolds then uses the uniform, low-quality character of the houses as a metaphor for all the people who inhabit them—"doctors and lawyers and business executives"—who were also turned out by universities in cookie-cutter fashion. Knowing the historical context of the lyrics, namely suburban housing developments, is key to understanding what the songwriter is critiquing and why.

When you're reading something that alludes to people, events, movements, or ideas, always ask yourself:

- How much background information do I know about this piece? Does it feel like I'm missing something critical?
- What events, ideas, or other forces have shaped the perspective of the author?
- Where does the author stand within the debates of his or her time?

Who is the intended audience? Sometimes, authors explicitly write to a very specific audience; at other times, the intended audience isn't obvious. For many academic writers, that audience might be colleagues in their academic discipline, who can be assumed to have a good deal of background in the subject. By contrast, textbooks are written for students whom the author can assume are learning a subject for the first time. Sometimes, the audience is specific to a certain publication. Readers of the *New York Times*, for example, tend to be more liberal than those who read the *Wall Street Journal*. Popular songs, on the other hand, are written for a broad, general audience. Sometimes, of course, an author may have more than one potential audience in mind. As a reader, you should always be on the lookout for any and all potential audiences of the readings you are assigned.

Many times, the readings you will be assigned are scholarly works originally intended for a group of experts in a specific field of study. Consider the following abstract of a scientific article:

Title: Relationship between Diet and Mental Health in a Young Adult Appalachian College Population

Abstract: Young adults in Appalachia may face poor nutritional status due to low access to healthy food and high mental health symptoms attributed to high stress and the college environment. A cross-sectional design was used to investigate the relationship between diet intake and mental health status of this population via surveys. Participant responses (*n* = 1956) showed students' mean number of depressed days over the past 30 days was 9.67 ± 8.80, and of anxious days, 14.1 ± 10.03. The mean fruit and vegetable intake was 1.80 ± 1.27 times per day and the mean added sugars intake was 1.79 ± 1.26 times per day. 36.7% of students were found to be food insecure. One-way ANOVA and Chi-Squared analyses were used to determine relationships between variables. Significant variables were placed into a full logistic regression model. Food insecurity and fruit and vegetable intake remained significant predictors of depression in males (odds ratio (OR) = 2.33 95% CI 1.47–3.71 and OR = 68 95% CI 50–89, respectively) and in females food insecurity remained a significant predictor of depression (OR = 2.26 95% CI 1.67–3.07). Food insecurity and added sugars intake were significant predictor [*sic*] of anxiety in males (OR = 2.33 95% CI 1.47–3.71 and OR = 1.09 95% CI 0.91–1.3, respectively) and for anxiety in females, added sugars intake and food insecurity were significant predictors (OR = 1.18 95% CI 1.05–1.32 and OR = 1.65 95% CI 1.27–2.16, respectively). Improving college student's [*sic*] diet intake through increased access to healthy foods could improve the mental health and well-being of students.[10]

This sort of text obviously assumes that the audience knows a good deal about methods of scientific analysis. As I said above, when you come across highly technical language, you may need to do some research on terms like *cross-sectional design*, *one-way ANOVA*, *chi-squared*, and *logistic regression*. But it helps that reports of scientific studies like this always follow a set format; knowing what these elements are will help you to quickly and accurately ascertain the most important components of the study and its findings. All scientific abstracts include the following elements:

- topic;
- research questions;
- methods;
- findings; and
- conclusions.

If you look for these elements, you should quickly be able to discern which question(s) the authors were asking, how they went about answering those questions, what they concluded, and what sorts of follow-up studies might be important to extend this research or answer new questions that emerged in the course of the study. Reading material written for an audience with far more background knowledge than you have doesn't need to be frustrating if you know what you're looking for and where in the abstract (and the article that follows) you can find it.

Whenever you read something, consider who the author's intended audience is.

- What assumptions are behind this piece of writing? In particular, what does the author assume that his or her audience knows or needs to know?
- What subgroups of people might have a particular interest in this writing (racial, cultural, religious, or professional groups, people of certain gender identities, sexual orientations, or socio-economic status)?
- How might the intended audience have influenced the author's message, tone, word choice, use of a particular idiom, or other aspects of the writing?
- How might it change the way you read something if you knew that the author never meant for it to be published (for example, a personal diary or letters to an intimate friend)?

What is the purpose? It's significantly easier to interpret a piece of writing when we know the author's purpose. While there are far too many different motivations to cover in this section, here are a few of the most common reasons why authors choose to put the pen to the page:

1. Sharing Information
   Much of what you read in college, especially in textbooks, is designed simply to convey information in the most direct and efficient way possible. When that information is new or complex, the challenge will be to comprehend and remember it.
2. Explanation/Theory
   Some selections will do more than provide information; they will attempt to explain why things exist or function the way they do. In these cases, the facts are embedded in some theory that explains those facts in terms of more abstract or general principles. The challenge here is to grasp the explanation and understand how the theory explains these facts.
3. Social or Political Commentary
   Many writers are attempting to make us see current events or social trends through their point of view. Sometimes, such commentary is designed to cast events or people in a particular light, frequently using openly laudatory or barbed language. Other times, authors' biases are more subtle, as when they omit arguments made by the opposing side. The challenge in reading this sort of material is to identify the author's assumptions so you can evaluate for yourself whether you agree with their assessment of the current state of affairs.
4. Inspiration/Motivation
   Many pieces are designed to motivate or inspire their audience. Often, this kind of writing includes language that encourages people to overcome obstacles or to focus on distant goals, emphasizing the righteousness of a particular cause or the inevitability of success. The challenge in reading such pieces is

that you need to try to inhabit the mindset of both the audience and the writer, feeling each of their respective motivations.

When you're reading, be sure to ask yourself:

- What is this piece of writing intended to accomplish? What appear to be the author's goals?
- How might these goals affect your stance in relationship to this writing? Am I being asked to passively take in the information provided, to evaluate the strengths of the author's argument, or to allow the author's passion to move me to action?

Exercise. For each of the following types of written texts, select what you believe the main purpose is—sharing information, explanation/theory, social or political commentary, inspiration/motivation:

1. your high school chemistry textbook
2. Martin Luther King's "I Have a Dream" speech
3. a newspaper editorial
4. a poster in a doctor's office demonstrating the signs of a stroke
5. Gordon Allport's 1954 paper in which he first laid out his intergroup contact hypothesis

Reading Visual Images

While language is the primary medium for communicating information and ideas, we also convey and absorb lots of information visually. Consider images in advertising or on websites, the logos used by companies, and the posters created to promote events. Like words, images can inform, persuade, incite, inspire, and explain. They can also be visually pleasing or disturbing, simple or complex, realistic or fantastical. Consider the following image, which I found on a website without any indication of its purpose.[11]

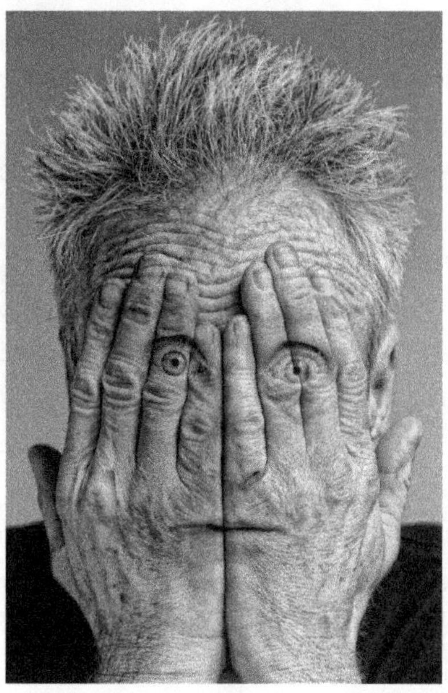

The components of this picture—a human face and human hands—are completely recognizable, of course, but here they have been superimposed and merged into a composite image to create a surrealistic effect. While we all cover our face with our hands at times, in this image, the face remains visible, so the hands become part of the face (or the face becomes part of the hands). The image is arresting precisely because it portrays something both familiar and impossible. As you ponder the meaning of such an image, keep in mind that it may not be possible to decode all of this image's potential meanings.

When you encounter a visual image, here are some questions you can ask:

- Who created this? What do we know about that person, their life, and their work?
- Who was the intended audience?

- What is the historical or physical context in which this image was created and/or displayed?
- What was the purpose or intent of the creator of this image?
- What are the most prominent features of this image?
- What feelings does this image evoke for you?
- Does the image cause you to rethink some aspect of your experience, in this case, the experience of covering your face with your hands?
- Is there anything symbolic in the image? What do those symbols represent, and how are they being used here (e.g., in typical or novel ways)?

There may not be a definitive interpretation of what an image is meant to convey or what reaction it aims to elicit from its viewers. But as you examine it more closely, you will notice details that might have escaped you at first, much as you do when you read a text over and over. The more time you spend looking at visual materials, the more adept you will become at observing their components and discerning why their creators chose such a composition.

Special Considerations for Internet Reading

Much of your reading is done on the Internet, unlike that of earlier generations of college students. While this gives you access to practically infinite information, it comes with a major challenge—assessing the accuracy of the information you find online. Because anyone can create a website or blog, you don't know immediately if the material you find is reliable, someone's uninformed opinion, or even an attempt to deceive you.

Recent research has shown that most students—and even some professors—are surprisingly bad at distinguishing fact from fiction on the Internet.[12] Fortunately, these same studies offer us some simple strategies for evaluating the truthfulness of what we find on the web.

Read laterally. Most people know that information found on a website can be misleading, so they will look for signs of bias in what they're reading. But think about it. If the question is whether this site is accurate and reliable, we aren't going to determine that just by looking at what's on the site, especially if the subject we're investigating is new to us (which is often why we went searching for this site in the first place). We can only determine the value of what we're looking at by looking at other sources of information that shed some light on this one.

So the first and most important way to evaluate the reliability of a site is to open other pages that tell us something about the organization or author that is the source of this primary site. For example, if the website appears to be official and to be providing objective information on a subject, open another search on that organization and then another on the names of the people who are mentioned on this site as its founders, officers, or promoters. This will often lead you to additional information not found on the first site, such as if the organization promotes a certain industry or supports a particular political agenda. You might think of this as the rough equivalent of checking references, which is done routinely by employers. You don't just assume that what someone tells you is the truth and the whole truth; you look to other sources of information that provide some background and context.

Look beyond the window dressing. Most of us are easily taken in by the look and feel of a website. If it looks professional, if the URL ends in .org, if it includes people with the title of Dr., or if it lists universities as partners or sponsors, then it must be reputable.

However, this is basically the same as trusting someone because they wear impressive clothes or because they sound like they know what they're talking about. Looks and sounds can be deceiving, especially on the Internet. In fact, if you think about it, anyone using a website to disseminate misleading or false information would want to make it look and sound as authentic and official as possible. So when you investigate a topic online, remind yourself that not everything you encounter should be taken at face value.

Seek out multiple sources. When you rely too heavily on a single source of information—whether on the Internet or elsewhere—you risk losing a critical perspective on the topic. This is especially the case in controversial issues—how would you even know it was controversial if you didn't read material composed by someone with a dissenting view? To get a fuller understanding of something, you need to look at a variety of sources. You then need to evaluate if those sources are skewed in some way or if the information they provide is reliable. Otherwise, you could just be collecting a range of biased sources, mistakenly believing that you were learning something valuable.

It follows from this that you should avoid clicking on just the first links that show up in an Internet search, which are the ones the search engine's algorithm has determined are most relevant to the words you searched for. Your goal in doing research isn't to look at the most popular or frequently searched sources of information but to look critically at numerous sources of information. This isn't to say that those top results are invariably disreputable and untrustworthy; they often contain valuable information. The key point here is just that it's impossible to glean the full spectrum of information on a topic from one or two sources.

Be aware of your own biases. When we investigate an issue, we almost never do so from a completely neutral stance. We have preferences and beliefs, assumptions and prejudices that influence how we take in and evaluate information. Many studies have shown that when we are presented with information that confirms what we already think, we assume it is true. By contrast, when we are faced with challenging evidence or arguments, we tend to be far more skeptical—or even to dismiss them out of hand. Psychologists call this "confirmation bias"; that is, we tend to trust information that confirms the biases we already have.[13]

One important element of becoming a critical thinker—and not just when we do Internet searches—is to bring some self-awareness to our preexisting views. If we do research with a predisposition to believe (or disbelieve) certain things, we are by default less likely to scrutinize the credibility of the content we find. As a result, we are least inclined to reference check a source precisely when we most need to. Cultivating greater self-awareness can reduce our chances of trusting a source just because we already agree with its message.

Run a reality check. The world is full of hoaxes and utterly unfounded conspiracy theories, many of which are spread through websites and social media that purport to be conveying news. For example, the website Infowars has spread the conspiracy theory that the Sandy Hook Elementary School shooting in December 2012 was staged by "crisis actors" interested in promoting anti-gun legislation (Alex Jones, the creator of Infowars, subsequently was found guilty of defamation and was forced to pay damages to the families, a ruling that resulted in the eventual bankruptcy of the website). Other common examples include conspiracy theories about the assassination of President Kennedy and the idea that the government intentionally caused the AIDS epidemic as a way to attack the African American community.

To be sure, outrageous things sometimes happen. But if you read something online that sounds preposterous, it probably is. At the very least, it should immediately raise your suspicion that someone might have an agenda to promote and that the supposed "news" is entirely fictitious. The more outlandish something sounds, the more you should activate your critical-thinking skills. And that means you want to investigate the author or source of this news, the reputation of that person or organization, whether the evidence supports the story, and who, if anyone, has fact-checked it.

When gathering information from the Internet, always ask yourself:

- What is the evidence for the claims that are made?
- Who is behind the information?
- What do other sources say?

In a world where anyone can claim anything and publicize that claim across the globe instantaneously, you need to take steps to protect yourself from being misinformed, or worse yet, being duped.

Conclusion

Reading, especially reading anything that is difficult, complex, or ambiguous, is demanding. It requires attending to key words, historical context, structure, and the author's purpose, among many other elements. As you tackle more and more reading assignments in college, you will improve your ability to analyze dense and unfamiliar writing, provided that you implement the techniques I've laid out in this chapter.

All this, of course, will require putting in a lot of time. You might well ask, Why bother? If I can get a basic grasp of something by reading superficially, what's the added benefit of all this extra work?

There are several answers to this question. First, reading is the way you engage with others' ideas. Reading what they have written closely and carefully shows that you are taking them and their ideas seriously. It's the way you demonstrate respect for others, including people with whom you disagree. In fact, if you disagree with them, it is especially important that you read their work carefully, since you might then come to understand and appreciate their point of view.

In addition, reading is one of the primary ways by which we take in information about the world around us. In college, you will be presented with vast amounts of new information that will expand and even transform your understanding of yourself, the natural world, society, and history. Reading that material in a cursory way will give you a cursory understanding of these things; reading more carefully will give you a more nuanced appreciation of the world around you.

Finally, reading critically is key to thinking critically. When you read with a questioning mind, you are really doing much more than trying to understand the words on the page (or the screen). You are seeing through that text to a world of meanings, contexts, questions, and implications that have both produced that piece of writing and will be generated by it. The text is no longer just an inert set of words but a window that enables you to see something in a new way and then to connect what you have seen with other things you have seen through other windows or texts. Developing a mind that is both open and critical, receptive and analytical, is among the most important benefits of a college education. And that is possible only by developing your skills as a critical reader.

Questions for Reflection

1. What sorts of reading do you find easiest? Hardest? Why?
2. What do you typically do when you read something that you don't understand? Skip over it? Reread it? Underline or make notes about it? Go to a reference book (e.g., dictionary) to look up unfamiliar words?
3. How do you interact with the text? Do you make annotations? Do you highlight? What kinds of annotations do you write down? Why do you think that helps? Are there any other ways you could interact with the text?
4. Have you ever made a conscious effort to become a better reader? What did you do? What could you do?
5. Try an experiment: the next time you're assigned to read something challenging, make a list of questions about everything you don't understand. After you finish the assignment, look over your questions and then reread the assignment with those questions in mind. Answer any of them that you can, even if you're not sure your answers are right.
6. Extra credit: try reading something deeply. As you come across words you don't know, look them up. When the author refers to an idea or person or place that isn't familiar, use your favorite search engine to learn more. If the author footnotes the same book or article two or three times (i.e., it seems like an important source for this reading), track down that source, and read it too.

ADVICE FOR THE ROAD AHEAD

Cultivate Curiosity

Curiosity—the desire to know something—is at the heart of all learning. It is the engine that drives us, pushing us to pursue a question or a problem, even a difficult one.

As children, we are naturally curious about the world around us. We constantly ask questions: Why is the sky blue? What does *sarcastic* mean? How does a car work? But for many of us, as we get older, we learn most of what we need to function in the world and no longer investigate everything we encounter for the first time. We have other priorities, and so asking and answering more questions feels less urgent.

As college students, though, you need to tap into that innate, childlike wonder once again. College can open you up to the intricacies and complexities of the world across a range of subjects, from the way atomic particles behave to the way societies are formed to the way individuals grow. Of course, few people are equally curious about all the subjects they're exposed to in college. And in general, college encourages you to focus a significant part of your work in an area, a major, that you choose, presumably because it's a subject you find interesting.

But you'll always have to take some classes in subjects you don't find fascinating. In these instances, the challenge is to stretch your imagination, to move beyond the initial "This is so boring" response and tap into your natural sense of wonder. Most often, this requires getting past the question "What do I need to know this for?" Instead of focusing solely on the practical application of this particular subject, focus on the intrinsic complexity and mystery of the topic. Allow yourself to notice what is peculiar or unexpected (like how we can't determine the location and speed of atomic particles at the same time). Take a broader view of something familiar so you can see it in a new light (like how social institutions such as marriage are not as stable over time as we usually suppose). Focus on what is extraordinary about even the most ordinary events (like how a child learns to walk).

If you can awaken your natural curiosity, even about those subjects that seem on the surface to be disconnected from your interests, you will enjoy your classes more and rediscover what every child knows: if you really pay close attention to the world around you, everything is amazing in its own way. If you have any doubts, just talk with someone who is fascinated by subjects that don't generally excite you. Cultivate your curiosity, and you will discover how much you have in common with people who are passionate about entirely different things. If you delve deeply enough, chances are you'll discover that there's more there to engage your curiosity than you had previously imagined. In that sense, curiosity isn't only natural. It's contagious.

CHAPTER SIX

Writing Well Is Thinking Well

Writing is both a process of doing critical thinking and a product that communicates the results of critical thinking.

—JOHN BEAN

Outline

In this chapter, you will learn how to approach writing as an integral part of your thinking process. When you approach writing as an opportunity to join a conversation—both with your audience and with others who have written about your topic—you will think more clearly, communicate more effectively, and enjoy it more.

■ ■ ■

Writing Is a Process of Refining Your Thinking

In writing this book, I faced several obstacles. I tried to synthesize the most important insights from teaching and advising students for forty years. I attempted to summarize succinctly the work of scholars in a number of fields, such as critical thinking, writing, and quantitative reasoning, in which I myself am not an expert. I needed to open to the (sometimes contradictory) advice of colleagues and students and then to decide what I thought the book needed to address in detail, what topics I could mention in passing, and what issues were simply outside the scope of what I could incorporate. I also needed to select examples and provide exercises that would illustrate the points I wanted to make. And I struggled to determine the best order of the chapters and the Advice for the Road Ahead pieces to ensure that the book flowed smoothly, without presuming that you would read this book from cover to cover.

While these challenges are unique in some respects to my experience and goals for this project, in other ways they are common to every writing project, whether you're a first-year college student or a senior faculty member. Writing is always about deciding what we think about a topic, which of those thoughts are worth sharing, and how best to share them, given the audience we're trying to reach. Rarely are the answers to these things immediately obvious. We work our way toward answers slowly, often laboriously, in fits and starts. We start off in one direction and then change course; we frequently change our minds about what we think just in the process of trying to write it down. We get feedback on a draft and discover that something we thought was clear actually isn't, which sends us back to the drawing board. This is what makes writing difficult and sometimes frustrating. But it also underscores just how much writing and revising (repeatedly) are essential to our own thinking process. In my case, it means that the book you are reading today is vastly different from the one I began working on years ago.

Here's the main point: writing well is not only a matter of creating a final product that captures our understanding of a topic accurately and effectively. *Writing is also a process of making sense of things, of discerning what you know and deciding how to organize your thoughts. Writing is not just something you do after you have finished thinking about a subject; it is integral to your thinking itself.*

All the knowledge in the world won't do you much good if you can't communicate it effectively. And while there are many modes of communication—images, charts and graphs, mathematical formulae, artistic media—the most common form of academic communication for most disciplines remains prose, or ordinary descriptive language (like this chapter). In addition to speaking, it is also the form of communication that you will use most often throughout your life to communicate your ideas, plans, and goals. This is why most colleges require a writing course, or some other way to assess and improve your writing skills.

Three Main Stages of the Writing Process

As I indicated above, the thinking/writing process has three components: deciding what you think, what you want to say, and how you want to say it. Be aware, though, that as you work on any writing assignment, you may cycle through these steps several times, and not always in this sequence. In the remainder of this chapter, I'll discuss these elements of the writing process in greater detail.

I. Writing to Figure Out What You Think

> As writing theorists often note, writing is generally not a process in which we start with a fully formed idea in our heads that we then simply transcribe in an unchanged state onto the page. On the contrary, writing is more often a means of discovery in which we use the writing process to figure out what our idea is.
>
> —GERALD GRAFF AND CATHY BIRKENSTEIN[1]

Experienced writers know how helpful it is to "write early and write often."[2] Rather than assuming you need to have figured out exactly what you want to say before you begin writing, it is far more productive to begin writing—recording information, ideas (even half-baked ones), questions for further investigation, and even tentative conclusions—as you go. There are several reasons for this.

First, *writing is a generative, creative process that yields new lines of thinking.* It is well-established that the act of writing itself stimulates your thinking.[3] As you put your thoughts into words, your brain is working to give those thoughts a concrete (verbal) form, and those words will be associated with other words, which will prompt your brain to generate other thoughts, and so on.

Second, *writing makes your thinking visible.* By externalizing your thoughts, writing enables you to see your thinking process in real time, as it unfolds. In this sense, writing at each stage of your thought process helps you track and retrace your thinking. You can go back and look at the path your thinking took you down and more easily notice where you may have hit a dead end or failed to develop an idea fully.

Finally, *writing helps you structure and clarify your thinking.* One of the challenges of writing a college paper is putting your ideas together in a coherent way. At times, you may feel as though you are trying to assemble a jigsaw puzzle with a thousand small pieces—only some of which fit together—but with no sense of what the completed picture is supposed to be. Writing those thoughts down can sometimes help you see connections that you didn't notice when all that information was just in your head.

At this early stage in the process, it is important to think and write freely, without judgment or self-censorship. This can be much harder than it sounds. Many of us are accustomed to feeling that what we put down on paper (or type into our computers) needs to be right. But when you postpone writing until you have completely worked out everything in your head, you end up stifling your creativity; you also make the writing process much more onerous and challenging. It's unrealistic to expect yourself to be able to put your thoughts together on paper in a way that is coherent, comprehensive, and clear on the very first attempt.

Free Writing

In this sense, writing prose should be like writing music. Composers generally don't wait until they have a fully formed musical score in their heads before they begin writing it down. They begin with a musical idea, perhaps no more than a short segment of a melody, which they write down in this raw form. Then they can continue playing with it—revising and refining it, adding to it, figuring out the instrumentation, adding the lyrics and harmonies—until they're satisfied. Your writing should be like that—provisional and playful, an extended, open-ended process. *Writing as a tool for thinking should be a very low-stakes activity.*

Writing instructors often call this process "free writing" to denote that this is a stage in which you want to unleash your creativity. Here are some practical suggestions for free writing:

- Familiarize yourself with the assignment before you begin writing. Read over the professor's instructions a few times. Note the key elements of the assignment and any parameters they have given you. Often, the assignment prompt or rubric will focus your thoughts in a particular way or caution you against moving in certain directions.
- Give your subconscious some time to start digesting the topic and generating thoughts. Don't underestimate the value of just musing and then jotting down a few key words, themes, or sources that will serve as guideposts for further thinking. Continue musing—drawing together what you know on this topic, what you've read, what the professor has presented in lectures—and then jot down more notes and partially developed

ideas. (Note: this is not to suggest that you procrastinate but rather that you dive right in as soon as you begin to have even half-baked ideas.)

- Some students also find it helpful to review their notes, especially if they have notes that are closely related to the topic of their paper. This can be a good way to remind yourself of issues previously discussed in this course or questions you had about that material, which often generates new ideas you can use as springboards.
- To jump-start the free-writing process, give yourself a set amount of time (maybe ten to fifteen minutes) to write down all your thoughts on a subject. Keep writing, without self-judgment, until you feel you have put down everything you can think of. The key here is to approach this in a carefree, playful spirit, without self-censorship. Then gather more information, take more notes, do more musing, and try more free writing. Continue until some of the thoughts begin to coalesce and you feel you are ready to begin outlining and writing your paper (see following section).

Here is an example of one student's free writing about how the media portray human-robot interactions:

> Human-robot trust relationships is a theme I'm interested in. . . . But how can I add something new to the conversation?
>
> I could incorporate analysis methods of media studies more generally, but how would that relate to human-robot interaction? We've talked a lot about people's attitudes toward technology this quarter. . . . Where could I find source material that touches on people's attitudes about the trustworthiness of robots? People reviewing robot movies likely have something to say on this matter . . . but what about the people making the movies themselves? Aren't all filmmakers somehow suggesting their own views when they make movies—producers of robot movies must make choices in representing their films' robots that could reflect the message they intend to convey about whether robots are trustworthy and what makes them so—maybe instead of

> reviewers' ideas I could analyze films to see what the filmmakers' salient intuitions are about human-robot trust relationships. . . . I would need to compare these attitudes with scientific literature, though, so my paper is based in empirical evidence and accepted data and not just a speculation about what non-scientists think. . . . Maybe I can compare the attitudes of the filmmakers (via analysis of whether or not they intended their robots to be trustworthy and the traits/characteristics they used to signal this) to the existing scientific literature about human-robot trust relationships to see if the natural intuitions people have about what makes robots trustworthy actually line up with the criteria that studies have proven to factor into people's judgements.

This student's free writing illustrates the way in which "thinking through writing" can help clarify and focus your thoughts. She begins with a general topic, "human-robot trust relationships," which she knows she wants to explore through films. This leads to a series of questions and musings—about where she might look for additional information relevant to this topic (in film reviews, in the reflections of filmmakers, in scientific literature) and then to some questions that might be worth pursuing (comparing the attitudes of filmmakers to the scientific literature). After this kind of exercise, she was able to begin gathering the material she needed to pursue this topic and then to pull it together into a paper.

The value of this sort of approach to writing is that it enables you to pull together your ideas gradually and to see where you are in the process at every point along the way. Before you begin to get invested in one very specific plan, you can let things remain fluid for a while and see where your writing leads you.

As you begin a writing project, always ask yourself:

- Do I clearly understand what the writing assignment is asking of me?
- What do I find surprising/interesting/contradictory about this topic?

- What is beginning to emerge—a focus of inquiry, a cluster of ideas, an organizational structure—as I gather information, take notes, muse, and review what I have written?
- What stage of the writing process am I at right now?
- Am I ready to move on to the next stage? Have I done enough background research? Have I organized my thoughts before beginning to write a draft?

Exercise. Now that you've seen an example of a student's free writing, it's your turn to practice. Set a five-minute timer and write as much as you can about your favorite hobby. Write as if you were trying to convince a stranger to make this activity their favorite hobby, too. Have fun with it!

II. Writing to Communicate What You Want to Say

Gathering Your Thoughts

Once you have settled on what you initially think about your topic, it's time to decide what you're going to say about it. Of all the thoughts you have generated, only some will make it into the paper you write. Moreover, the order of your points in the paper may be different from the order in which they occurred to you. For example, you might have jumped from point A to point X while free writing, but your reader wasn't involved in that messy, open-ended exploration of the topic—and they don't want to be! *Your reader wants a clear, coherent, well-organized presentation of your thoughts on the subject.* That's why the key challenge in this stage of writing is one of organization, imposing some order on what might have begun as random and disconnected thoughts.

The first step in doing this is to *keep your audience in mind.* Consider what your audience already knows and what requires explanation. Think about how you can connect your topic to your audience's interests. In most cases, the actual audience for your paper is your instructor; that's likely the only person who will be reading and grading it. But it is generally helpful to imagine your classmates as your audience when you write. If you imagine that you're writing to them—maybe even visualizing them across the desk from you when you sit down at your computer—you will be able to gauge accurately what level of background they have on your subject and also how your subject connects with things already covered in the course. Partly for this reason, some of your professors might even include a peer-review process as part of your assignment. Looking at a classmate's writing often helps them see things they missed, and it also improves your own writing when you imagine a classmate reading it.

But in determining what you're going to say, there's a second, equally important audience to keep in mind: the people who have already written things about this subject. You never write in a vacuum; you've read the products of other people's thoughts, so you need to present your thoughts as being in dialogue with theirs. In fact, organizing your own thoughts is often easier when you consciously consider how your ideas agree with, differ from, build on, modify, or extend the ideas of others.

It follows from this that one of your challenges in college writing is to assemble and engage with other sources—books, articles, data sets, visual materials—basically, whatever is relevant to your subject.[4] (This process will be covered in more detail in chapter 8 on research.) These will generally be the sources you encountered in your courses or those that you found during your research. They will now figure into your presentation in a number of ways:

- as background information that captures what is known about a subject;
- as evidence you will cite to support the thesis, or main point, of your paper; and
- as viewpoints in relation to which you will present your own views.

In each case, you will want to carefully acknowledge the sources that you have used in developing your ideas. This requires you to

- provide accurate citations for all information that you draw upon, and

- clearly distinguish your voice from the voices of others with whom you have been in conversation. (These issues of proper citation and avoiding plagiarism will be dealt with further in chapter 8.)

Formulating Your Thesis

At the core of most academic writing is the formulation of a **thesis**, a succinct statement of the point(s) you want to make, what you came to understand about your subject at the conclusion of your long process of thinking about it. In *Problem-Solving Strategies for Writing*, a thesis is defined as

> an assertion about a topic that you believe to be true and that you intend to support and explain in your paper. If we could follow the thinking process of a writer, we would see that it often follows this path from topic to problem to thesis. Faced with a topic or situation, the writer first looks for a felt difficulty that seems worth thinking about. This leads to a clearer definition of the problem or conflict, which leads to an analysis of that problem, which ends up with some form of conclusion. The conclusion, in turn, becomes a thesis the writer is willing to support.[5]

In an academic context—unlike a casual conversation with friends, perhaps—you will be expected to provide evidence and reasons to support your thesis. *College thinking is about more than just sharing your opinions about a subject. It is about explaining, supporting, and defending those opinions with reference to facts, data, and the views of experts who have studied that subject extensively and carefully.* Your writing, then, needs to capture your best, most careful thinking.

One of the main criticisms that professors make of student writing is that it is purely descriptive, lacking analysis or an overarching thesis. Summarizing a lot of information you have assembled rarely satisfies the requirements of a writing assignment in college, unless you were asked simply to describe a phenomenon or to summarize the views of others without attempting to take a stand or render a judgment. Because critical thinking is at the center of college learning, usually your job is to take a stand on a topic and defend it.

Here are some pointers that should be helpful in developing your thesis.

- **Narrow the scope of your topic.** Students often make the mistake of biting off more than they can chew. Writing about the migrations of birds in North America is such a broad topic that you probably won't be able to learn enough about it to develop a meaningful thesis. Narrowing it to a particular species, and then further to a particular geographical area, will make it easier to wrap your head around the subject and to decide what you have to say. Naturally, in that early stage of "writing to figure out what you think," you probably had to cast a broad net to determine what materials were available to you and then what aspect of the subject was interesting to you. But a good rule of thumb is that *the broader the subject you're writing about, the shallower (and less important) the thesis you can develop about it.* Your thesis is sure to be more nuanced and interesting if it focuses narrowly on just one aspect of the subject.
- **Follow your interest.** It is typically harder to write about something you're not really interested in. As you explore your topic, notice what issues excite you and pursue them. Sometimes this will require more work, as the things you're most interested in may not be the things about which you can easily find the most information. At the same time, you want to be careful not to lose sight of the original prompt. You may end up with a fascinating paper but one that didn't respond to the assignment you were given.
- **Seek out controversies.** Where there is a large body of well-established facts or a substantial consensus among scholars, it can be difficult to find something interesting to say. When you come upon issues where scholars disagree, on the other hand, there are almost always opportunities to explore those disagreements, compare alternative explanations, and take sides within an academic dispute. Another way to develop a meaningful thesis is to find scholars from different fields who

have contrasting perspectives on your topic. Comparing these perspectives will often give you opportunities to make a claim that one offers insights that the other lacks, or that they complement one another in some way.

Finding a good thesis is more than just knowing what you want to say; it is knowing why you want to say it and why it matters. A thesis, to be worth defending, needs to be something about which someone could reasonably disagree. That, after all, is why you're bothering to state it and defend it! Your thesis doesn't need to be novel, and it certainly doesn't need to be groundbreaking, but it does need to be significant—clear, specific, arguable. And you can only know that your idea is significant if you have spent enough time exploring a subject to be able to put your thoughts in conversation with others.

Finally, it is best to think about your thesis not as the last word on a subject, or even your last word, but as an invitation to further exploration. In college, you are being invited to participate in an intellectual conversation with others (both scholars and classmates) who are trying to understand something better. Step into that conversation modestly. Your goal is to contribute to a conversation, not put an end to it. Accordingly, it is always better to state your position as something you believe and are willing to defend but also as something you hope will invite others to think more deeply about this subject. When they do, they may have other things to say that will prompt you to revise your initial conclusions.

As you're developing your thesis and argument, always ask yourself:

- What is my main point? Can I state it clearly and succinctly?
- What is my argument, and how well do I understand it? Can I give a clear summary of it to a non-expert?
- Is my argument interesting? Is it original? Why do I care about this interpretation?
- Why is my argument significant, either to people within this discipline or to those who may not specialize in this subject? Is

there any chance that someone will read my thesis and respond, "So what?"

- Have I presented my thesis firmly but modestly, in a spirit that invites further conversation about this topic?

Organizing Your Paper

Once you have a thesis, the body of your paper will generally be dedicated to defending it. This is where you need to assemble your evidence, explain how it supports your thesis, and make a case as to why it matters. As a writer, you want to help your reader understand (a) each individual piece of your argument, (b) how all those pieces are connected to each other, and (c) how, all together, these pieces support your thesis.

This is fundamentally a question of organization. You can have a lot of great evidence to support your thesis, but if you present it as a hodgepodge of material, your reader will likely have a hard time seeing how that material constitutes an argument. The challenge here is somewhat like constructing a jigsaw puzzle—except that there isn't one predetermined way to assemble the pieces. You need to decide which pieces connect with which others and how they together create a whole, coherent picture. Sometimes you'll be lucky, and the pieces will just seem to fall together naturally. In those cases, it will just be obvious which pieces of evidence support which claims and how you want to weave different perspectives into your own discussion of the material. But more often, you will struggle to see how it all fits together and how best to make your case to your reader. Here are some things you'll want to think about at this stage in your writing.

- **Look for relationships.** When you're faced with a lot of material, perhaps many pages of notes and a jumble of ideas, you want to focus on the connections among these things. How do the different viewpoints you encounter relate to one another? Do they agree, disagree, build on one another, or talk past one another? If you're having trouble doing this, you can use an online concept-mapping program that helps you visualize how the pieces of your paper are connected. Or if you prefer a low-tech approach, try putting each important piece of information (data, quotes, key ideas, etc.) on a separate index card and lay all the cards out on a table. Then you can play with different ways of arranging them until you have an organizational plan that makes sense. Here, referencing your earlier notes from the exploratory stage can help to remind you of how you arrived at a certain train of thought or how connections between segments of your argument emerged.

- **Find an arc or a direction for your presentation.** If you're writing about historical development, you might organize the material chronologically (or in reverse chronological order). If you're writing about the cause and effect of a phenomenon, you might make those causal connections the framework around which you organize the material. Or perhaps you're comparing and contrasting two things (e.g., two works of literature or two methods of solving a problem), in which case, the structure of your presentation will be dictated by the key similarities or dissimilarities on which you have chosen to focus. The specifics of your writing structure are less important than just having one and making sure the reader knows what it is.
- **Neither too much nor too little.** In writing, this means avoiding the tendency to add so many details that the reader is overwhelmed and can no longer see the forest for the trees. But it is equally important to avoid being so terse or so general that the reader can only see the forest from a great distance and can't make out any individual trees at all. The happy medium is to include a balance of general statements, principles, and broad claims together with detailed evidence, data, or illustrations. In this way, you enable your readers to see how the details add up to something bigger and how that larger whole (the main point you want to make) is supported by those details.
- **Cut what's unnecessary.** You may be tempted to try to find a place in your paper for everything that you learned about the subject. After all, you spent all that energy assembling all that information; not including it could make you feel that you wasted

a lot of time. Avoid that trap. Inevitably, in the process of studying something, you will learn a lot of information that may very well be interesting and worth knowing but doesn't make it into the final presentation. Don't be afraid to leave some things on the cutting room floor. Or to the extent that some of these extraneous things are related to, but not central to, your main point, put them in footnotes or endnotes.

Once you have a clear sense of how the pieces fit together, what the overall structure of the presentation will be, how much detail you need to include, and what you can safely leave out or move to the notes, you can construct an outline. The point of an outline is just to have a written road map for how you will proceed to put the paper together, something to remind you which pieces belong where, so that you don't get lost in the process of writing. As with all plans, sometimes you need to tweak your outline as you go—for example, when you realize that something you want to say actually fits better in one place than another. Creating this outline will not only help you plan and organize your paper in a logical order but it will also help ensure that you can clearly signal to your reader the various components of your argument within the body of the paper itself.

Here's an example of one outline for a paper comparing Federalist and anti-Federalist views among early American political thinkers:

Background: Federalists supported ratification of the United States Constitution. Anti-Federalists did not. But Federalist and anti-Federalist sources reveal broad agreement on many issues. Where, then, do they disagree, and why?

Outline

1. Introduction
    - A. Federalist and anti-Federalist writings share many goals.
    - B. The bulk of disagreement is about whether the proposed Constitution will achieve these goals.
    - C. Question: What is the basis of their differing assessments?

2. Road Map and Argument
   Reconstruct the anti-Federalist apprehension of unlimited government and identify one assumption that drives this worry.
   A. Anti-Federalists think constitutions should prioritize restraint. They worry about flexibility that gives the government powers before they are truly needed because of concerns about consent and abuse of power.
   B. They believe that people, not officials, should decide what is "necessary and proper." (explain Art. I, sect. 8 gives Congress open-ended powers to do what is "necessary and proper" to execute the power expressly delegated to it.)
3. Avoiding abuse of power
   A. One role of constitutions is to restrict future abuse of power.
   B. Anti-Federalists wanted a bill of rights to protect people from the abuse of governmental power.
4. Flexibility, but when?
   A. Restricting future uses of power isn't always straightforward, since we have imperfect knowledge of the future and government needs to respond to changing circumstances.
   B. Both parties favor some flexibility, but disagree on whether the flexibility should be offered preemptively to Congress or whether powers should be delegated as needs arise.
   C. Concerns about preemptive flexibility are based on the concern that ambiguous power is a threat to liberty
5. Undermining the social contract
   A. For anti-Federalists, ambiguous power undermines the consent that underpins the social contract.
   B. Constitution essentially deprives future generations of their opportunity to determine the scope of the social contract by preemptively appropriating powers.

6. Conclusion

   A. Federalists and anti-Federalists share beliefs and concerns.
   B. Their disagreements center on different empirical predictions.
   C. These predictions differ partly because anti-Federalists believe it makes little sense, in principle and practically, to delegate powers before they are needed.
   D. Their concern is about arbitrary misappropriation of power, made possible by the necessary and proper clause of the Constitution.

Even if you're not familiar with the views of Federalists and anti-Federalists in the eighteenth century, it's easy to follow this outline. This student has articulated a very clear question at the outset and then proceeds to provide several factors that influenced the anti-Federalists' concerns about adopting the US Constitution. Notice how each of these points follows logically from the one before it, so that the reader is introduced step by step to the anti-Federalist position and the logic behind it. In a well-structured paper, each paragraph is clearly linked to the one before it, so that readers are never left wondering, "Why is the author telling me this, and what does it have to do with what they were just saying?"

As you build your outline, always ask yourself:

- Does the structure of my argument make sense? Does it build logically?
- Is each piece of my presentation in the right place?
- Who is reading this? How well does my presentation address what my readers need or want to know?

III. Writing to Refine your Communication

Revision is one of the exquisite pleasures of writing.
—BERNARD MALAMUD[6]

Students often feel that the writing process ends when they've typed the last sentence and the paper is "complete." But experienced writers know that the first complete draft is never the final version. In between the first complete draft and the final paper, there are likely a few rounds (sometimes more than a few!) of revision. Rewriting or revising is that point in the writing process when you review and refine your draft until you're certain that you have a clear, precise, fluid, and grammatically correct paper. Producing a polished final draft takes a good deal of work, and it comes late in the process, when you may feel tired of the paper and more than ready to move on. But this process of revision is necessary in that it creates a fully polished piece of prose for your reader. (Think of how many times musicians practice the same piece of music to get every aspect of the tempo and phrasing just right.)

Review the Assignment

One important step in the process of revising is to go back again to the assignment you were given and double-check to make sure your paper fully responds to the prompt. Often, your instructor will ask you to include certain elements in your paper (such as references to readings covered in class or a certain number of external sources), as well as other guidelines (such as compare X and Y, or discuss the implications of this author's position). A paper can be great in all respects, but if it doesn't address the required elements, you will probably not get the grade you were expecting.

Here is an example of a paper topic, together with some guidelines for a writing assignment, followed by the first section of one student's paper.

> Statement: On the Internet, community and factory (a place of production and exchange) are one and the same.
>
> You may agree with this statement, disagree with it, or take a position in the middle.

Grading Criteria:

The strongest response papers will

- frame their arguments in terms of the course readings and discussions;
- make a single case and explore its ramifications thoroughly (rather than, say, surveying multiple possible points of view); and
- demonstrate a command of the course materials, an ability to synthesize them and in the best papers, an ability to move beyond them toward an argument of one's own.

Virtual Community: Virtually Factory

At its core, the early Internet was about communion and consumption and as its interface was evolving in the 1990s and 2000s, so too were its users' complex ideas about the relationship between cyberspace and the multifaceted interactions that occurred there. One element of the Internet that underwent intense scrutiny was its propensity to foster virtual communities; to some, this feature was unifying and humanistic, while to others, networked community merely symbolized an exploitation of true connection—such that goods, and not people, were its true focus. While these assessments were disparate, the claims mirrored in each imply something essentially true about the Internet: it is a locus of exchange. It was this sentiment that, as early as 1988, led Howard Rheingold to explain of his reciprocity with fellow Internet users, "This unwritten, unspoken social contract, a blend of strong-tie and weak-tie relationships among people who have a mixture of motives, requires one to give something, and enables one to receive something" (Rheingold 1992). Though his overall attitude was optimistic, Rheingold's language points to a more pragmatic understanding of how resource allocation works in a virtual community: taking part in community requires a kind of requital.

This paper, on the Internet as both a place of community and a place of production and exchange ("factory"), needed to include several elements.

It had to refer to course readings, make a case and explore its ramifications, and synthesize a number of readings and perspectives into an argument. As you reread your paper, if you discover that you haven't quite addressed some aspect of the assignment, you should correct that problem in your final revisions.

Once you're sure that your paper has fully responded to the assignment, there are many other things to attend to in the process of revision. Here are just some of them:

Observe disciplinary conventions. Different academic disciplines have developed different standards for communication. Be aware of these expectations, and make sure that your paper conforms to them. For example, science papers generally require a very specific structure and format—a paper with an introduction, hypothesis, methods, results, discussion, and conclusion.

Usually, these expectations will be communicated in the instructions for the writing assignment. If you're unclear about these, ask your instructor. Different disciplines also employ citation methods according to the conventions of different style guides. These style guides (e.g., the *Chicago Manual of Style* and the *MLA Handbook*), can be found easily online, and you should refer to them regularly. In chapter 8, I'll discuss citation styles more fully.

Tone. Academic writing is more formal than other forms of writing you are accustomed to, such as tweets or emails. Sometimes, students feel that writing an academic paper is unnatural, as if they were being asked to speak a foreign language or some form of English that is completely unfamiliar. It may even be tempting to think that academic prose is supposed to be obscure or full of jargon (and to be sure, lots of academic writing has these qualities!). But actually, you don't want to sound like someone else; you want to sound like yourself, only a version of yourself that uses language carefully. In the words of one writing handbook, "Mastering academic writing does not mean completely abandoning your normal voice for one that's stiff, convoluted, or pompous, as students often assume. Instead, it means creating a new voice that draws on the voice you already have."[7]

Concision. You don't want to use ten words to say what you can say equally well in five. Your readers will be frustrated if you force them to wade through wordy phrases, awkward expressions, or circumlocutions (roundabout ways of saying things). Once you've figured out what you're trying to say, find the most precise and concise way of saying it.

Fluidity. You want your prose to flow, which means that you want to avoid abruptness and choppy sentences. You also want to vary the sentence structures rather than relying on repeated simple subject-verb-object constructions. No one expects your prose to be a work of art or a candidate for a prize (especially as a first-year student), but neither should it be wooden and boring. As a test, check how many times the main verb in your sentences is a form of *to be*—*is*, *am*, *are*, *was*, or *were*. If you can find more colorful verbs to use, it will both enliven and condense your prose.

Grammar, and all the rest. There are lots of conventions about the proper use of English vocabulary, punctuation, and syntax. If you didn't have a high school English teacher who drilled these into you, now is the time to brush up. (There are many style guides to choose from, and you can find some in the resources section at the end of this book). Have one at your fingertips, and refer to it often. And of course, double-check your spelling, and carefully proofread everything you write before you turn it in.

It's helpful to think of this last stage of writing and rewriting as more than just attending to technical and stylistic issues, important as those are. This is your chance to take a step back, review what you've written, and think again about your thesis, your argument, your organization, your audience, and your presentation. That's because if your tone or word choice is off, your writing is wordy, or your prose is flat, it's likely your thoughts are not yet fully clear. To *revise* literally means "to see again," so spending enough time in the editing stage doesn't just allow you to refine your work as much as possible; it also provides you with an opportunity to see your draft—and your thinking—more clearly as you iterate and polish.

As you do your final revisions, always ask yourself:

- Is this easy to read? Am I making my reader do a lot of work to make sense of what I'm trying to say?
- Is this enjoyable to read? Have I used language in a nuanced and interesting way?
- Does my paper follow the structure appropriate to my discipline?

Some Practical Tips for Becoming a Better Writer

Writing is effortful, as even the most successful writers will attest. Over time, you will learn what techniques work best for you. Some students will insist that they write best when they have their headphones on and are listening to loud music. (Personally, I need absolute quiet.) Some writing assignments will prove more challenging than others, at times for no apparent reason. But eventually, most writers develop strategies that facilitate this uniquely human process of using the written word to formulate, refine, and communicate their thoughts. Here are just a few of the strategies you might consider:

Write, write, write. It sounds trite, but it's true—the more you practice, the better you'll get. Even the most famous writers produce many times more pages of material than they ever publish. But those pages that don't see the light of day aren't wasted effort; they are essential to honing one's thinking and writing skills. If you approach the writing process as an ongoing work-in-progress rather than an all-out effort to produce a masterpiece, you'll be much less frustrated and a much more adept writer.

Read, read, read. Make a point of setting aside time to read, especially to read the work of well-regarded writers. As you do, *pay close attention to the qualities of their writing.* When you are struck by the power of a particular phrase or the force of a well-argued essay, stop and take note of the ways in which the writer formulated their thoughts and chose their words carefully for maximum impact.

Divide and conquer. Writing assignments can be daunting. There can be so much material, so many issues to think through, so many choices to make. It often helps to break down the process into several discrete steps. As you complete each step, you'll feel yourself making progress, which will motivate you to tackle the next piece of the project. Thinking of your paper as several smaller parts and not pressuring yourself to write it all in one go can help relieve some anxiety and rid yourself of writer's block by making the task more manageable and less intimidating.[8]

Ask for help. Most colleges have a writing center or an office staffed with people whose job it is to help you improve your writing (and often your speaking skills, too). Use them. They are experts in the teaching of writing, and they will help you when you're feeling stuck. If you share a draft with them, they will give you concrete suggestions for refining it. Even your professors, who write and publish all the time, share drafts with colleagues to get feedback. (If you have any doubts about this, just look at the acknowledgments section of any book.) If a writing-center tutor isn't available, ask a classmate or roommate to read over your work and to tell you if there are things that don't make sense to them. Be sure to be specific about the kind of feedback that will be most helpful to you.[9]

Read your draft aloud. When we hear our own voice, we can sometimes notice problems in our writing that would escape our attention if we were just reading a draft to ourselves. Awkward or ambiguous phrasing will become much more apparent when you find yourself orally stumbling over long clauses, and convoluted sentences will jump out at you when your own intonation alerts you that you've misunderstood your own prose.

Create fake deadlines. If your paper is due on Friday, make Wednesday the due date on your calendar. Even though you know the real deadline, scheduling your work as if you had to finish sooner will leave you extra time at the end for that final stage of revising. You'll also have given yourself a cushion so that if things don't come together quite as quickly as you had planned, you're not working up until the last minute. (This also applies to all the stages of writing; setting deadlines helps you make progress on your paper.)

Take breaks. Our brains can work for only so long before we hit that point of diminishing returns. Anyone who has tried to pull an all-nighter knows this experience. We rarely do our best work when we're exhausted, and while extra caffeine may keep us alert, it does nothing to promote critical thinking or creativity.[10] But just before you step away, take a minute to identify where you are in the writing process, what you're working on, and what the next step will be. That way, while you're off doing something else, your subconscious mind will still be working in the background. When you return to your writing, you'll be surprised at the progress you have made—without even trying!

Conclusion

It is best to think of writing not as a means to an end but rather as an ongoing process of self-improvement. Through the writing process, we discover what we think and how to share those thoughts in a way that will inform, entertain, and persuade. And just as critical reading develops over time, writing, too, continues to evolve and improve through repeated practice, constructive feedback, and reading what others have written. As this book emphasizes, college is a time to develop your critical-thinking skills, and writing (and rewriting) are among the very best ways to do that. After all, your writing is nothing other than your thinking made visible.

The ability to write—clearly and persuasively—is also among the skills you are likely to use most often throughout your life, both in your professional pursuits and in your personal relationships. Employers often identify the ability to communicate clearly, both in writing and orally, as among the skills they value most in potential employees.[11] So even if you don't aspire to become a professional writer, you absolutely need to become a proficient writer.

Finally, writing is often the way in which you find your voice, in more than one sense. Over time, if you work at it, your writing will develop a distinctive style. Certain words and phrases will begin to come naturally, and your writing will develop a kind of personality—your personality. You will begin to take a certain pleasure in your ability to express yourself in a way that feels authentic and distinctively your own. In this sense, your writing will become one more way in which you can express your individuality.

But you find your voice through writing in another, deeper way, too. Because writing is so integral to thinking, as you write more, your ideas become more defined, and you become more invested in them. You come to understand that your thoughts matter and that sharing them with others is one important way in which you leave your mark on the world. In this way, writing isn't just a means of self-expression; it is a means of self-formation. We can actually write ourselves into being—that is, into being different people than we were before we made writing a focus of our education. And if you leave college with just one new conviction, it should be that you believe in the power of your own mind. If you do, it will be because you took your thinking—and your writing—seriously.

Questions for Reflection

1. How would you describe your relationship with writing? What is your current writing process? What writing experiences have been the most positive? The most negative? Why? What could you have done differently?
2. If you wanted to focus on writing as a process of thinking, rather than just as a way to produce a paper, what would you do? What would it take for you to change your mindset?
3. Think of something you've written that you feel proud of. What made it special? How did you approach it?
4. One writing expert has written, "Fear of badness is probably what holds people back most from developing power in writing. . . . If you care too much about avoiding bad writing, you will be too cautious, too afraid to relinquish control. . . . If, on the other hand, you really seek excellence, if you seek to write things that others might actually *want* to read, you need to stop playing it safe: go for it, take

the plunge, jump over the edge. You won't know where you are going. You will write much that is terrible. It will feel like a much longer path to tread than if you just want to get rid of badness. But you will get rewards."[12]

How fearless are you as a writer? What is holding you back? What rewards do you imagine you'd reap if you stopped playing it safe?

ADVICE FOR THE ROAD AHEAD

Take Risks

People naturally have varying levels of tolerance for risk. Some people love the thrill of skydiving or bungee jumping, while others are terrified by the idea. Some are drawn to unfamiliar places and foods, while others prefer to stick with what they know and like. Apart from risk-taking behaviors that potentially harm others, there are no rules that dictate which risks are worth taking; it's a matter of taste and preference.

But we can and should consider the potential costs and benefits of the risks we take. If we go to a party with people we don't know, we might be uncomfortable, but we also might meet a new, fascinating friend. If we buy a product we've never tried before, we might discover that we really like it, or we might feel disappointed and regret that we wasted our money. Every day, we face small choices about what sorts of risks we're prepared to take and which ones we'd rather pass up. Risk is an opportunity for trial and iteration, growth and learning.

The same is true of your education, except that the stakes here may be higher than you realize. Until now, your high school education has probably followed a pretty standard curriculum—English, history, math, natural sciences—and perhaps some room for electives. Those subjects are quite familiar to you, so when you register for college courses, they are relatively safe. You know what to expect, and if you've done well in them before, you will have some confidence that you can handle them in college. But there will always be far more choices in college than you had in high school, including subjects that may be utterly unfamiliar—linguistics, anthropology, neuroscience, or electrical engineering. Taking one of those courses may well feel risky in that you are venturing into unknown intellectual territory. This is the point at which you want to ask yourself, "How *intellectually* risk-averse am I? What might I gain by moving outside my comfort zone and exploring a subject that is entirely new to me?"

Again, there's no single right answer to this question. Much will depend on what you hope to get out of your college education, how clear you are about your career goals, and how concerned you are about your GPA, among other factors. But there are more benefits to pushing yourself to explore new subjects than you might imagine. Also, remember that most colleges permit you to take a certain number of courses on a "pass/no credit" basis, precisely to allow you to experiment without putting your GPA at risk.

When we learn something new, we expand our horizons. We discover dimensions of human experience and of the world around us that we never knew existed. Sometimes we learn to think in a different way, which can be both challenging and exhilarating, because each academic discipline exposes us to specific ways of thinking (see chapter 3 of this book). In short, we widen our perspective on the world, which inevitably enables us to see that the concepts we thought we understood are more complex than we realized. In the process, we may also learn something new about ourselves, see ourselves in a new light, or free ourselves from previously unexamined assumptions.

Sometimes, that subject we never imagined we'd find interesting turns into a new passion. I have known many students over the years who avoided a subject—like religion—because they thought they knew what it was (after all, they had attended Sunday school their whole lives and mostly hated it). What they discovered when they took a college course on religion was that it wasn't anything at all like what they expected. Religion suddenly became something fascinating and very relevant. Sometimes, this led them to major in the subject and even to pursue graduate work on this newfound passion. But even those students whose lives were not changed by exploring a new subject were excited by the discovery of a new interest and appreciative of the ways it expanded their horizons and perspective on life.

In college, you will face many pivotal decisions. You will have many opportunities to either try something new and unfamiliar or to stay with what feels comfortable or what comes easily. This is one of the most important aspects of college, and while no one will fault you if you play it safe, you will learn more and grow more as a person if you take some risks—in the courses you take, the assignments you choose, the people you seek out (including your instructors), and the activities you join. It is, after all, a once-in-a-lifetime adventure.

CHAPTER SEVEN
Knowing How to Count What Counts

Be able to analyze statistics, which can be used to support or undercut almost any argument.
—MARILYN VOS SAVANT

Cognitive psychology tells us that the unaided human mind is vulnerable to many fallacies and illusions because of its reliance on its memory for vivid anecdotes rather than systematic statistics.
—STEVEN PINKER

Outline

In this chapter, you will be introduced to the basics of quantitative reasoning—how to think with and about numbers. Knowing how to make sense of statistics and how to represent numerical data will be essential for many of the classes you take in college. It is also a skill you will need throughout your life to evaluate the information presented to you.

- Thinking about Data
  - Types of Variables
  - Visually Representing Data
  - Standard Deviation
  - Relationships between Variables
- Making Inferences about a Population from a Sample

▪ ▪ ▪

Consider the following questions:

In 2016, most pollsters predicted that Hillary Clinton would win the US presidential election over Donald Trump, and in 2020, they predicted that he would lose to Joe Biden by a far larger margin than he did. Why were they wrong?

On an almost daily basis, reports of medical research outline the effectiveness of various drugs and treatments for diseases or the risks and benefits of adopting a particular diet. Frequently, emerging reports challenge or contradict what other experts have said in the past about the same things. How reliable are these new reports?

▪ ▪ ▪

Wherever we turn, we are surrounded by data of all kinds. Throughout your life, you will need to make decisions—about whom to vote for, what medical treatments to accept, what diets work best, and where to invest your money, to name but a few. Knowing how to assess the meaning of the numerical data connected to these decisions has never been more important. And yet the math classes you likely took in high school were focused more on abstract formulae and theorems than on solving real-world, quantitative problems.

Among the many learning challenges you will confront in college is how to think about numerical problems in specific contexts—economic trends, psychological experiments, or probabilities of future events. The ability to do this is often referred to as "quantitative reasoning" (QR), and many colleges now have QR requirements.[1] The ability to reason quantitatively requires more than just computational skills; *it requires knowing something about the tools we use for analyzing and interpreting quantitative data.*

In this chapter, you'll learn some of these competencies, as well as how they can help you make sense of real-world problems. You'll be introduced to just a few of the key concepts in quantitative reasoning, such as the relationships among variables, making inferences from samples to a larger population, statistical significance, and distinguishing causality from correlation. Each of these topics has associated mathematical formulae and derivations that we will not discuss—to learn more, consider taking a statistics course! This chapter emphasizes building intuition for quantitative reasoning skills that are fundamental to the sciences and the social sciences (e.g., psychology, sociology, or economics). But growing interest in the "digital humanities" means that such skills can also be used to analyze literary texts or historical artifacts.

Thinking about Data

Suppose you are given the task of summarizing data on your high school's senior class. For each student, you obtain data on a variety of factors: race/ethnicity, gender, height, GPA, household income, and so on. You now have all this data in a large spreadsheet. However, especially if the student body is large and diverse, this spreadsheet alone is unlikely to be useful to you—it's nearly impossible to glean any meaningful information by merely scrolling through the spreadsheet.

Types of Variables

The first step in working with this data, using it to answer some question, is to notice that there are different types of data—some are **categorical**, and some are **numerical**. Club membership, for example, is a categorical variable. All students can be tagged as members (or nonmembers) of one of the available clubs at their school. Height and household income, on the other hand, are numerical data because there are not a set number of types or groups from which to choose. You could plot the height or household income of each student in the class along a spectrum from lowest to highest.

When you're working with categorical data, much depends on the way you define your categories. For example, the United States census uses a set of categories for classifying individuals' racial identity (e.g., white, African American, Native American, Alaska native, etc.), and leaves some space for respondents to add racial categories that they haven't listed or for people who identify as mixed race to check two or more categories. But these categories have changed over time, so anyone relying on this information will need to be cautious about how comprehensive and consistent these classifications have been. By the same token, different scholars may analyze the same data but use different categories to do so.

Visually Representing Data

Once you've identified the categories you will be analyzing, you want to think about how to appropriately visualize the data. Categorical variables are often visualized in bar graphs, in which the height of each bar is proportional to the number of items in the respective category, or pie charts, in which the area of each slice corresponds to the proportion of the matching category (figure 1). Having visualized the distribution of items, or data points, across categories, we might ask why some categories are more numerous than others. Consider the pie chart below showing the racial composition of a high school—white students are in a clear majority. Does this reflect the demographics of the surrounding community, or is there possible bias in the school's enrollment practices?

Quantitative analysis of your high school's student body also reveals ways in which presentation of data can be manipulated to stretch or alter our perceptions of a situation. So, for example, saying that 90 percent of the students in your high school graduate sounds pretty positive, while

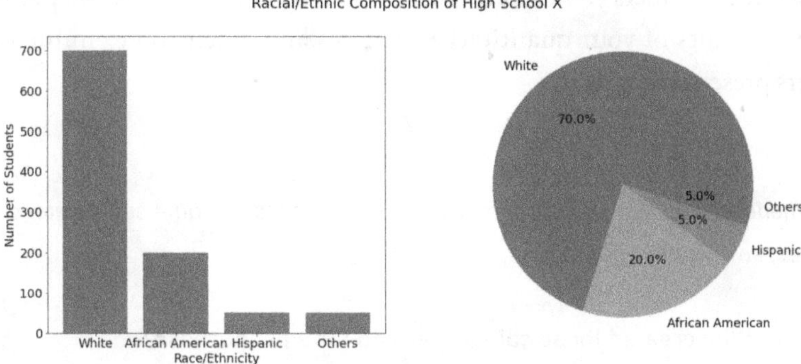

Figure 1: An example of a bar graph (left) and a pie chart (right) for visualizing a categorical variable.

saying that 10 percent of students in your school don't graduate may create a different impression, even though those statements are mathematically equivalent.

As another example, suppose you wanted to graphically report differences in graduation rates among male students (say, 40 percent) and female students (45 percent) at your high school. This sounds like a small difference, right? Notice, however, how the bar graph on the left visually exaggerates the difference in graduation rates by using a narrower scale on the *y* axis (figure 2):

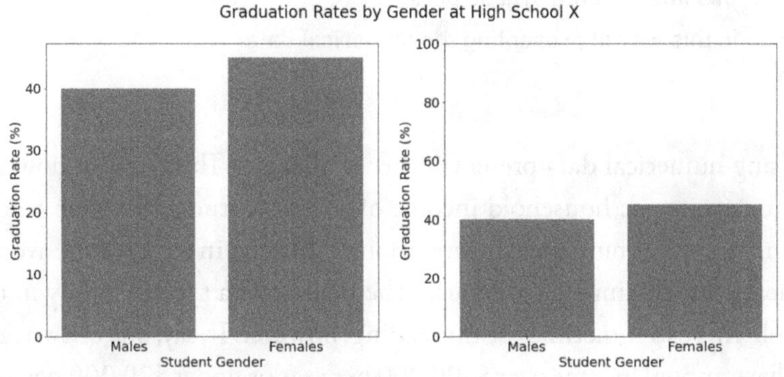

Figure 2: Changing the scale of the y *axis can either exaggerate or reduce perception of the differences in categories.*

These examples show that you can express the same mathematical reality in different ways, depending on which numbers you focus on and how you convey the numbers you use. Keep this in mind both when you are presenting the results of your quantitative analyses and when you examine how others present their data.

Whenever you use statistical information that relies on some set of categories, always ask yourself:

- Who created these categories, and for what purpose?
- How consistently have these categories been used for analyzing this data?
- Would we draw different conclusions from this data if we defined the categories differently or used different categories entirely?
- How can we visualize the distribution of counts across categories, and what useful information does this provide us?

More generally:

- How has the data been presented? Does this represent a particular focus or even a desire to create a certain reaction to this information? Whose perspective or interests are reflected in this way of presenting the numerical data?

Using numerical data presents other challenges. Think about how you might capture the household income of a typical student at your school. Often, we express numerical information of this sort in terms of the average or **mean**, which aims to summarize the income of a typical family in our school. This can sometimes be misleading, however. If, say, one or two families have annual income over $500,000 per year or under $20,000 per year, it will skew the average either higher or lower. Either way, this results in the mean being a poor representation of the typical family income for most students in your school.[2]

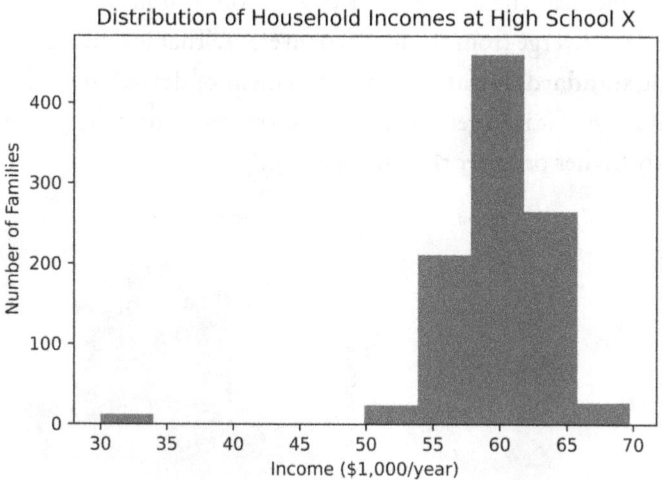

Figure 3: Using a histogram to represent visual data.

This is one reason why it is essential to present visual representations of your data alongside the averages. A **histogram** (figure 3) shows us the numbers of families whose incomes fall in a particular range. Perhaps a typical family makes between $55,000 and $68,000, but a few families appear to have much lower incomes relative to the rest. Examining the histogram thus gives us a more nuanced sense of the *distribution* of incomes across the students in your high school. But even this can be tricky. What cutoffs will you use to cluster the data? You will get different snapshots of the income profile of your high school depending on how many subgroups you use and how you define the upper and lower bounds of each group.

Standard Deviation

The distribution of data is very important in other ways, too. Consider two schools, one in which everyone has an annual family income right around $50,000 (figure 4, left) and another in which the average is $50,000 but where incomes range widely from very low to very high (figure 4, right). In both cases, the average is $50,000, but while that gives you a good summary of the families in the first class, fewer families in the second class actually have an income near the average. For this reason, you need to know how widely the data diverge from the mean, or average. That is captured in what is called the **standard deviation**, a measurement of deviation, or distance, from the average; if it is larger, then the values range more widely, with some significantly higher or lower than the average.[3]

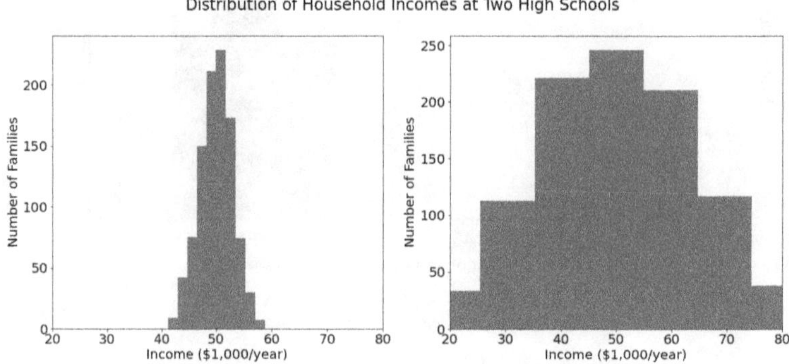

Figure 4: Examples of two data sets with the same mean (center) but widely differing standard deviations (spread).

Whenever you are dealing with numerical data, always ask yourself:

- What is a "typical" data point like in the data set?
- Beyond looking at the average of the data, how widely dispersed are they? Do they cluster around certain numbers, or are they spread more evenly across a whole range of numbers? Are there exceptionally high or low data points?
- How have these data been clustered into subgroups, and is there some reason why the cutoffs are where they are?

Relationships between Variables

Some of the most interesting quantitative questions involve combinations of categorical and numerical data. For instance, we might be interested in whether students at high school X have a higher average GPA than students at high school Y. In that case, we are using both categorical information (which high school they attend) and numerical data (average GPAs). Or we might be interested in comparing two categories, as when we investigate whether male students drop out more frequently than female students (categories: male/female, and dropouts/non-dropouts). Finally, we sometimes compare two numerical sets, for example, if we look at the relationship between family income and student GPAs.

When we're analyzing the relationship between sets of data, or two variables, we are always exploring how differences in one set explain variations in the other. The variable that we believe does the explaining is called the **independent variable.** The variable that responds to the independent variable's changes is called the **dependent variable**. So in the examples above, high school (independent variable) might explain differences in GPA (dependent variable); gender (independent) might explain dropout rates (dependent); and family income (independent) might explain GPAs (dependent). Of course, many times, we don't know which variable is affecting the other, so in that case, we simply guess. If we end up being wrong about the relationship, we can always go back and test for the opposite relationship. Let's take a closer look at how we would analyze these sorts of relationships.

Let's suppose that male students are more likely than female students to drop out of high school. We begin with the proportion of males who drop out (let's say 10 percent) versus the proportion of females who drop out (let's say 8 percent). How should we describe this difference? Often, people are interested in the relationship between the two groups, which is called **relative risk**. In this case, that would be calculated as 10 percent (0.10) for males divided by 8 percent (0.08) for females, or 1.25. This is useful if we're looking for a way to express the relative proportions of men and women who drop out. Males are 1.25 times more likely to drop out than females.

Similar statistics are often used in clinical medical trials, where people attempt to measure the effects of a certain medical treatment, meaning people who receive it are more (or less) likely to have a certain outcome. Likewise, we use statistics to express whether people who engage in certain risky behavior (say, vaping) are more or less likely to develop a certain medical condition. But it is important to recognize that these sorts of reports can easily be misinterpreted.

Let's say that people who vape are, relatively speaking, three times as likely to develop lung cancer over the next twenty years as those who don't vape. That sounds pretty bad, right? But the relative risk has to be considered in the context of the **absolute risk**, that is, the total number of people who will ultimately be affected by vaping. Suppose that three people in a thousand who vape develop lung cancer, but only one person in a thousand who doesn't vape develops cancer. That's three times as many. But expressed in terms of absolute risk, that's the difference between a one-tenth of 1 percent risk and a three-tenths of 1 percent risk—three times as high, but still extremely small.

It's also important to note that not all differences are meaningful in the ways we might assume. Suppose we find that the average GPA is higher at high school X than at high school Y. Does this mean that the students at high school X are, on average, smarter or better students than their peers at high school Y? Not necessarily. It's possible that classes are just easier at high school X or that the grading scale (i.e., what counts as an A, B, or C) differs between the schools, or that students at high school X have more tutoring services available to them, or even that they regularly cheat on exams. Any one of these factors could explain a difference. There's a world of difference between noticing a discrepancy between two sets of data and knowing how to explain those differences and interpret their significance.

Whenever you're comparing two or more sets of data, always ask yourself:

- What inferences can reasonably be drawn by looking just at the relationship between two sets of data? What other factors, besides the one that has been used to analyze this data, might explain the differences you see in the comparative results?
- When analyzing relative risks, what are the absolute risks involved in this comparison? You want to know not just how much more likely one outcome is compared to another; you want to know how likely it is altogether.

Sometimes, we want to investigate the relationship between two numerical sets of data. For example, we could test the assumption that students from wealthier families do better in school. Here, household income is our independent variable, and student GPA is the dependent variable. One common and relatively simple way to represent this would be to create a scatter plot, where each point represents a single student with a specific household income (on the *x* axis) and GPA (on the *y* axis), as follows (figure 5):

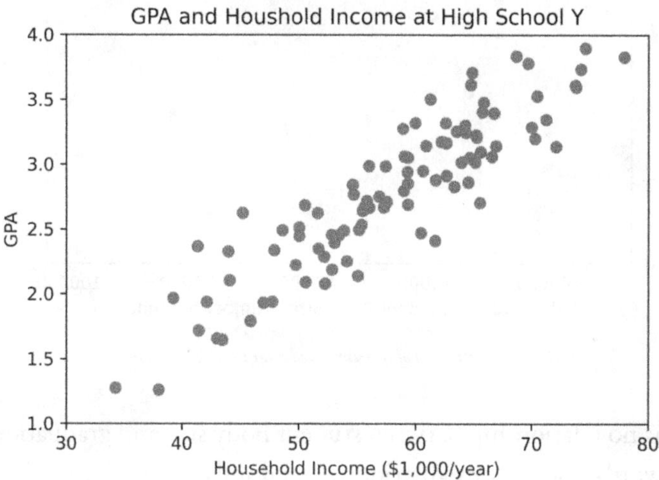

Figure 5: A scatterplot showing the relationships between two quantitative variables.

When we plot the data in this way, we can see a certain trend, namely, that in general, GPAs go up along with household income. Moreover, it's also clear that while students with the highest GPAs, say 3.0 and above, cluster at the top of the income distribution, it's also true that students with lower GPAs, say 2.0–3.0, come from both less affluent and more affluent families.

Social scientists are often interested in analyzing sets of data to see what sort of relationship exists between them, if any. Suppose we are interested in determining the relationship between the size of a university's undergraduate student body and the graduation rate at that university. We want to know how the number of undergraduates affects graduation rate, so our independent variable is the size of the student body, the dependent variable is graduation rate (0–100 percent). In the scatterplots below, each dot represents one university with a specific graduation rate and average student body size.

Here are some possible outcomes:

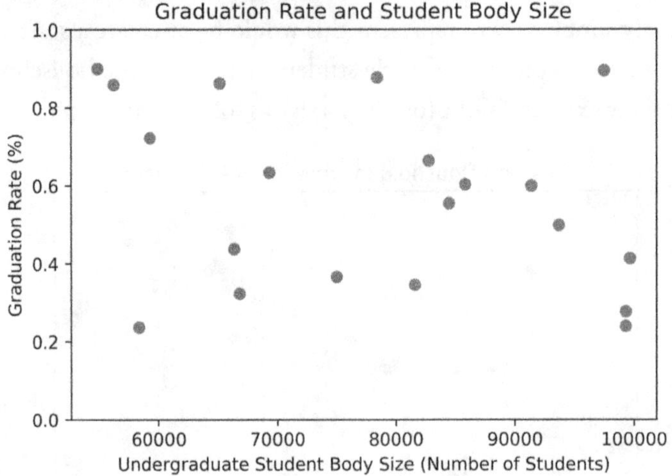

Figure 6: A scatterplot of two unrelated quantitative variables.

There is no relationship between student body size and graduation rate. In other words, the dots are distributed randomly across the graph, which means that there is no correlation (mutual relationship) between the two variables.

But let's consider another possibility.

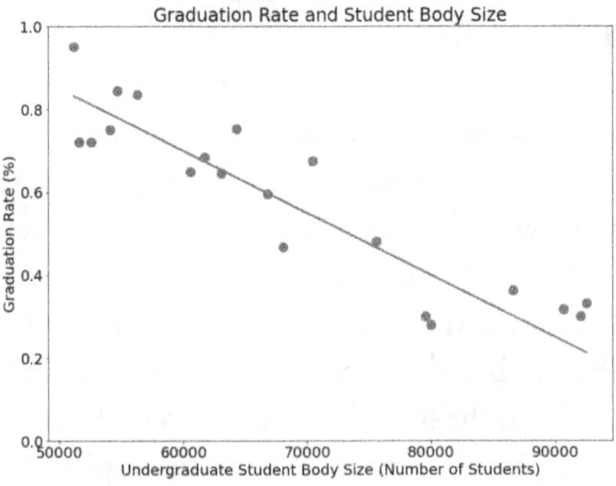

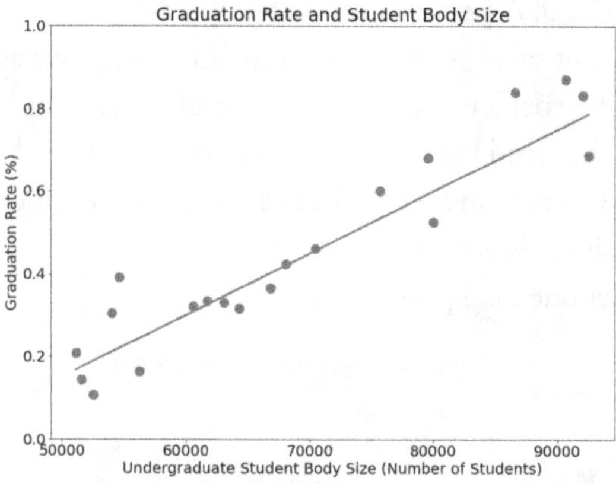

Figure 7: Scatterplots with negative (previous page) and positive (above) linear relationships.

The data here are linear; that is, there is a consistent rate of change in the relationship between the number of undergraduates and the graduation rate. In other words, graduation rate responds to increases in student body size in the same way throughout the range of student body sizes—either consistently increasing (a positive relationship) or decreasing (a negative relationship). The graph on the previous page shows a negative relationship, in that universities with larger student bodies have lower graduation rates, while the graph immediately above shows a positive relationship, in that universities with larger student bodies have a higher graduation rate. But in both cases, as shown below, the line showing the trend is steady, equally steep, across all student body sizes.

We should also observe how strong the linear relationship is. If the correlation between student body size and graduation rate is very strong, the points will be tightly clustered around a line. (A perfect correlation would mean that, given an undergraduate student body size, we could exactly predict what the graduation rate would be. In that case, every dot would fall exactly on the line.)

We can measure the strength of the relationship between quantitative variables—how closely they group to that line marking the trend—using a number, called the **correlation coefficient**. If there is no relationship between the variables, as in the random scatterplot above, the correlation coefficient will be 0. A perfectly linear positive association will have a correlation coefficient of +1, while a perfectly linear negative association will have a correlation coefficient of −1. Since not all data points in this example fall exactly on the trend line, the correlation coefficient in the earlier graph (negative) is between 0 and −1, while the correlation coefficient in the second graph (positive) is between 0 and +1.

Let's consider one final possibility.

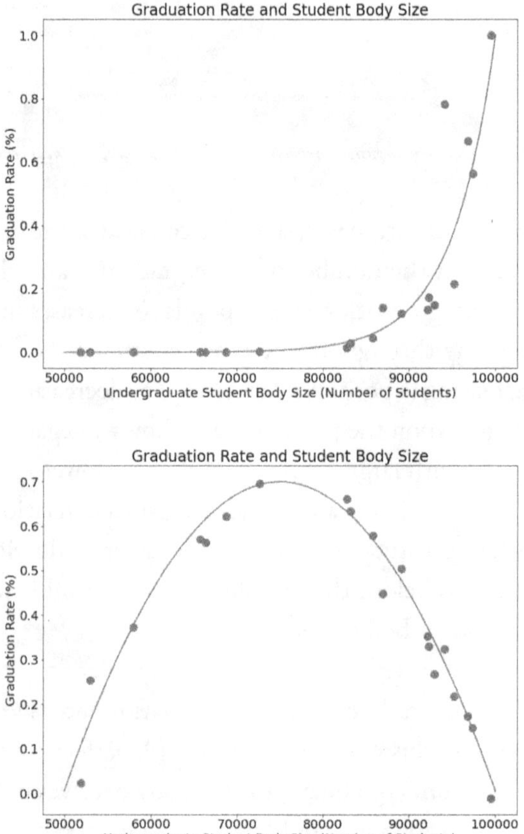

Figure 8: Scatterplots with possible nonlinear relationships.

The data here are nonlinear; the relationship between graduation rate and size of the student body may vary depending on the size of the student body. Perhaps graduation rate doesn't change much as we move from very low to moderately sized student bodies but then dramatically increases in universities with the most undergraduates (figure 8, top). Or perhaps graduation rate rises dramatically from low to moderately sized student bodies, peaks, and then begins to drop off for the largest student body sizes (figure 8, bottom). Can you think of other possible nonlinear relationships?

So far, all these potential results are simply ways of depicting the relationships between two variables: student body size and graduation rates. Getting the data and putting them into a form where we can see the trends (if there are any) is just the first step. Then we have to begin interpreting those data. Sets of data like this describe reality, but they don't explain that reality. For that, we need to look at the social circumstances and attitudes of the people whose data we have aggregated in this exercise. We might, for example, need to interview people in different universities to find out how they think the study body size at their university affects their experience. Or we might need to collect more data—say, on the correlation between these two things in a single university where student body size changed significantly over a decade or so. These additional inquiries would enable us to begin to explain why the data are what they are.

Finally, the lines on these graphs that mark the trends we've been discussing are known as "lines of best fit," meaning they follow as closely as possible the data points we have. The line is drawn in such a way that it minimizes the distance to each data point; it represents a trend or prediction based on the data we have about actual reported student body size and graduation rates. It also enables us to do what social scientists call an **interpolation**, namely, a calculation, based on this trend line, of what graduation rate we would expect to find in a university with a given student body size. These lines can be easily calculated on spreadsheet software, like Google Sheets or Microsoft Excel.

Whenever you want to analyze the relationship between two sets of numerical data, always ask yourself:

- Are there trends that we discern in the data, or is it random?
- If there are trends, how strong are they? Is the relationship between the independent variable and the dependent variable

consistently positive or negative, or does it change depending upon the independent variable?

- What additional information would you need to gather to interpret the significance of any trend that appears in the data?

Making Inferences about a Population from a Sample

Another important quantitative skill involves drawing conclusions about a large group of things by looking at just a small sample. We do this in many contexts. Every time we read about a political poll—what percentage of the voting population views a particular candidate favorably or supports a particular referendum—we are looking at the results of statistical sampling. We might also want to draw conclusions about the population of fish in a lake, or the prevalence of a particular medical condition in a certain country's population. In each case, it is impractical to look at every single member of the target group (every voter, every fish, or every person in a country). So we take a small sample and try to generalize from that sample to the characteristics of the group as a whole. But how can we be sure that our sample is representative of the whole? And how do we know if our inferences from this sample are valid?[4]

Sampling Procedure

The key here is often the sampling procedure and whether it results in a sample that is genuinely representative of the target population. For example, if you wanted to sample voters, you could stop people randomly on a college campus and ask them about which candidate they supported. But, note that the people on college campuses are likely to be more educated than the overall population of voters, and this might create an inadvertent bias in the results of your sampling.[5] Similarly, let's say you are interested in determining the weight of fish in a lake. If you collect your sample from just one spot, which might be shallower or deeper than the lake as a whole, the fish you collect there might not be representative of all fish in that lake at that time. Of course, if you were only interested in the views of college-educated voters or the weight of fish in a particular section of the lake, then these would be perfectly appropriate ways of sampling.

To get a truly random sample, think of the process of drawing names out of a hat. To get a truly random sample of political views within a population of voters, you would try to get voter registration lists, scramble those lists, and then choose every hundredth name to contact with your survey. Even then, you might need to think about the procedure for contacting them. If you send a survey in the mail, you might not get responses from less affluent people, who tend to move more frequently and might not have a current address in your registration list. If you tried to contact people based on their home phone numbers, you might miss younger people, who tend to have only cell phones, not landlines.

The size of the sample you choose also matters. No one would suppose you can gain reliable information about a million voters by asking just ten of them, even if you chose them at random. It's just too small a sample to be a reliable indicator of how the larger group thinks. The range of variation, or standard deviation, within the group that you're examining is also a key factor. Imagine a lake in which all the fish weigh about the same, say between 3.25 and 3.75 pounds. If you sample just ten fish, and they all fall into this range, then it turns out that you have good reason to infer that most other fish will as well. On the other hand, if you find a diversity of weights in your ten-fish sample, you'd have to sample many more of them to capture and confirm this diversity; weighing just a few would likely not reveal the full range of variation within the fish population.

Confidence Intervals

As these examples demonstrate, even randomly collected samples always have room for error, whether from limited size, high variability, other biases, or just from chance. We can't be certain that our sample mirrors the larger population perfectly. That margin of error is captured in what statisticians call a **confidence interval**: a range of possible values including the sample mean within which we might reasonably assume the true population mean is found. For instance, a confidence interval for a sample of fish with a mean of 4.5 pounds might be 4.0–5.0 pounds. To use what might be a more familiar example, political polls regularly report that they have a "margin of error" of "plus or minus x percentage points." Because pollsters can sample just a percentage of the voters, the poll can tell us within a certain range what the larger population of voters thinks but not a precise percentage of voters who think that way.

To understand why we need an interval of values to capture error, consider fish samples collected at lake A and lake B. Both the lake A sample and the lake B sample have a mean weight of 4.5 pounds, but the lake A sample had one hundred fish, while the lake B sample had just ten. Moreover, almost all the lake A fish weighed around 4.5 pounds (i.e., low sample standard deviation), while some fish in the lake B sample were smaller than one pound and others larger than twenty pounds (i.e., large standard deviation). Under these circumstances it would not be reasonable to simply report an estimated population mean of 4.5 for both samples. We have much greater confidence in our inference of lake A's mean than lake B's mean, due to the greater sample size and lower variation in our lake A sample. Instead, we should factor in our sample mean, standard deviation, and size to construct a range of possible values in which the mean might lie. This interval should be broad if, due to some combination of small sample size and standard deviation, we are uncertain of our inference, and narrow if we are more confident. Although the formulas for calculating confidence intervals are beyond the scope of this book, we can intuitively understand that lake A should have a narrower confidence interval (say, 4.0–5.0 pounds) than lake B (say, 3.0–6.0 pounds).[6]

Whenever you want to draw inferences from samples, you should always ask yourself:

- How clearly defined is the group you're trying to analyze? When you do a political poll, for example, are you looking for the opinions of all potential voters, only those who have registered to vote, or only those who say they are likely to vote? Your analysis will be quite different depending on how you define the group you're interested in.

- How was the sampling conducted? Is the sample representative of the target population or is there any possibility that the sampling process introduced unintended biases in the data you collected?
- What is your sample size, and how variable are the measurements within your sample? How does this affect your confidence in your inferences about the broader population?

Statistical Significance

As noted above, we are often interested in assessing the relationship between two variables. For example, we might begin with a hypothesis that smokers see health-care providers more often than nonsmokers. Here, we have a hypothesis of a relationship between a categorical independent variable (smoker/nonsmoker) and a quantitative dependent variable (number of visits to health care providers in a year).[7] We randomly sample groups of smokers and nonsmokers and ask them about the frequency of their health-care visits. We calculate the average number of visits per year among the nonsmokers as 5.5 and the average number of visits among the smokers as 7.0. We might be inclined to jump to the conclusion that there is an actual difference between smokers and nonsmokers.[8] But given the random error inherent in the sampling procedure, it is very possible that we obtain two samples of different means even if the underlying populations have the same mean!

Our question then becomes, how likely is it that we would obtain these two sample means—5.5 annual visits for nonsmokers, 7.0 for smokers—if there were actually no difference in the population average number of doctor's visits for smokers and nonsmokers? It helps to think of this by analogy to flipping a coin and seeing how often it comes up heads. Suppose we were testing the hypothesis that the coin is weighted so that it comes up heads more often. We flip the coin three times and get three heads. The probability of this occurring with a fair coin is 50 percent x 50 percent x 50 percent = 12.5 percent, which is not so unusual, so it makes sense to accept that the coin is fair. If, however, we flip the coin a hundred times and get all heads, the probability of this occurring with a fair coin is 50 percent (or $0.50)^{100} = 7.8 \times 10^{-31}$ (an infinitesimally small percentage likelihood). We now have significant evidence that the coin is weighted.

Returning to our example of smokers and health-care visits, the question is whether our sample populations of smokers and nonsmokers accurately mirror the larger populations of those groups. We can begin by plotting the means of the two groups and 95 percent confidence intervals on a bar graph (indicated by the length of the vertical lines) to represent the potential uncertainty as to whether the difference in our samples is significant or not (figure 9):

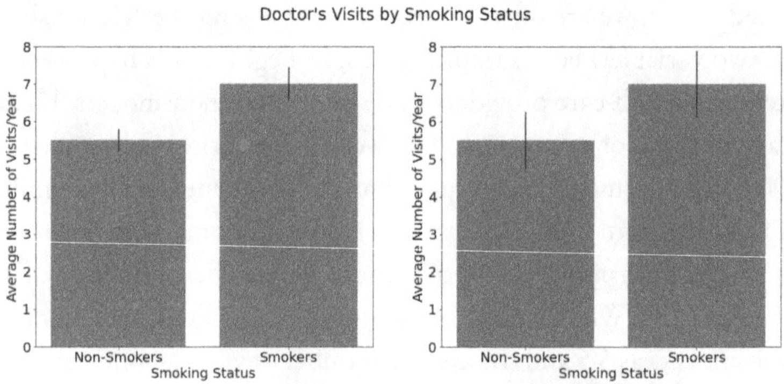

Figure 9: Bar graphs showing significant (left) and nonsignificant (right) differences in a numerical variable in different categories.

Notice that there is substantial overlap in the confidence intervals for the graph on the right, while the intervals on the left are more clearly delineated. So it is less likely that the population means are the same for the samples in the graph on the left than the graph on the right. We can quantify the likelihood that the population means are the same using a ***p* value** (probability value), which can be obtained using a statistical test. For instance, a *p* value of 0.10 means that there's a 10 percent chance of getting sample means as different as ours if the underlying population means were the same. Low *p* values indicate a more significant result—it's less likely that the differences are the result of chance differences in our samples. The difference in the means in the graph on the left has a lower *p* value than the difference for the graph on the right. Most disciplines use a *p*-value cutoff, or significance level, of 0.05, meaning a statistical test with a *p* value less than 0.05 is deemed a statistically significant result. (Though it is worth noting that some disciplines have recently adopted a threshold of less than 0.01 for statistical significance.) If the *p* value for the comparison of average doctor's visits is 0.03, we would conclude that there is a statistically significant difference in the mean number of doctor's visits for smokers and nonsmokers.

Remember that our inference of statistical significance is still drawn from a comparison between samples, so it is still subject to uncertainty from sampling error. When a *p* value is lower than our cutoff, we decide that the probability of observing such a difference due to random chance is low enough to reasonably conclude that it likely did not occur due to random chance. But with any non-zero *p* value, there is some chance, however small, that the observed differences are the result of random chance. In this context, if the *p* value for the comparison between number of doctor's visits is significant (< 0.05), there is still a 5 percent chance that the mean number of doctor's visits is the same for the smoking and nonsmoking populations. It's also possible that we failed to perceive a significant difference in our sample means (the *p* value is not less than 0.05), when there is, in fact, a difference in the mean doctor's visits within this population. Thus, statistical analysis gives us a systematic way of dealing with uncertainty in sampling, but it does not eliminate this uncertainty entirely.

Finally, we must be careful not to conflate statistical significance with real-world significance. There may be a statistically significant difference of one average doctor visit per year for smokers and nonsmokers, but does this translate to a relevant difference in medical costs or quality of life? Statistical significance tells us that we have reason to believe that these two populations do indeed have differing levels of medical treatment. However, this doesn't necessarily mean that this difference creates a health disparity. The latter needs more research and expertise.[9] Statistical analysis should always be connected back to the problem's original context to assess real world significance.

When you attempt to analyze the statistical significance of difference among samples, always ask yourself:

- What is the probability (*p* value) that such differences would be observed due to random chance rather than a true difference in the underlying populations?
- Is this *p* value low enough to be considered significant (lower than a predetermined significance level)?
- If the observed difference is statistically significant, is it also practically significant?

Establishing Causality

In the last section, I described how we might find evidence of a statistically significant association between two variables, smoking and number of doctor's visits. But as we'll see, this is not the same as proving that smoking causes an increase in doctor's visits.

Distinguishing Causation from Correlation

To understand the distinction between association and causation, consider whether engaging in community service lowers stress levels. Suppose we sampled a group of individuals who engage in community service and a group who do not, and we observed that the community service group had significantly lower stress levels (as measured using a questionnaire). Does this necessarily mean that engaging in community service causes lower stress? To put it another way, is it possible that the group with lower stress would've been lower even if they had not engaged in community service?

The issue here is whether there could be some other explanation for this difference. Maybe individuals who do community service are of higher socioeconomic status, and that—not community service itself—lowers stress. In this case, socioeconomic status is a **confounding variable**. If we are trying to establish a relationship between variables X and Y, a confounding variable is a third variable that affects both X and Y, leading us to falsely conclude that changes in X cause changes in Y or to misjudge the strength of the causal relationship between X and Y. In this case, socioeconomic status might affect both community service and stress levels. Here's another, peculiar example of confounding. Pedestrian accidents might be more common on days when people eat more ice cream. Is it likely that eating ice cream causes more pedestrian accidents? Here, weather is a potential confounder: when the weather is warmer, people are more likely to eat ice cream *and* spend time outdoors (increasing the risk of accidents).

Exercise. Now that you've learned a bit about confounding variables, think of two potential confounds for the association between doctor's visits and smoking. Jot down the first ones that come to mind.

____

____

____

____

Thus, confounding is one reason why *observing an association between two variables does not imply that changes in one cause changes in the other.* For example, observing that stress levels are lower in a group that does community service does not mean community service lowered stress levels. Finally, consider the possibility that higher stress levels actually cause people to be less likely to do community service—maybe stress makes people less eager to help others. In this case, we would still observe the same association: stress levels would be higher for the non-community service group than the community service group. Yet drawing the conclusion that community service causes lower stress levels would clearly be backward here. This is an example of **reverse causation**, when an association between X and Y is interpreted to mean that X causes Y, when in fact, Y causes X. As another example, consider that schools with more experienced principals perform better on statewide tests. This might mean that more experienced principals are better able to prepare their students for the tests. Alternatively, more experienced principals might be attracted to highly performing schools.

Whenever you're attempting to draw causal claims from associations between variables, always ask yourself:

- What other (confounding) variables could influence the observed relationship?
- Could reverse causation be a factor?
- Have possible confounding variables been controlled in the study?

Experimental Design

Considering the problems with drawing causal inferences from associations, how would we definitively prove that doing community service causes lower stress levels? The key is to perform an experiment in which we directly change the independent variable and then observe any difference in the dependent variable, rather than looking for preexisting associations. So we might recruit a study sample of individuals who do not engage in community service and randomly assign individuals to one of two groups: one that is paid to do community service (the experimental group), and another that is paid to do a non-service activity, such as reading.

We need to have a group that is paid to do a non-service activity because it is possible that just being paid, or being recruited into a study itself, has some effect on stress levels. In medical clinical trials, merely believing you are being treated often improves health outcomes. So to ensure that they are measuring the effects of the independent variable rather than these other factors, experimenters include a control group—which is the same as the experimental group in all regards except the independent variable—as a basis for fair comparison. For instance, in clinical trials, researchers avoid the imbalanced effects of participants believing they're receiving treatment by also giving the control group a placebo, or fake pill. Therefore, to show that community service (and not some other feature of being in the experiment) lowers stress, we need a control group to serve as a basis for comparison (in our service example, the control group would be composed of the participants in the reading condition).

In addition, it is essential to randomly allocate individuals to the experimental and control groups. Ideally, the treatment and control groups should be identical in all factors except for community service (the independent variable). Of course, this is not always possible, since people differ in gender, race, genetics, background, and so on. Variability between our control and experimental groups might cause us to observe a difference between the groups that is not attributable to the independent variable. If women have different stress levels from men, we would not want to have all women in the experimental group and all men in the control group, as our observed differences might be more attributable to the confounding variable of gender than to community service. Therefore, to minimize systematic differences between the control and experimental groups, we should randomly assign subjects to groups.

Since we can only establish a causal relationship by directly manipulating the independent variable with appropriate controls and randomization, what is the purpose of associational studies, as in the relationship between smoking and doctor's visits? Sometimes, for practical or ethical reasons, it is impossible to directly manipulate the independent variable in a randomized, controlled experiment. For example, knowing the risks of smoking, it would be unethical to ask the experimental group to begin smoking. Instead, we might match smokers with demographically identical nonsmokers (same race, gender, socioeconomic status) and compare doctor's visits across these matched pairs. Or, if we suspect that drinking behavior is a confounding variable, we might match smokers and nonsmokers by alcohol consumption levels. This allows us to be more confident that observed differences are due to smoking itself and do not reflect confounding variables of race, gender, and so on. While such adjustments represent an improvement over pure observation, the gold standard for establishing causal relationships is a controlled experiment. You should be more skeptical of causal claims made from observational rather than from experimental studies.[10]

Whenever you're designing or interpreting experiments to assess claims about causality, always ask yourself:

- What control groups are needed to show that the independent variable, and not a confounding variable, is what affects the dependent variable?
- Have research subjects been randomly allocated to groups?
- Is experimental manipulation practical and ethical? If not, what confounding factors should be considered in an observational study?

Exercise. For each of the following hypothetical study findings, indicate whether you think these findings suggest a causal or correlational relationship between the independent variable and the dependent variable:

1. Educational researchers examining the average SAT scores of a California high school found that girls tended to score higher (by fifteen points) than boys.

   Independent variable: Gender

   Dependent variable: SAT score

2. Kinesiology researchers found that participants who were randomly assigned to practice a particular physical therapy routine saw reduced knee pain compared to participants who were randomly assigned to a control activity (basic stretching).

   Independent variable: Type of physical activity

   Dependent variable: Knee pain

3. Psychologists found that participants who were randomly assigned to do fifteen minutes of gratitude journaling every night for two months saw significant increases in self-reported happiness compared to participants who were assigned to fifteen

minutes of neutral journaling (describing what happened to them that day) every night.

Independent variable: Type of journaling

Dependent variable: Self-reported happiness

4. Two doctors survey a group of two hundred patients. One hundred of these patients run three days per week, forty-five minutes each run. The other one hundred of these patients run five days per week, thirty minutes each run. The five-day running group has significantly lower blood pressure than the three-day running group.

   Independent variable: Frequency of running (i.e., runs per week)

   Dependent variable: Blood pressure

Conclusion

Mark Twain allegedly said that there are three kinds of lies: lies, damned lies, and statistics.[11] This disparaging view of statistics likely stems from the widespread perception that they can readily be used to deceive people. And no doubt, sometimes they are. Just look at how frequently PolitiFact or other fact-checking sites rank a politician's statement as "true, but misleading." Quite often, such statements involve a fast and loose use of statistics.

But the deeper truth is that our society is awash in numerical information. The Internet has made it easier than ever to promulgate blatantly false information, or partial truths, that test our ability to think critically about data. In this context, it is more important than ever that you develop the quantitative reasoning skills to be a careful consumer of this information. This involves asking the sorts of questions raised throughout this chapter—how data was gathered and categorized, how confident we can be that it accurately describes the real world, and whether the form in which it is presented exaggerates or minimizes its significance. It also involves being attuned to unfounded inferences that are frequently made about the significance of a particular numerical finding. Sometimes, a result appears to be meaningful but on closer analysis turns out to be just random. Similarly, sometimes we jump to the conclusion that two numerical findings demonstrate a cause-and-effect relationship when in fact, they just appear in tandem, but not because one is the cause of the other.

In this chapter, we have been able to cover just a few of the skills of quantitative reasoning that will likely play a role in your college education. But acquiring even a few of these skills will help prepare you to think critically about numbers, which will be important in many areas of life, even outside the classroom. Becoming a competent quantitative reasoner will enable you to evaluate the claims of advertisers ("75 percent of dentists recommend this brand of toothbrush") but also claims of potentially far-reaching significance, such as the effectiveness of particular medical treatments you are considering. In the context of your academic work, quantitative reasoning will be essential to your success in evaluating the research you encounter in class assignments and will ultimately help you present your own research results in precise, compelling ways.

In a very real sense, quantitative reasoning enables you to transcend your personal experience and say something about a whole group of people. To refer to the earlier example about the wealth of the students who attend your high school, you may well have your own perceptions about that, but it is only if you gather and analyze the data that you know the income distribution for a fact. It also enables you to make comparisons across high schools, which enables you to ask still other questions that can only be addressed by looking at large data sets.

Being able to think well with numbers also improves the quality of your thinking. You will often read material in which the author says that "many" or "some" or "most" people behave in a certain way or believe something to be true. But how many is "many?" Without more precise numbers, it is more difficult to assess the significance of those assertions. Using your quantitative reasoning skills, you will find that your thinking becomes more precise. You will begin to avoid those vague approximations in your own writing, and to consider them more carefully when you encounter them in the work of others.

Becoming proficient in quantitative reasoning, then, is a crucial part of thinking critically about the world, at least those aspects of life that are quantifiable. It enables you to evaluate the strength of evidence that is offered to support claims, which we have already noted is a key skill expected of you in college. It also enables you to gain a broader perspective on the world by providing you with bases of comparison and reference points outside of your own experience. Thinking in a sophisticated way about numerical data will enhance your appreciation of the complex world in which we live.

Questions for Reflection

1. Where have you encountered quantitative thinking in your coursework? In everyday life? (Think beyond the boundaries of traditional math and science courses; quantitative reasoning is everywhere.)
2. People often make bold claims without sufficient backing from quantitative evidence, or "fudge" quantitative measures with words like *many*, *some*, *lots*, or *almost all*. Over the course of a week, try to keep track of claims you or others make that could be better supported with quantitative measures. What sorts of data would you collect to support these claims? How would you visualize and analyze these data?
3. Even when people support claims with quantitative evidence, they often knowingly or unknowingly use this evidence in misleading ways. Drawing on ideas presented in this chapter, can you think of examples of the misuse of quantitative reasoning?
4. Mistaking association for causation is one of the most common and dangerously misleading statistical fallacies. The next time you're watching the news, listen for implicit or explicit causal claims (e.g., "diet Y prevents disease X," or "X government program improves Y outcome"). Are the causal claims drawn from a controlled experiment or an associational study? If the latter, consider what

factors other than a direct causal relationship might explain the observed association. Could reverse causation be at play? Can you think of possible confounding variables?

5. A second common mistake is making inferences about a broader population from a nonrepresentative sample. The next time you encounter a political poll or opinion survey, try to track down the researchers' sampling procedure. What is the target population in the study (e.g., all voting-age adults in California, all first-year students at your university)? Do you think the researchers' sample represents this broader population? What sort of biases might the sampling procedure have introduced (e.g., would all people in the target population respond to a phone call)?
6. Think back to the last time you encountered a statement about probability, test results, or other statistical information. How well did you understand the claims being made? Did you skim over these details, or did you stop and really question how those conclusions were reached? Knowing what was covered in this chapter, what questions would you want to ask now?

ADVICE FOR THE ROAD AHEAD

Get Engaged, Remain Detached

It's easiest to learn something new when we feel excited about it, and frequently, we're most excited to learn about things to which we have a personal connection. For example, you may want to study a particular religious tradition or cultural practice that has been influential in your own life. Or you may be interested in exploring a musical genre because you love listening to that type of music. It is simply natural to be more interested in things that are personally relevant. We feel particularly motivated to learn—especially if the material is difficult to master—when we can see the payoff. Because there's something in it for us, we become engaged.

But academic work also requires that we maintain a certain kind of distance from what we study. We attempt to understand things, as much as possible, from a neutral perspective. We need to follow the evidence wherever it leads us, and we need to present our findings in ways that are persuasive to others in this academic field. College is designed precisely to teach you to identify and apply common standards for weighing evidence and defending your conclusions. In this sense, you need to avoid skewing your data, or your presentation of it, in ways that simply confirm your prior beliefs or commitments—the very beliefs and commitments that may have led you to study this subject in the first place.

The goal is not to steer clear of any subject in which you feel personally invested. Rather, it is to find a balance between being (emotionally) engaged in your learning and, at the same time, (intellectually) detached enough to examine it without letting that personal connection influence your conclusions. This is difficult, and it will likely take you some time to find this balance.

Being personally connected to the subject matter can make it a challenge to evaluate the information you find in a scholarly way. It may even be difficult to notice the ways in which your personal beliefs color your perspective, since they seem completely natural to you. When you choose to study something you care about personally, be especially vigilant about looking for information that may challenge your own personal beliefs and values. And if you find some, pay close attention to that natural tendency we all have to minimize or dismiss it. Try instead to open up to the possibility that your studies may actually require you to reconsider long-held beliefs and values. While this can be unsettling, it can also lead to some of the deepest and most important learning you will do in college. In short, allow your personal stake in this particular material to drive your interest but not your perspective or your conclusions.

CHAPTER EIGHT

Doing Research: From Consuming Knowledge to Creating It

If we knew what it was we were doing,
it would not be called research, would it?
—ALBERT EINSTEIN

Research is formalized curiosity.
It is poking and prying with a purpose.
—ZORA NEALE HURSTON

Outline

In this chapter, you will learn what research is, as well as how to design and conduct your own research project. You will be introduced to the common challenges that arise when doing research, and how to tackle them. Doing research is one of the best ways to hone the critical-thinking skills you have practiced throughout your college education.

- How to Think about Research
- Types of Research
- The Challenges of Research
  - Finding a Topic
  - Asking a Question

▪ ▪ ▪

I began the discussion of disciplinary thinking (chapter 3) by inviting you to imagine wandering around a large room and eavesdropping on various conversations among scholars discussing topics distinctive to their academic discipline. Often, especially in your first year or two of college, just understanding more about those disciplinary (and interdisciplinary) conversations will be challenging enough. But at some point, you will likely move beyond just understanding those conversations; you will begin contributing to them. Generally, you will do this through some focused research in that field. At some schools, doing an independent research project in your field will be one of the requirements for completing your major (or receiving honors in your major). Many of you may get involved in doing independent research much earlier in your college careers.

How to Think about Research

But what is research, actually, and why is it so important? *Research represents the frontier of knowledge; it is the way in which we discover new things about the world or expand and refine the current state of our knowledge.* Depending on your field of study, this may involve new ways of understanding how the natural world functions, how societies are organized and evolve, or how human beings make meaning in their lives, individually and collectively.

None of these subjects will be entirely new to you. But at some point, you will be asked to become an active participant in the production of new knowledge, which requires you to engage in research. You might think of doing research, then, as an opportunity to join the academic community by expanding our knowledge about your chosen subject. It may also be one of the most daunting aspects of your college education.

Whether it is exciting or daunting (and, very likely, it will be both), doing research is valuable not only because of the contributions you may make to a field of study. Doing research is also a chance to expand and sharpen the critical-thinking skills you have been developing throughout your college years. Moreover, studies have shown that research is a "high-impact practice," one that gives students increased confidence in their skills, increased independence as thinkers, deeper relationships with faculty, and leads to more active engagement in their learning.[1] Of course, if you pursue education beyond the undergraduate level, doing research is also excellent preparation for graduate programs, where you will be required to engage in more extensive and sophisticated research. In addition, many careers now require you to have some basic research skills, so these will be valuable to you even if you don't pursue a graduate degree.

Before turning to the specific challenges you will face in doing research and how to address them, it is worth thinking a little more about what research is.

Research is a conversation. As the metaphor above indicates, doing research involves participating in an ongoing disciplinary conversation. Within that conversation, there will be some things that all (or nearly all) researchers agree on, and many other topics on which they disagree. Clearly, before you can contribute in any meaningful way to that conversation, you need to understand what intellectual disputes are alive, as well as what issues haven't been fully addressed (or addressed at all). But most fundamentally, you must appreciate that when you do research, you are stepping into a conversation in which differences of opinion are valued and encouraged.

Research is human. The advancement of knowledge through research is a human endeavor—among the noblest of human endeavors, some would say.

But precisely because knowledge is created by people, it has many of the qualities and limitations of human beings. Despite our best efforts to make our research objective, the human quest for knowledge is often tainted by personal biases, cultural assumptions, the state of our technology, and many other factors. There are myriad examples of "well-established knowledge" in one era that is overturned by later scholars.[2]

Research is exploratory. Since research, by definition, is the effort to discover or understand something, we don't generally do research into things that are well-known and widely understood. While some research projects aim to refine well-studied concepts, most researchers will say that they are driven to research by their innate curiosity or sense of wonder. In this sense, the possibilities of research are limited only by human curiosity, which is boundless.

Research is inquiry. As I have emphasized frequently throughout this book, critical thinking—including research—is driven by questions. So when you go looking for a topic to research, you will want to begin with some questions. Whatever your topic, you'll want to ask:

- What issues do you think current research overlooks?
- Where can the work of others who have already studied this be challenged, supplemented, or improved on?
- Which aspects of the current scholarly conversation on this topic feel most urgent, relevant, or troubling?

Research is iterative. The process of engaging in research involves several steps, which will be discussed below. But it is important to realize that these steps are rarely just sequential, like the steps involved in baking a cake. Rather, you will cycle through these steps several times, and not always in the same order, in the course of pursuing answers to your questions. This is because research is messy, and it often requires us to resolve issues with our study or its results by returning to earlier phases in the process and double-checking our work or assumptions.

That said, in general, the process consists of defining your topic, finding sources, gleaning information, deriving new insights and viewpoints, seeing what new questions all this generates, sketching your argument, and then returning to expand or narrow the scope of your research. Then you will repeat this cycle, in whole or in part, as you continue to learn new things, raise new questions, and home in on the thing(s) you most want to say about this topic.

Research is challenging. Research is difficult because there is virtually no end to what you could learn about a topic if you pursue it hard and long enough. That's why the process of sifting the information, refining your questions, adjusting the scope of your research—the steps in the iterative process described above—are so important. There are vast bodies of knowledge already out there, and as a college student, you are going to be able to find and absorb only a fraction of this as background to your own research.

In addition, research is sometimes frustrating when your initial hypothesis is not supported by the data or information you find. While this can feel like a failure, it isn't. Actually, whatever you discover is important, even if it requires you to revise your proposed conclusion. This is one more example of how research is often iterative.

Finally, research is challenging just because *contributing intelligently and meaningfully to a scholarly conversation requires bringing your best college-thinking skills to bear on the problem.* All the critical-thinking skills covered in the earlier chapters of this book will come into play when you launch your first research project in college—which is why this chapter has been saved for last.

Types of Research

It's important to realize that not all research is directed toward the same kind of problem. In some cases, your research will aim to solve a practical problem, while at other times, the problem you want to address is conceptual. No doubt, you have done the first type of research many times, like when you have read restaurant reviews on Yelp or product reviews on Amazon. Much research within an academic context is also motivated by a desire to solve practical problems (though not generally a search for the best restaurant). Consider these examples:

- A chemist researches a new antidepressant by looking at its impact on selective serotonin reuptake inhibitors (SSRIs). The problem is that the new drug may not be the most effective way to treat depression, and small adjustments may make the treatment better.
- A music historian studies many of Beethoven's manuscripts and those of his contemporaries to determine whether a particular piece of music was actually written by him. The problem is that we have a music manuscript not attributed to any composer, and we want to know who wrote it.
- A web developer creates a new script that reduces search time on a website by 33 percent. The problem is the website is too slow, and a faster website would attract more users.

Conceptual research, by contrast, addresses gaps in knowledge or understanding about the world. Though sometimes conceptual research will have implications for solving a real-world problem, this is not its primary purpose. With conceptual research, the problem is just that we don't understand something or don't understand it as well as we would like. Here are some examples:

- A researcher analyzes the impact of SSRIs on brain function. The problem is the lack of knowledge about the connection between SSRIs and brain function.
- A music historian studies Beethoven's work to understand the evolution of his distinctive style.
- A computer scientist examines when a computational prediction model fails in order to understand its limitations.

In addition to categorizing research in terms of its purpose, we can also classify it in terms of the sources it draws on.

Primary research involves the collection of new data or source material from the field or from experimentation. This includes most research typically associated with the sciences and social sciences, including experimentation, observation, interviews, and surveys. For example, a researcher might conduct surveys asking people for views about capital punishment and then compare the results to past surveys to see if attitudes have changed over time. While primary research is traditionally associated with such fields, it's important to remember that primary research occurs in all fields.

Secondary research, by contrast, involves the use of existing data and source material, together with the researcher's own ideas, to develop new ways of thinking about a topic. This often includes new interpretations of cultural artifacts or developing new theories to explain phenomena that are already well-known. An example would be an analysis of trends among urban and suburban populations in a specific area between 1980 and 2020 using census data.

Because different disciplines investigate different kinds of questions and utilize different types of evidence, they naturally use different methods to pursue their research. While it is difficult to generalize across the many dozens of disciplines you might be exposed to in college, there are some broad differences you will find among research methods. In the natural sciences and engineering (biology, chemistry, physics, computer science), researchers generally design an experiment with controls, run the experiment repeatedly, analyze the data they obtain, compare their results to existing studies, and draw new conclusions. In the humanities (history, art, music, literature, philosophy, religion), it is common for researchers to examine sources (primary or secondary), do close readings, analyze them using a variety of theoretical frameworks, compare interpretations, and synthesize ideas and perspectives from a range of sources. In the social sciences (psychology, economics, sociology, political science, anthropology, linguistics), researchers will often design an interview, observational study, social experiment, or survey based on existing methods, analyze the data from such a study, compare their results to existing studies, and draw new conclusions. Keep in mind that this is by no means an exhaustive list; scholars in all fields employ a variety of methods to answer the questions that interest them. The important point is this: *whatever subject you're researching, be sure you're familiar with the generally accepted forms of research conducted in that field.*

The Challenges of Research

No matter what topic you choose, doing research will involve certain challenges. It is important to recognize these challenges up front, so you can anticipate them and be better equipped to address them.

The overall structure of a research project has been captured succinctly and elegantly by Wayne Booth, Gregory Colomb, and Joseph Williams in their classic book, *The Craft of Research*. In their words:

> Your aim is to explain
>
> 1. what you are writing about—your topic: "*I am studying . . .*"
> 2. what you don't know about it—your question: "*because I want to find out . . .*"
> 3. why you want your reader to know about it—your rationale: "*in order to help my reader understand better . . .*"[3]

This framework reveals the underlying structure of every research project. You need to have a topic or subject, a question (or questions) that you are asking about that subject, and a reason for asking those questions, or what you might think of as the response you would give to the "So what?" question. But it's not just a good idea to check your finished research project to ensure that it addresses these three points; it's also valuable to use them to plan your research (even if you won't always follow these steps in precisely this order). Let's now examine these elements, one by one.

Finding a topic. Assuming that the topic hasn't been chosen for you by the instructor in your course, your first challenge is deciding what you want to learn about. Often, it is easiest to begin by reviewing things you've learned, either from previous courses or from your own independent exploration, and thinking about what especially aroused your curiosity. Ask yourself, "What would I really enjoy learning more about?" If you're having some trouble deciding whether a potential topic would be worth pursuing, check with your professor.

Don't be surprised if you need to do a bit of research in order to decide what you want to research. You may need to do some preliminary poking around to get a sense of what's out there. As you do, you may well stumble across something that helps you determine a direction (or entices you to change direction, if you already had one). At this stage, it may help to approach your potential subject like a photographer with a wide-angle lens. Take in as much as you can until you feel comfortable narrowing the focus, and then as you get further into your work, narrowing it again. On the other hand, sometimes reading just one article will stimulate your interest and motivate you to pursue the topic further. However you go about it, finding a good topic is likely to take some time and a bit of brainstorming. For example:

> *After reading an interesting article about African American identity in the early twentieth century, you decide you want to write your research paper about Black children during the 1920s for your course on the Harlem Renaissance.*

After learning about the placebo effect in your psychology course, you decide you want to explore ways in which people's mental states contribute to their health.

Asking a question. This is a crucial step in designing your research project. Knowing which questions are worth asking and which may lead to dead ends is central to your learning in college. How you formulate your research question will determine where you look for material, what you find, and often, how you put that material together into a compelling argument. Even small variations in the question can lead you in different directions. But how do you know when you have formulated a good question?

In general, your research question should follow the SOFA rule: it should be **succinct, open-ended, focused,** and **arguable**. It's worth considering each of these in turn.

Succinct. Ideally, you should be able to articulate your key question in a sentence or two (if your question has multiple parts). Try focusing clearly on what you don't know but wish you did, and then attempt to complete the sentence, "I want to know why/how/if/to what extent . . ."

Bad Example: What are the impacts and effects of population growth and development on the urbanization of rural and suburban areas of the Minneapolis metropolitan area and its surroundings during a period of increased immigration and increased birth rates? (This question is both repetitive—"impacts and effects"—and includes what may be extraneous elements—"rural and suburban areas" and "Minneapolis area and its surroundings.")

Exercise. How could you make this research question more succinct?

____

____

____

____

Open-ended. Your question should also not be answerable with a simple yes or no, nor should the answer be implied in the question itself. A good open-ended question will require you to engage in some significant analysis and complex reasoning.

Example of a simple question: Are the impacts of anthropogenic biodiversity loss significant in the Amazon Rainforest? (The question is answerable with a yes or a no, and since scholars overwhelmingly agree that the answer is yes, answering this question would not require deep reasoning or analysis.)

Example of a leading question: What environmental and social disasters will result when biodiversity suddenly collapses in the Amazon? (The question implies extremely bad occurrences and a sudden loss of biodiversity, which suggests that the person asking the question already knows the answer. This question appears to look for evidence in support of a thesis rather than a thesis that emerges from the evidence.)

Exercise. How could you make this research questions open-ended?

____

____

____

____

Focused. The scope of your question should be neither too broad nor too narrow. Finding just the right focus can be tricky; it will depend in part on what material is available to you on your topic. If it's too broad, you might end up producing generalities, and if it's too narrow, you may not be able to find enough material to say anything at all. Consider limiting the scope of your topic to a specific geographical area, culture, time period, discipline, or population. Here are some examples:

Overly broad: In your business management class, you want to write about the impact of pandemics on businesses.

Overly narrow: You want to write about the impact of COVID-19 on the beef supply chain for McDonald's restaurants in southwestern California during May of 2020.

Exercise. How could you make these research questions properly focused?

____

____

____

____

Arguable. For a question and its answer to be interesting, it needs to be something about which people could reasonably disagree. Finding a worthwhile question in this sense will require that you know something about what other scholars have said about your subject. As you do your initial research, keep an eye out for those scholarly disagreements and/or issues that scholars have identified as deserving further investigation.

Not arguable: You want to research whether police arrests and shootings disproportionately target citizens of color. (All available evidence makes it clear that this is true, so there isn't much to argue about here.)

Exercise. How could you make this research question arguable?

____

____

____

____

Articulating your rationale. All good research projects have broader implications. That is, they reach some conclusion that is significant because it contributes to our understanding of some larger topic or issue. You might think of your specific, focused project as a window that enables you to see something outside more clearly or in a new way. This is the part of your project that answers the third part of the research structure presented above, namely, what will your research help your reader to understand better? To get a handle on this, ask yourself:

- What is that larger concern or topic to which your research contributes?
- What contribution does your research make to the scholarly conversation about this topic?
- What are the implications of your research?
- What further questions does it help us to ask?

When you know the answer to one or more of these questions, you elevate your research from just a good question about an interesting topic to something that has real significance for your readers. Often, when you begin your project, you may not have a clear sense of what the implications are. But as you delve into the issues further, you want to look for those larger questions and think about how your research connects with those questions. Frequently, the greater implications of your work will be presented in your conclusion.

The process of developing your research, then, might look something like this:

> *You're interested in children during the Harlem Renaissance. In order to find a question worth asking, you search in academic databases and find a scholarly book called* Children's Literature of the Harlem Renaissance, *which argues that children's poetry during this period reflected debates about the meaning of Blackness. You narrow in on one specific aspect of those debates: How did children's poetry during the Harlem Renaissance mirror and respond to the disagreement between W. E. B. DuBois and Booker T. Washington? In the course of your*

research, it occurs to you that children's literature would not engage with social issues if its writers didn't believe that how we teach children could be important in the struggle to change society. Thus, this study could illuminate the way writers in early twentieth century Black society imagined the relationship between child-rearing and social change.

Overall research summary: You are studying children during the Harlem Renaissance (topic) because you want to find out how children's poetry reflected the debates about racial identity between DuBois and Washington (question) in order to clarify the role of educating children in promoting social change (rationale).

The Process of Research: Working with Sources

With this framework for designing a valuable research project in mind, it's important to introduce you to some of the logistics. What work will you do in the process of selecting your topic, refining your question, and determining its significance? Again, the various steps in this process are all essential, though you may need to do them more than once, and not necessarily always in this order. All of them, as you will see, involve how you work with sources.

Finding your sources. As we noted earlier, doing research involves participating in a scholarly conversation. To do that, you need to know what those scholars have been saying about your topic. There are a number of ways to do this, all of which involve reading widely to get a handle on what scholars call "the state of the question."

Often the first step is to conduct a literature review, which involves scanning bibliographies, finding relevant databases, doing searches within your library's collection, looking for academic journals that cover your topic, and employing other methods to find what's out there. At this stage, you are really just collecting information that will establish the basis for your decisions about how broad or narrow your topic should be, what sorts of issues have been identified by scholars, and what questions they regard as worth exploring. It can also help you zero in on gaps in the research that has already been done, differences in the methods scholars have used, and those larger questions of significance that will help you articulate the ultimate value of your work.

As you do your literature review, it is important to look at various sources, in different mediums, with varying views. The point of the literature review is not only to find sources that you think will support your argument but also to understand the knowledge in the field, the conversation, and the range of scholarly opinion. You may approach the literature review with a thesis already in mind, but you should be willing to change course as you encounter new evidence. Because a literature review can be so helpful in formulating your thesis, it is common practice in some fields to write up the results of this review as its own separate stage in the research process.

As you explore various sources, be aware that not all sources are created equal. The gold standard in academic publications are those that are peer-reviewed. This means that the author had to submit this work to a group of other scholars who anonymously reviewed it to ensure that the methods, analysis, and argument were up to the quality expected in that field. Some premier academic publications are known to have exceptionally high standards, which means that they publish only a small fraction of the pieces submitted to them. So when you look at a publication, you will want to know whether it was subjected to this sort of rigorous vetting process. By contrast, think about the range of materials you can find on websites or in blogs, as well as materials published by organizations with a particular agenda, or other self-published materials. While these sources may well include valuable information and perspectives, if you choose to use them in your research, you will want to proceed cautiously and take extra steps to make sure they are accurate and responsible, with an eye to spotting unacknowledged biases. Refer back to chapter 5, where I offered some advice on how to check on the source and reliability of materials found on the Internet.

In terms of finding sources, it is generally best to begin by searching online databases, which you can most likely access through your college library. Databases attempt to catalog the available academic materials in a particular subject (or set of subjects) for easy retrieval. They generally focus on academic articles but can include books, magazines, journals, archival materials, photographs, multimedia, microfiches, and other materials. You may want to begin by searching general databases, like Academic Search Primer and ProQuest, or by using Google Scholar. But you will likely also want to look for more discipline-specific databases. Talk to a reference librarian to find out what databases you can access that focus on your specific area of interest (you may be surprised to discover just how many of them there are).

Searching databases is a bit of an art, and at first, you may find that it takes you a while to get to the materials that are most helpful to you. In addition to searching by author and title, you can search by keywords. These are the words scholars in the field have selected as helpful ways to tag and sort the whole range of books and articles in their discipline. Some of these will not be immediately obvious to you, and some may not look like they're related to the title of an article. For example, the keywords for the 2018 article "Globalization and Labor Force Participation," by economists Stacie Beck and Soodong Park, include *fiscal policy*, *tax competition*, and *compensation hypothesis*.

Sometimes you can find your way to the sources you want by looking at the index or bibliography of a book on your subject. There you will find the names of authors cited and a list of other books and articles that this author referred to in writing this book. Following the trail of references from one book to an article, and from there to something written by an author quoted in that article, and from there to another book mentioned in a footnote, is a bit like embarking on a scavenger hunt—and it's best if you can approach it with a similar sense of adventure.

Finally, if you prefer a high-touch, low-tech approach, you can just look through the shelves of your college library. Since books are always catalogued by subject, once you find one book that's relevant to your topic, the books shelved nearby are likely to be related. Start browsing and see what you find!

A Note on Wikipedia

Wikipedia is a great source of information when beginning your research, especially when you are still in a topic-finding phase, but you should be wary about using it as a source for your final research.

Wikipedia is often very up-to-date, allows you to ask questions on forums, makes it easy to leapfrog to related articles and sources, and has unparalleled amounts of information on many subjects.

However, Wikipedia has varying levels of quality and unpredictable biases, and it can be vandalized with incorrect or misleading information.

Wikipedia is also always being edited and updated, and it can be edited/updated by nearly anyone on the Internet. There are quality controls, but there is never a "final" product, as there is in print sources.

Look at the sources, understand the biases of any article, find what other sources link to the article, and examine the history of an article.

Remember to cite information from Wikipedia (and other websites) via permalink to ensure that the version you used gets remembered correctly.

Tracking and citing your sources. As you gather sources for your research project, you'll need to keep track of them so you can refer to them correctly in your final project. Listing the sources you referred to in your notes and providing a complete list in a bibliography at the end of your paper is important for a few reasons. Now that you are part of a scholarly conversation, you need to acknowledge and recognize the contributions of others and indicate where you have relied on their work. This is both a way of showing you have done your homework and of preserving your academic integrity. You don't want to mislead your reader into thinking that what you wrote is original when it's not. (I'll come back to the issue of plagiarism later in this chapter.)

There are many different formats for citing sources (books, articles, films, websites, etc.) that vary by academic discipline. The most commonly used formats are MLA (Modern Language Association), Chicago (based on the

University of Chicago's *Chicago Manual of Style*), and APA (American Psychological Association). Typically, MLA is used for most of the humanities, Chicago is used for history, most of the arts, and some sciences, and APA is used for social sciences and other sciences. There are also various other styles used in specific disciplines, so you should always check with your professors about what style they prefer (or require).[4] Here are just a few examples of variations of the bibliographic citation formats for books and journal articles according to these three most common style guides:

MLA	Suzuki, Koji. "Approximating the Number of Integers without Large Prime Factors." *Mathematics of Computation*, vol. 75, no. 254, 2006, pp. 1015–1024. (Journal Article)
	Curran, Kevin, editor. *Renaissance Personhood: Materiality, Taxonomy, Process*. Edinburgh University Press, 2020. (Edited Book)
APA	Suzuki, K. (2006). Approximating the number of integers without large prime factors. *Mathematics of Computation, 75*(254), 1015–1024. (Journal Article)
	Curran, K. (Ed.). (2020). *Renaissance Personhood: Materiality, Taxonomy, Process*. Edinburgh University Press. (Edited Book)
Chicago	Suzuki, Koji. "Approximating the Number of Integers without Large Prime Factors." *Mathematics of Computation* 75, no. 254 (2006): 1015–24. (Journal Article)
	Curran, Kevin, ed. *Renaissance Personhood: Materiality, Taxonomy, Process*. Edinburgh: Edinburgh University Press, 2020. (Edited Book)

Note: These are the formats used when you're listing your sources in a bibliography; the formats for notes (footnotes or endnotes) or in-text citations are different.

Finally, you will sometimes be asked to produce what is called an annotated bibliography. This is a list of the sources you used with short (usually two- or three-sentence) notations after each one to indicate what you found there and how it was relevant to your work. This is a service to your reader, who may want to use your bibliography to help them find their way to the sources that will be most useful to them. (It is also a way to let your professor know you really read those sources and aren't just listing them to pad your bibliography.) If you know that this is a requirement for your research project, you'll want to keep notes about the content and value of all your sources as you read them. Even if it isn't required, you may want to annotate the sources you use in your notes, just to make it easier to keep track of what is, or might be, useful in your research. Here is an example of an entry in an annotated bibliography:

> **Davidson, Hilda Ellis**. ***Roles of the Northern Goddess.* London: Routledge, 1998.**
> Davidson's book provides a thorough examination of the major roles filled by the numerous pagan goddesses of Northern Europe in everyday life, including their roles in hunting, agriculture, domestic arts like weaving, the household, and death. The author discusses relevant archaeological evidence, patterns of symbol and ritual, and previous research. The book includes a number of black-and-white photographs of relevant artifacts.[5]

Managing your sources. The sources you find will shape your thinking about the subject, help you to narrow your focus, and contribute to your final research paper or poster. There are a variety of ways in which these sources will contribute to your work.

Some sources provide general background on your subject. They will help you get a handle on the subject, providing context and giving you an overview of how your particular topic fits within a broad field of inquiry.

> *For your course on ecology, you've decided to write about the impacts of the invasive cheatgrass on the local flora and their resilience. A field guide on local plants and their characteristics would be a background source. This source will give you general information you will use in your paper.*

Often, background sources will also be useful in providing bibliographies or lists of other sources you might find relevant to your topic.

Sometimes, a source will be useful as evidence for a claim you're making. It might provide data that supports your conclusion about the efficacy of a particular medical treatment, or it might contain historical facts that help you build an argument that certain events influenced the development of a particular phenomenon, like capitalism. In some cases, the source is its own evidence, as when you focus on the interpretation of a particular short story.

Rainfall data from the last five years that you will interpret as correlated with cheatgrass growth provides you with crucial evidence for your argument. You'll analyze it, along with other sources.

Sometimes, sources help you build or refine your argument. These are typically sources where the author has taken a position that you want to either affirm, dispute, qualify, or extend in some way. In essence, you are using these sources to engage in a dialogue with the other experts in the field.

An article describes the impacts of cheatgrass on the wildfire cycle and local flora in the macro-ecological system. You'll use this in your own argument, affirming its validity or highlighting the study's shortcomings.

Finally, sometimes a source is helpful because it illustrates a particular method for studying something. Think of a method as just a distinctive way of thinking, a procedure for analyzing something, or a way of categorizing things. In some cases, your source may offer a method for studying a topic that has no relationship to yours—it's just a method that you think can help answer your research questions. (In fact, some of the most creative research involves importing methods used in one field and applying them in another.[6])

You found a source that describes the impact of kudzu on temperate forests in Illinois. You like the methods it uses to measure the impact of kudzu, so you use that same method to analyze the cheatgrass problem you're working on.

It's important to remember that sources don't come prelabeled in ways that tell you how to use them. Part of the intellectual challenge of doing research is determining which sources are useful for your specific purpose and then how to use them. It's not uncommon to use the same source (or parts of it) for more than one purpose within the same research project.

You find a United States Geological Survey report on soil quality in your county and its impact on plant growth. You can use the results of that study in your own analysis of cheatgrass to further your argument or use the data in that study as evidence that enables you to make a point about the relationship between soil quality and invasive species.

And as your needs or the focus of your research change, you may find that you use old sources in new ways.

You want to do a comparison of the impact of invasive species on native flora in the continental United States. You find extensive experimental field logs on the impact of kudzu in the Ozark National Forest but can't find anything on cheatgrass. Since you liked the experimental methods of the kudzu study, you decide to do your own experiment on cheatgrass in your university's biology lab. In this case, the original researcher's studies contribute both to your argument and to your methods.

Note: A solid research project depends on having sources that both provide evidence and contribute to your argument; that is, they give you material to interpret and engage with. If all your sources are providing just background or methods, you are probably summarizing information from others rather than developing your own ideas.

A Note on Libraries

Even in this age of the Internet, libraries remain essential places of information access and research. University libraries generally have an incredible selection of materials that are well catalogued, including special collections, microfiches, traditional books, periodicals (both academic and popular press), DVDs and other electronic mediums, and government documents. They also generally offer free access to databases, software, and sometimes equipment.

Librarians are research professionals. They know about research procedures and resources and can help you at every step of your research process. They also love helping students take full advantage of the library's resources, so consult with them early and often!

Integrating your sources into an argument. Now that you have lots of sources, ideas, and arguments, you'll have to combine all this knowledge into one coherent, clear, concise presentation. The writing process has been discussed at length in chapter 6, and you should refer back to the guidelines offered there about how to tackle all writing assignments. Here, we'll focus on some of the questions you need to ask yourself as you pull together the results of your research.

You want to make sure the sources you've assembled will give you what you need to make your case, that is, to answer the question you posed and explain why it's significant.

Whenever you're working with sources, always ask yourself:

- Do I have enough sources?
- What is promising (or problematic) about the sources I have gathered?
- Do I have the right kinds of sources, ones that will provide background, evidence, arguments, and methods?
- Do I need to broaden or narrow the topic?
- Do my conclusions need to be adjusted to reflect what I've learned from my sources?

If you're confident that you have the right number, range, and quality of sources, then you'll need to organize them in some logical fashion so they help your reader understand the questions you've asked and the ways you have tried to answer them.

Whenever you're organizing your sources, always ask yourself:

- How do the sources relate to each other?
- Do some sources shed light on others?
- What is the general flow of ideas from source to source?
- How will this affect the overall structure of my presentation?
- What are my conclusions?

At this point, you should be ready to summarize your thesis, or main point, and outline your research presentation. This will involve putting the pieces together in a way that flows, which means you have told your readers what they need to know at just the right point in your presentation. In the end, all the connections among the pieces of your argument should be explicit, so readers don't have to work to make those connections themselves. *Be clear about how your evidence supports your claims, how your thesis answers your question, and how your conclusions contribute to a larger conversation surrounding your work.*

An important part of assembling your sources into an argument is to distinguish your voice from the voices of the scholars whose work you have relied on in all the ways discussed above. You will quote some of those sources directly because their exact words capture something you want to say or because you want to include their voices in your presentation. Sometimes, you will glean ideas or evidence from a source but paraphrase or summarize it. And still other times, you will have used a source for general background that you don't actually include in the paper but that you used as a guide. In all these cases, you need to provide citations in footnotes, a bibliography, or both, depending on the specific requirements of this project.

Failing to correctly identify the sources you used in your research is considered a form of academic dishonesty, since you have misled your reader to believe that someone else's work is your own. In college, your professors may be stricter about acts of plagiarism than teachers were in high school. In egregious cases, there can be strict penalties—losing credit for that assignment, failing a course, or even being sanctioned by the college's committee on academic integrity.

Needless to say, directly quoting another scholar's work without citing it, turning in someone else's work as your own, and buying an essay through the Internet are unacceptable. But you also need to be aware of more subtle forms of plagiarism:

- Self-plagiarism is when you submit a past assignment (in whole or in part) as if it were new, thus getting credit twice for the same work. This can be avoided by writing a new essay for each assignment, unless your professor has explicitly permitted you to reuse older work.
- Mosaic plagiarism, also called "patchwriting," is when you blend paraphrased material and direct quotes without distinguishing them. This can be avoided by quoting the original text exactly if it contains notable, uniquely important language, or paraphrasing it completely if you simply wish to summarize its primary argument.
- Accidental plagiarism can occur when you take notes in a sloppy way, forgetting to indicate when your notes include quotes. This can be avoided by clearly identifying direct quotes in your notes with color coding, underlining, or highlighting.

Products of Research

When you have finished doing all this work of finding, tracking, using, and integrating your sources, you're ready to begin creating the final product that will convey the results of your research to your audience. After all, the point of all this work is not just to learn new things, valuable as that is, but to share what you have learned with others. This is done in a number of forms.

Research papers. Most often, the results of your research will be shared in a paper or an article. Professors often read their research papers at academic conferences (where they gather to share their work and learn from one another) and publish them in academic journals or books. While there are some conferences and journals devoted to undergraduate research, it is more likely that your research will be shared with your professor, your classmates, or perhaps in a public presentation.

Posters. In many fields, especially in the natural and social sciences, research results are shared in the form of posters. The poster is a visual representation of the work you did. It summarizes very succinctly the research questions you asked, the methods you used, and the conclusions you reached (and sometimes also questions to be pursued in future research on this topic). Posters are usually shared in large settings that offer people an opportunity to circulate and take in the results of many research projects in one session (many academic conferences include poster sessions). Typically, researchers stand alongside their posters and give brief talks to those circulating around the room and learning about a range of research on display.

Designing an effective poster is challenging. Many students make the mistake of trying to include too much detailed information on their posters, which results in something that is difficult for the viewer to absorb.

The special challenge of creating a research poster is that it requires both a certain aesthetic sense, an appreciation of what will look appealing, and an ability to effectively communicate a lot of complex information succinctly in a visual format. Here is an example of a good research poster:

Freshwater Security in Fresno County, California

Alexander Li | Stanford University

This study highlights the freshwater issues in Fresno County and projects its consequences into the future.

Introduction

Fresno County is located in the San Joaquin Valley and is an urban center for much of the agricultural industry in Central California. With a population of 975 000, the county spans 15 600 km²(6 000 mi²) and faces major water challenges.[9] A changing climate, low water quality, and overdrafting will present Fresno County with hard choices to come.

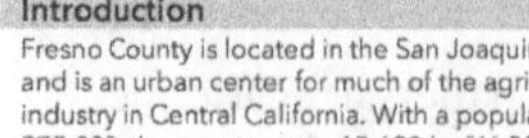

Fluxes In

Precipitation in the County is seasonal and varies from year to year (see Fig 2). Because of this, the county needs storage capacity to stabilize supply.

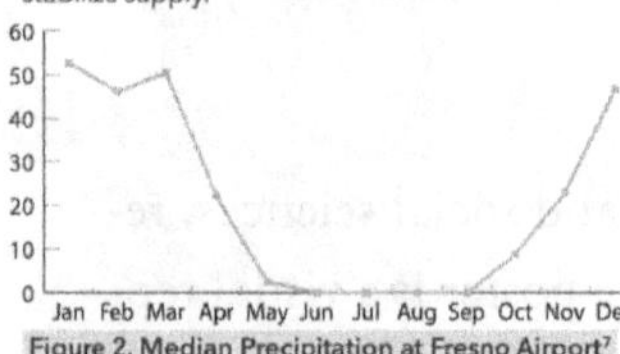

Figure 2. Median Precipitation at Fresno Airport[7] in mm/month

The **Delta-Mendota Canal** and mountain **streams** bring important supplements for the region.[8] They provide high quality water from upstate and' support recreation and wetlands.

Stored Water

Reservoirs provide continual water supply throughout the year. They also provide recreation, electricity, and spaces for wildlife. The three major reservoirs are *Pine Flat, Millerton,* and the *Big Creek Complex.*

Groundwater provides an important water "bank" for the county. However, years of overdrafting have led to lower water quality, land subsidence, and possible collapsed aquifers.[2]

References

1. Allen R, Pereira L, Raes D, Smith M. 1998. Food and Agricultural Organization of the UN. Crop Evapotranspiration: Guidelines for computing crop water requirements FAO Irrigation Drainage Paper 56. Chapter 6. 01 Feb 2018.
2. Bertoldi GL, Johnston RH, Evenson KD. 1991. Groundwater in the Central Valley, CA-A Summary Report. USGS. USGS Professional Paper, Vol 1401-A. 10 February 2018.
3. 2014. CA Dept. Water Resources. CADWR Land Use Viewer. 25 January 2018.
4. 2015. CA State Water Resources Control Board. Geotracker GAMA. Water Quality Summary for Fresno County. 04 March 2018.
5. 2018. Environmental Working Group. EWG's Tap Water Database. 04 March 2018.
6. 2017. NOAA. Climate Resilience Toolkit. 18 January 2018.
7. 1995. NOAA. Fresno/Air Terminal CA Climate Variable Descriptions. 10 January 2017.
8. 2017. U.S. Bureau of Reclamation. Central Valley Operations. Reports of Operations Monthly Delivery Tables. 19 Feb 2018.
9. 2017. U.S. Census Bureau. Quick Facts: Fresno County, California. 11 January 2018.
10. 09 December 2016. U.S. Geological Survey. Estimated Use of Water in the U.S. County Level Data for 2010. 22 February 2018.

Figure 1. Box Model of Fresno County
in millions of cubic meters/year

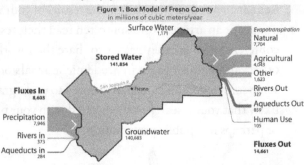

Surface Water 1,171
Stored Water 141,854
Groundwater 140,683
San Joaquin R.
Fresno
Fluxes In 8,603
Precipitation 7,946
Rivers in 373
Aqueducts in 284
Evapotranspiration
Natural 7,704
Agricultural 4,043
Other 1,623
Rivers Out 327
Aqueducts Out 859
Human Use 105
Fluxes Out 14,661

Fluxes Out

Natural Evapotranspiration (ET) makes up most of the water lost in the county. However, **Agricultural ET** also creates a large water loss. In recent years, the increase of water intensive crops has lead increase ET (see Fig 3).

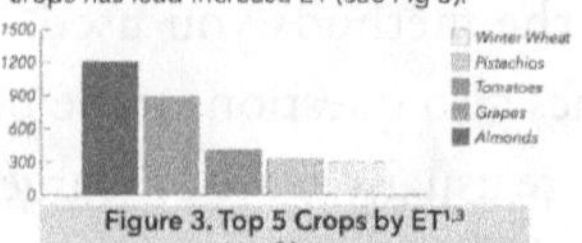

Figure 3. Top 5 Crops by ET[1,3] in m³/year

The **Friant-Kern Canal** takes water from the Millerton Reservoir southward to the ag-heavy Tulare and Kern County, which also have water shortages.[8] The **San Joaquin River** flows northward where it will eventually reach the San Francisco Bay.

The **Human Urban Use** does not account for most of the water use, but does account for most of the population. *Public* and *Domestic* use is approx. the same (see Fig. 4).

Figure 4. Urban Water Use[10] in millions m³/year

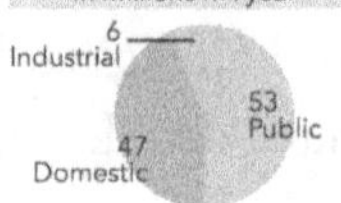

Water Quality

The natural water quality has suffered due to agricultural pollution, overdrafting, and improper waste disposal.

Water Quality Grade
C+

Common contaminants include:[4,5]
- Uranium, Radium
- Arsenic, Chromium, Manganese
- Chlorine Byproducts
- Volatile Organic Compounds
- Nitrates, Pesticides, Salts

The Future

Fresno County is looking at a growing population and a **hotter, more extreme climate.**[6] This will lead to more urban water use, higher ET, and less dependable precipitation.

Conclusion

Fresno County's freshwater security is at risk in the near future. Without efforts to stabalize water usage, prevent water pollution, and adapt to a changing climate, the county could have a water crisis within a generation.

The county has a net flux of - 8 181 million m³/year. It will run out of water on

Wednesday, August 14, 2041

The poster clearly identifies the research question (introduction), key elements of the project (highlighted with section headings), the conclusion, and references. The conclusion of the research is driven home by a box, highlighted in the bottom right corner, which indicates the date when the water in Fresno County will run out.

Whenever you're creating a research poster, always ask yourself:

- What is the most important/interesting finding from my research?
- How can I visually share my research? Should I use charts, graphs, photos, or images? How can I arrange the text and visuals in a way that best conveys the work I did?
- What can I do to make my poster visually engaging, so that people are drawn to it and can easily find the information they want?

Other formats. Depending on the discipline, the scope of your research, and the requirements of a particular assignment, the results of your research could take a number of other forms. These include lab reports, case studies, news stories, art projects, videos, PowerPoint presentations, and lectures. Different sorts of subjects, and different sorts of audiences, will dictate the medium best suited for your particular research project.

At the end of your project, you'll want to double-check to make sure your final presentation includes all the following elements.

- Title: a short description of your topic. Titles are most effective when they are brief and clearly signal to the reader what your project is about.
- Abstract: a brief summary of your work. This should include everything essential about the research: the question, the methods you used, and your results. Readers will look to an abstract (as you may have done in your own research) to determine if this article is relevant to their interests.
- Introduction/Literature Review: a brief overview of the question being addressed and the existing literature on the subject. This is where you explain what drew you to this topic, provide background information your reader will need to make sense of your research, and present the relevant contributions of previous

researchers. Many of you will have done a version of this if you were ever asked to write an annotated bibliography.

- Argument/Experiment/Study: this is the heart of your paper, where you pull together your sources to provide evidence for your thesis and present your argument.
- Methods: an explanation of how you answered your research question, including the methods for gathering and analyzing data, the assumptions you made, and the interpretive framework you brought to this material.
- Conclusion: a summary of your results and their significance. You may want to include applications of the results and/or questions that merit further study.
- Bibliography: the list of all sources—cited and uncited—that you used in your research.

In some cases, these components of your research will appear in distinct sections and may even be identified with subheadings. But whether you adhere to such a strict organizational scheme or not, all successful research projects will have these elements (though not necessarily in this order).

Conclusion

At the beginning of this chapter, I noted that research represents the pinnacle of your college learning. It requires you to draw upon all the habits of mind and critical-thinking skills you have honed in previous college work and then produce something that demonstrates your comprehension, analytical skills, and communication skills. Engaging in research really does involve making the transition from consuming knowledge to producing it. No wonder, then, that it is so demanding.

But the rewards can be equally great. As a researcher, even a novice one, you will come to appreciate, from the inside, what it takes to produce all those books and articles you have read and learned from all these years. Almost certainly, it will also lead to a deeper understanding of how *knowledge is both constructed and contested,* since you will have experienced all the challenges of identifying a question, assembling and weighing evidence, considering alternative points of view, and assessing the implications of your findings. You now know that scholars who do these things are exercising choice and judgment at every point, just as you did.

As with so many other things in life, as you practice the skills of researching, you will improve—through critical feedback from your professors, of course, but also through self-reflection on your own experience. As you move through your college career, you might occasionally take the time to go back and reread work you submitted earlier, considering how you might improve it if you were doing it now. In all likelihood, you'll quickly see places where you could have deepened your analysis, gathered a different kind of evidence, made your conclusion bolder, or just expressed yourself more clearly. Research is the ultimate training ground for thinking critically. Each new research project gives you an opportunity to demonstrate how well you know how to learn.

You would do well, then, to approach each research assignment in a spirit of adventure and humility. Not every adventure unfolds as planned; often you encounter unexpected obstacles and get lost along the way. But if you are prepared for that, you need not get flustered or frustrated. Some of those dead ends and misadventures are precisely where you learn the most. And if you adopt a humble stance toward your learning, you will find that research is your opportunity to join the conversation that scholars in your field began long before you were born and that will continue long after you are gone. You may not leave an indelible mark on that conversation, but you get to make your own small contribution to it.

Remember that none of your professors expects you to be an expert, just as a high school basketball coach wouldn't expect her players to play like professionals. She would expect them to use all the skills at their disposal to play the game as well as they could. And that is what research in college invites you to do—get out on the court and play to the best of your ability, knowing that the point is not whether you win or lose but how much satisfaction you can derive just from being in the game.

Questions for Reflection

1. Try this exercise:
   A. Pick any article you have been assigned for a class, read through the citations (quotes or notes), and ask yourself, "From where does the author draw their evidence? What kinds of sources does the author draw upon?"
   B. Select at least two citations and take the time to trace them back to their original source. This will most likely require a trip to the library. When you find the original quotation, passage, or statistic, consider its context, which might require skimming the article or chapter from which the citation is drawn.
   C. Finally, evaluate how the author uses these sources in the development of his or her argument. Consider these questions:
      - Have they cited their source properly?
      - Why have they inserted a citation here, as opposed to elsewhere in their text?
      - Do you think the author uses his/her source carefully?
      - Do you have critiques or reservations about their interpretation of the source material? Could the source reflect a particular bias that may influence their findings or make their conclusions less reliable?
      - In what way do the sources function as evidence? Do you think the sources support the author's claims and help to convince you of the author's argument? If not, are there types of sources you think might have helped make their argument more convincing?
      - If the citations are not used as "evidence," what types of evidence does the author employ in crafting their argument?[7]

2. How has research impacted your life? Think of times when you have benefitted from some piece of research you encountered through the media. How do you imagine those researchers did their work? How long might it have taken them, and what challenges might they have faced?

3. Imagine a history student a hundred years from now who is taking a course on the history of American education and writing a research paper about student life in the twenty-first century. What could a potential research question be? What kinds of present-day sources do you think would be useful to them? How would they use such sources? What larger issues might motivate their research?

4. Try mapping a research conversation. Find a scholarly article that interests you, and summarize its topic in the center of a piece of paper. Then, pick another scholarly source from its cited literature, summarize that new source, and draw a line connecting the two summaries. Pick another source cited in the second article, summarize it, and continue the process. What unexpected connections do you stumble upon? How many separate disciplines or authors can you connect?

5. What's your process for taking notes and tracking sources when researching? How can you refine it to be more efficient and protect against accidental plagiarism?

6. Producing your first research project in college can be daunting, especially when you begin reading work by experts in the field and try to imagine producing something that measures up. Remember that those published books and articles were likely written by experts who spent years studying their subject. Try locating a journal of student research, even if it isn't relevant to your topic. What inspires you about the articles you find there? What aspects of their work could you learn from, or even imitate?

ADVICE FOR THE ROAD AHEAD

Offer Critique, Not Criticism

College is designed to teach you critical-thinking skills. Often, college students assume that that means the goal is to be critical, that is, to look for the weak point in everything you read and to poke holes in the views or arguments of others, including one's classmates. But the point of college is not just to become more critical. It is to become a more careful and subtle thinker, to learn to look at things from multiple perspectives, and to weigh the persuasiveness of various answers to the same question. To be sure, sometimes this involves seeing the shortcomings of someone's position or comparing two views and arguing that one is stronger than the other. But this doesn't mean that learning to be a better critical thinker is the same as learning to be more negative.

Typically, your professors will ask you to offer critique, not criticism. What's the difference? To critique something—an article or book, a work of art, or an experimental protocol—is to *consider its strengths and weaknesses in a balanced way.* This requires explaining why certain aspects of this material are stronger (more persuasive, or artful, or better designed) than others. A critique commonly includes some appreciation for the positive elements and may even include suggestions for how the author could have made this work better. If you provide just a list of the shortcomings of a work, you are actually leaving yourself open to the charge that you are biased against it, since you didn't really see it as a whole.

And a critique, when it is careful, considers the relative importance of those errors or shortcomings that you do identify. It's possible that the author has made a mistake or has overlooked something, and critiquing that person's work requires you to note this. But it requires you to do something else: indicate just how important that particular failing is. After all, in academic work as in life, not all mistakes are equally serious.

You can think of this by analogy with a physical structure. Some beams in the structure may be weight-bearing in that they support the roof of the structure; others are just decorative. So, too, some shortcomings touch on the essence of what the author is attempting to do; others may play a less important role. To critique something is to notice just how significant a problem is or the extent to which it is a fatal flaw rather than a minor one.

In short, critique is not about finding fault, and certainly not about assuming that the more faults one can find, the better. Rather, it is about looking closely at something and evaluating its merits in an evenhanded, sophisticated, and careful way. To do this requires critical-thinking skills of the sort discussed throughout this book. But it also requires using those skills in a way that demonstrates you can discriminate between more important and less important aspects of an argument (or of a work of art, or of a procedure). A really smart critique is one that recognizes shortcomings but as part of a wider assessment, including strengths that are unaffected by these particular shortcomings.

Which brings me to the final point about feedback: when it is your work being subjected to critique, it may be hard not to take it personally. Negative feedback may strike you as a judgment on how smart you are, or how hard you worked on the project, or simply as unkind. But just as it is important to learn how to give a critique in a constructive way, it is important to learn how to receive it in a spirit of openness and appreciation. In this way, too, college is good preparation for life. Whatever you do, you will be subject to someone who will have judgments about your work. College is a great time to practice receiving critical feedback from others in an environment where the stakes are relatively low.

CONCLUSION

The Final Frontier: Becoming an Educated Person

I believe that education is a process of living
and not a preparation for future living.
—JOHN DEWEY

When people learn, they don't take on new
knowledge so much as a new identity.
—JULIE LINDQUIST

There are many reasons to go to college. For some of you, the motivation is entirely practical—college is a prerequisite for getting the job you want. Some of you may not know what job you want, but you know that college graduates on average earn far more over their lifetimes than those without college degrees.[1] Some of you may have the luxury of not worrying too much about your future earnings, so college is about expanding your intellectual horizons and perhaps studying a subject that really interests you. Or perhaps you are going to college simply because it's what your family expected. Since college was required, not optional, it isn't something you've been asked to justify or explain.

College does convey all these benefits—career opportunities, greater earning potential, and broader intellectual horizons, among others. But the premise of this book has been that while all these are valid reasons for attending college, *the most distinctive and long-lasting benefit of college is that it teaches you to think in more complex, rigorous, and sophisticated ways.* And this ability to think critically will enhance your life no matter what career you choose, how much you make, or what interests you ultimately develop.

A college education is designed to foster critical discernment, a willingness to probe and question information. Even a cursory reading of the news reveals that the world is full of gullible people who espouse unfounded conspiracy theories, fail to think through illogical views, or refuse to critically examine their own beliefs. There is even a widespread failure to recognize the difference between personal preferences (e.g., your favorite flavor of ice cream) and issues where there are reasoned arguments for and against a point of view. How many times have you heard someone defend their not-very-well-considered view by appealing to the idea that "everyone is entitled to their own opinion." Of course we are. But that doesn't mean that all opinions should carry equal weight! Knowing how to distinguish well-reasoned opinions from poorly reasoned ones is a key skill you will develop in college.

No matter what you do in life, our increasingly complex world will bombard you with information you need to process. In addition, you will encounter people whose experiences, beliefs, and values will be very different from yours. You will also inevitably face various challenges as you move through life (e.g., adversity, moral dilemmas, and social problems) that will require you to think deeply and creatively about the kind of person you are becoming, about your responsibilities, about the kind of society and world you want to live in, and about your legacy. You will need to respond to these novel challenges and to adapt to changing social, economic, political, and ecological circumstances. In short, both intellectually and personally, you will need to be able to solve problems you haven't yet faced. How prepared will you be to do this?

A college education is among the best ways to prepare for these challenges. Its goal is ultimately *to train you to think more clearly, analyze information more carefully, engage with the views of others more deeply, and examine your own assumptions more honestly*. Of course, there is no guarantee that simply earning a college degree will confer these benefits; we can probably all think of college graduates who continued to be prejudiced, opinionated, or gullible. Sometimes, even a good college education can't overcome our human susceptibility to these shortcomings. But if you really buy in and acquire the habits of mind college is designed to teach you, you will emerge from these years with a set of skills that will serve you well for the rest of your life. It will change the way you think and, as a result, the way you live. As Julie Lindquist says in the epigram above, it will involve taking on a new identity and really becoming a different person.[2]

What I am describing here are the benefits of what is generally called a "liberal education." Though the exact scope and purpose of liberal education have been debated for centuries, it is generally agreed that it is designed to "liberate" you from confusion and prejudice and to free you to fully explore and understand the world—both the external world and the internal one. This liberal education will make you a better citizen, insofar as you are asked to weigh in on the great social, economic, and political issues of your society. But it will also give you the tools to cultivate tolerance, to combat prejudice, and to make decisions more thoughtfully.

College is at least as much about the habits of mind you acquire as it is about the subjects you study. If you talk to college graduates, you will likely discover that decades after graduation the information they learned is out of date and the particulars of what they studied (their major or concentration) are not what they remember and value most. Instead, they will tell you that what they learned was a way of thinking, communicating, and collaborating that has served them in ways they never anticipated when they were in college. In fact, corporate leaders regularly report that what they look for in potential employees is less the expertise they bring or the content knowledge they have than their ability to think clearly and to communicate effectively.[3] That's because employers know that these skills are transferable and broadly applicable to any work situation or project to which you might be assigned. And unlike concrete skills and bodies of knowledge that become outdated, these skills are endlessly relevant. *Knowing how to think well is an asset that never loses its value.*

Many students think of college in an instrumental way—it will get you where you want to go, to a secure job or to graduate school. It's as if a college education were a plane ticket to the destination of your choice. And certainly there's nothing wrong with using your college education to get you to a specific goal. But few students who think of their education this way have considered this: a plane ticket is a single-use item, and it is good for just one destination. When you arrive, the ticket has served its purpose and is now useless, obsolete. That's why we throw away used plane tickets after we arrive.

But I encourage you instead to think of your college education as a passport, which can be used again and again. When it expires, it can be renewed. And it can take you to any destination. It even has within it the record of all the places you have visited, the stops on your journey where you have had meaningful experiences. That's why many people hold onto their old passports long after they have been replaced by newer ones.[4] Your college education is your passport, which will take you to destinations you haven't been to or even heard of, or maybe to places that don't even exist yet.

But there is a sense in which your college education is even more powerful than your passport. After all, it's possible to have a passport but never use it. You can opt to just stay home and avoid any of the challenges (and forgo any of the benefits) that come from international travel. But this is where the metaphor of education as travel reaches its limit. Once you acquire the critical-thinking skills college gives you, you will find it nearly impossible not to use them. Wherever you go, you will take your mind with you. And your mind will forever be shaped by the habits of thought and tools of analysis college teaches you.

▪ ▪ ▪

It is common knowledge that our world is changing at an unprecedented pace. We simply cannot know what new challenges we will face in another generation or two. But notwithstanding this uncertainty, there is one thing we can be certain of: facing those challenges will require people who have the skills to think about complex problems in rigorous and creative ways. For precisely this reason, college is undoubtedly one of the best investments you can possibly make in your future. It is also an excellent investment in the future of our world, for we will never exhaust our need for people who are adept at thinking critically.

RESOURCES/SUGGESTIONS FOR FURTHER READING

Introduction. Pack Your Bags: College as Intellectual Adventure Travel

Bader, John. *Dean's List: 11 Habits of Highly Successful College Students*. Baltimore: Johns Hopkins University Press, 2011.

Light, Richard J. *Making the Most of College: Students Speak Their Minds.* Cambridge, MA: Harvard University Press, 2001.

Chapter One. Learning How to Learn

Brown, Peter C., Henry L. Roedinger III, and Mark A. McDaniel. *Make It Stick: The Science of Successful Learning.* Cambridge, MA: Harvard University Press, 2014.

Doyle, Terry, and Todd Zakrajsek. *The New Science of Learning: How to Learn in Harmony with Your Brain.* Sterling, VA: Stylus Publishing, 2013.

Hacker, Douglas J., John Dunlosky, and Arthur C. Graesser, eds. *Metacognition in Educational Theory and Practice.* Mahwah, NJ: Lawrence Erlbaum Associates, 1998.

Perkins, D. N. *The Mind's Best Work.* Cambridge, MA: Harvard University Press, 1981.

Chapter Two. Critical Thinking 101

Bailin, Sharon, Roland Case, Jerrold R. Coombs, and Leroi B. Daniels. "Common Misconceptions of Critical Thinking." *Journal of Curriculum Studies* 31, no. 3 (1999a): 269–83. doi:10.1080/002202799183124.

———. "Conceptualizing Critical Thinking." *Journal of Curriculum Studies* 31, no. 3 (1999b): 285–302. doi:10.1080/002202799183133.

Barnet, Sylvan, and Hugo Bedau. *Critical Thinking, Reading, and Writing: A Brief Guide to Argument.* Boston: Bedford/St. Martin's, 2014.

Bers, Trudy, Marc Chun, William T. Daly, Christine Harrington, and Barbara F. Tobolowsky, eds. *Foundations for Critical Thinking.* Columbia, SC: University of South Carolina Press, 2015.

Browne, M. Neil, and Stuart M. Keeley. *Asking the Right Questions: A Guide to Critical Thinking.* 2nd ed. Englewood Cliffs, NJ: Prentice-Hall, 1986.

Chaffee, John. *Thinking Critically*. 9th ed. Boston: Houghton Mifflin, 2009.

Forte, James M., and Christopher P. Horvath, eds. *Critical Thinking*. New York: Nova Science Publishers, 2011.

Haber, Jonathan. *Critical Thinking*. Cambridge, MA: MIT Press, 2020. https://doi.org/10.7551/mitpress/12081.001.0001.

Kurfiss, Joanne Gainen. *Critical Thinking: Theory, Research, Practice, and Possibilities*. Washington, DC: Association for the Study of Higher Education, 1988.

Lewis, Arthur, and David Smith. "Defining Higher Order Thinking." *Theory into Practice* 32, no. 3 (1993): 131–37. doi:10.1080/00405849309543588.

Moon, Jennifer A. *Critical Thinking: An Exploration of Theory and Practice*. London: Routledge, 2008.

Moore, Tim John. *Critical Thinking and Language: The Challenge of Generic Skills and Disciplinary Discourses*. London: Continuum, 2011.

Mulnix, Jennifer Wilson. "Thinking Critically about Critical Thinking." *Educational Philosophy and Theory* 44, no. 5 (2012): 464–79. doi:10.1111/j.1469-5812.2010.00673.x.

Paul, Richard, and Linda Elder. *Critical Thinking: Tools for Taking Charge of Your Learning and Your Life*. Boston: Pearson, 2012.

———. *The Miniature Guide to Critical Thinking Concepts and Tools*. Dillon Beach, CA: Foundation for Critical Thinking Press, 2010.

Vaughn, Lewis. *The Power of Critical Thinking: Effective Reasoning about Ordinary and Extraordinary Claims*. 5th ed. New York: Oxford University Press, 2016.

Wisdom, Sherrie, and Lynda Leavitt, eds. *Handbook of Research on Advancing Critical Thinking in Higher Education*. Hershey, PA: IGI Global, 2015. http://doi:10.4018/978-1-4666-8411-9.

Chapter Three. What Am I Doing in This Class, Anyway?

Buehl, Doug. *Developing Readers in the Academic Disciplines*. Newark, NJ: International Reading Association, 2011.

Donald, Janet Gail. *Learning to Think: Disciplinary Perspectives*. San Francisco: Jossey-Bass, 2002.

Pace, David, and Joan Middendorf, eds. *Decoding the Disciplines: Helping Students Learn Disciplinary Ways of Thinking*. San Francisco: Jossey-Bass, 2004.

Schwartz, Daniel L., Jessica M. Tsang, and Kristen P. Blair. *The ABCs of How We Learn: 26 Scientifically Proven Approaches, How They Work, and When to Use Them*. New York: W. W. Norton, 2016.

"Scientific Reasoning" and "Scientific Method." Boundless. March 5, 2021. https://bio.libretexts.org/Courses/Chemeketa_Community_College/Cell_Biology_for_Allied_Health/01%3A_The_Study_of_Life/1.01%3A_The_Science_of_Biology/.

Wineburg, Sam. *Historical Thinking and Other Unnatural Acts: Charting the Future of Teaching the Past*. Philadelphia: Temple University, 2001.

Chapter Five. Reading 2.0

Adler, Mortimer J., and Charles Van Doren. *How to Read a Book: The Classic Guide to Intelligent Reading.* New York: Simon & Schuster, 1940.

Klayman, Joshua. "Varieties of Confirmation Bias." In *Decision Making from a Cognitive Perspective*, edited by Jerome Busemeyer, Reid Hastie, and Douglas L. Medin, 385–414. San Diego: Academic Press, 1995.

Miller, Susan. *Rescuing the Subject: A Critical Introduction to Rhetoric and the Writer.* 2nd ed. Carbondale, IL: Southern Illinois University Press, 2004.

Nickerson, Raymond S. "Confirmation Bias: A Ubiquitous Phenomenon in Many Guises." *Review of General Psychology* 2, no. 2 (1998): 175–220. doi.org/10.1037/1089-2680.2.2.175.

Chapter Six. Writing Well Is Thinking Well

Arapoff, Nancy. "Writing: A Thinking Process." *TESOL Quarterly* 1, no. 2 (1967): 33–39. https://doi.org/10.2307/3585751.

Bean, John C. *Engaging Ideas: The Professor's Guide to Integrating Writing, Critical Thinking, and Active Learning in the Classroom.* 2nd ed. San Francisco: Jossey-Bass, 2011.

Burke, Kenneth. *The Philosophy of Literary Form: Studies in Symbolic Action.* New York: Vintage, 1957.

DaFoe, Nancy. *Breaking Open the Box: A Guide for Creative Techniques to Improve Academic Writing and Generate Critical Thinking.* Lanham, MD: Roman & Littlefield Education, 2013.

Elbow, Peter. *Writing with Power: Techniques for Mastering the Writing Process.* 2nd ed. New York: Oxford University Press, 1998.

Flower, Linda. *Problem-Solving Strategies for Writing.* New York: Harcourt Brace Jovanovich, 1981.

Graff, Gerald, and Cathy Birkenstein. *They Say / I Say: The Moves That Matter in Academic Writing.* 4th ed. New York: W. W. Norton, 2018.

Hacker, Diana, and Nancy Sommers. *A Writer's Reference.* 10th ed. New York: Bedford/St. Martin's, 2021.

Harvey, Michael. *The Nuts and Bolts of College Writing.* 2nd ed. Indianapolis: Hackett, 2013.

Huck, Geoffrey. *What Is Good Writing?* New York: Oxford University Press, 2015.

Klein, Perry D., Pietro Boscolo, Lori Kirkpatrick, and Carmen Gelati. *Writing as a Learning Activity.* Leiden, Netherlands: Brill, 2014.

Levy, Mark. *Accidental Genius: Using Writing to Generate Your Best Ideas, Insight, and Content.* 2nd ed. San Francisco: Berrett-Koehler, 2010.

Menary, Richard. "Writing as Thinking." *Language Sciences* 29, no. 5 (2007): 621–32. https://doi.org/10.1016/j.langsci.2007.01.005.

Oatley, Keith, and Maja Djikic. "Writing as Thinking." *Review of General Psychology* 12, no. 1 (2008): 9–27. https://doi.org/10.1037/1089-2680.12.1.9.

Rosenwasser, David, and Jill Stephen. *Writing Analytically.* Fort Worth, TX: Harcourt Brace College Publishers, 1997.

Strunk, William, Jr., and E. B. White. *The Elements of Style*. 4th ed. Needham Heights, MA: Pearson, 2000.

Woodford, F. Peter. "Sounder Thinking through Clearer Writing." *Science* 156, no. 3776 (1967): 743–45. https://doi.org/10.1126/science.156.3776.743.

Chapter Seven. Knowing How to Count What Counts

Bock, David E., Paul F. Velleman, and Richard D. De Veaux. *Stats: Modeling the World*. Boston: Pearson, 2007.

Elrod, Susan. "Quantitative Reasoning: The Next 'Across the Curriculum' Movement." *Peer Review* 16, no. 3 (2014): 4–8.

Khan, Salman. "Statistics and Probability." N.p.: *Khan Academy*, 2020. www.khanacademy.org/math/statistics-probability.

Spiegelhalter, David. *The Art of Statistics: How to Learn from Data*. New York: Pelican, 2019.

Chapter Eight. Doing Research

Bizup, Joseph. "BEAM: A Rhetorical Vocabulary for Teaching Research-Based Writing." *Rhetorical Review* 27, no. 1 (2008): 72–86. http://dx.doi.org/10.1080/07350190701738858.

Bock, Peter. *Getting It Right: R&D Methods for Science and Engineering*. San Diego: San Diego Academic Press, 2001.

Booth, Wayne C., Gregory G. Colomb, Joseph M. Williams, Joseph Bizup, and William T. FitzGerald. *The Craft of Research*. 4th ed. Chicago: University of Chicago Press, 2016.

Collins, Jill, and Rodger Hussey. *Business Research: A Practical Guide for Undergraduate and Postgraduate Students*. 4th ed. Basingstoke, UK: Palgrave Macmillan, 2013.

"Conducting Primary Research." *Online Writing Lab (OWL), Purdue University*. https://owl.purdue.edu/owl/research_and_citation/conducting_research/conducting_primary_research/index.html.

Maree, Kobus, ed. *First Steps in Research*. Pretoria, South Africa: Van Schaik, 2007.

Thody, Angela. *Writing and Presenting Research*. Thousand Oaks, CA: Sage, 2006.

"Wikipedia: Researching with Wikipedia." *Wikipedia*. 2020. https://en.wikipedia.org/wiki/Wikipedia:Researching_with_Wikipedia.

Conclusion. The Final Frontier

DeNicola, Daniel R. *Learning to Flourish: A Philosophical Exploration of Liberal Education*. New York: Continuum International, 2012.

Freedman, James O. *Liberal Education and the Public Interest*. Iowa City: University of Iowa Press, 2003.

Gamson, Zelda F. *Liberating Education*. San Francisco: Jossey-Bass, 1984.

Hadzigeorgiou, Yannis. "Reclaiming Liberal Education." *Education Sciences* 9, no. 4 (2019): 264. https://doi.org/10.3390/educsci9040264.

Nussbaum, Martha. *Cultivating Humanity: A Classical Defense of Reform in Liberal Education*. Cambridge, MA: Harvard University Press, 1997.

Roth, Michael S. *Beyond the University: Why Liberal Education Matters*. New Haven, CT: Yale University Press, 2014.

Sullivan, William M. *Liberal Learning as a Quest for Purpose*. New York: Oxford University Press, 2016.

Wimpey, John A. "Value Perspectives in Liberal Education." *Peabody Journal of Education* 38, no. 5 (1961): 285–91. http://www.jstor.org/stable/1491324.

Zakaria, Fareed. *In Defense of a Liberal Education*. New York: W. W. Norton, 2015.

ANSWER KEY TO CHAPTER EXERCISES

Note: Not all chapters have exercises that require answers.

Chapter Two. Critical Thinking 101

Page 44

Passage from Lincoln's famous Gettysburg Address.

1. Historical circumstances: The United States is in the midst of a civil war. The people gathered to hear this address are standing at the location of the highest-casualty battle in that civil war.
2. Questions the author is trying to answer: "whether that nation, or any nation so conceived and so dedicated, can long endure." He's arguing that despite all of this animosity and bloodshed, the United States can survive as a country.
3. Assumptions the author is making: That the people in the audience also wish to honor the fallen troops. Also, that the audience wants this nation to last. And that they subscribe "to the proposition that all men are created equal."

Pages 56

Question: Identify the fallacy represented in the statements.

1. Hasty generalization
2. Appeal to popularity
3. Appeal to authority

Page 59

Real-world implications of the second law of thermodynamics:

When we recycle material, a small percentage of usable material is lost every time. We have not yet developed the capability to recycle glass, metal, and so on with 100 percent efficiency. Means of capturing renewable energy (e.g., solar panels, wind turbines, etc.) are on the rise, and they are becoming increasingly efficient. One major issue standing in the way of converting all our energy sources to renewables is that we do not yet possess batteries that can store energy well enough for times when renewable energy is not available (e.g., winter months, non-windy periods). As batteries sit unused, a significant amount of energy is inevitably lost every day.

Page 59–60

Implications of "mutual toleration" and "institutional forbearance":

One implication is that democracy relies on the voluntary actions of political actors to sacrifice power for the continuation of the system as a whole. They must sometimes choose to not be self-serving, at a cost to themselves. Also, that democracies are pretty vulnerable, as they can erode when individuals or political parties choose to prioritize their interests over the political system's health.

Chapter Three. What Am I Doing in This Class, Anyway? An Introduction to Disciplinary Thinking

Pages 81–82

Question: Physics problem.

Step 1: Represent the problem.

$\epsilon = 2.0N$
$mg = (40kg)\ (9.8m/s^2) = 9.8N$

Step 2: Identify knowns, unknowns, and assumptions.

Given: Forces, time, mass of objects
Unknowns: Velocity
Assumptions: On earth, particle (i.e., no rotation)

Step 3: Select the appropriate principles or equations to solve this problem.

Kinematics under constant acceleration: $v(t) = a \bullet t$
Newton's 2nd Law: $F = ma$
Resultant Force (Distance Formula): $F = \sqrt{F_x^2 + F_y^2}$

Step 4: Apply the selected principles and/or equations.

$$F = \sqrt{(2N)^2 + (9.8N)^2}$$

$$= \sqrt{100.04}$$

$$\approx 10N$$

$$a = \frac{F}{m} = \frac{10N}{1.0kg} = 10m/s^2$$

$$v = (10m/s^2)\ (10s) = 100m/s$$

Step 5: Assess your answer.

The answer seems reasonable as gravity is the dominant force.

Page 90

Quantitative or qualitative:

1. Quantitative
2. Qualitative
3. Qualitative
4. Quantitative
5. Qualitative and quantitative

Pages 99–100

Extrinsic or intrinsic approach:

1. Extrinsic. Using the biographical or psychological dimensions of an author's or artist's life to connect the meaning of their experience to the things they created.
2. Intrinsic. An effort to understand a creative work by looking solely at the formal elements that constitute it.
3. Extrinsic. Looking at the relationship between the music that young adults listen to and their identity development.
4. Intrinsic. Examining how grammar and syntax connect individual words to deeper meanings.
5. Extrinsic. Looking at the institutions or social conditions that gave rise to this specific piece of work.
6. Extrinsic. Considering how the work fits into a history of ideas.

Chapter Five. Reading 2.0: How to Read the Words That Aren't on the Page and Really Understand the Ones That Are

Page 148

Identify the purpose of the texts.

1. Sharing information
2. Inspiration/motivation
3. Social or political commentary
4. Sharing information
5. Explanation/theory

Chapter Seven. Knowing How to Count What Counts

Page 211
Confounding variables for the association between doctor's visits and smoking:

> One possibility is stress. People often smoke because they're stressed, and smoking calms their nerves. Chronic stress is associated with a host of medical issues. Perhaps smokers are more likely to engage in other risky behaviors, like excessive drinking, which contribute to the need for more medical care.

Pages 214–215
Causal or correlational relationship:

1. Correlation
2. Causation
3. Causation
4. Correlation

Chapter Eight. Doing Research: From Consuming Knowledge to Creating It

Pages 230–232
Make sentence succinct:

> How will the population growth that results from increased immigration and birth rates influence the development of the suburbs surrounding Minneapolis?

Open-ended:

> What are the impacts of anthropogenic biodiversity loss in the Amazon Rainforest, and who will bear the consequences?

Properly focused:

> You decide to write on the impacts of COVID-19 on the hospitality industry in the United States in the spring of 2020.

Arguable:

> You want to research the factors that contributed to the drop in violent crime rates in large American cities in a recent five-year period. (Criminologists have long-standing debates about what factors influence crime rates.)

PERMISSIONS

From *The Lancet*, vol. 395, Yeming Wang et al., "Remdesivir in Adults with Severe COVID-19: A Randomised, Double-Blind, Placebo-Controlled, Multicentre Trial," no. 10236 (2020): 1569–78. Used with permission from Elsevier.

From *Conversations by Myself*, by Nelson Mandela. Copyright © The Nelson Mandela Foundation, courtesy Blackwell & Ruth Ltd. Used with permission.

From Fran Landesman, *The Collected Poems*. Copyright ©2015 The Permanent Press. Used with permission.

From the song, *Little Boxes*. Words and music by Malvina Reynolds. Copyright ©1962 Schroder Music Co. (ASCAP). Renewed 1990. Used by permission. All rights reserved.

From Rachel A. Wattick, Rebecca L. Hagedorn, and Melissa Olfert, "Relationship between Diet and Mental Health in a Young Adult Appalachian College Population," *Nutrients* 10, no. 8, 2018. Used by permission of the authors.

From Linda Flower, *Problem-Solving Strategies for Writing*. Harcourt, Brace, Jovanovich, 1981. Used by permission of the author.

Gerald Gribbon, "Steve," March 15, 2012. Photograph available at https://500px.com/photo/5890333/Steve-by-gerald-gribbon/. Despite best efforts to secure permission from photographer, author received no response prior to publication.

NOTES

Foreword

1. "Even Einstein Struggled: Effects of Learning About Great Scientists' Struggles on High School Students' Motivation to Learn Science," Xiaodong Lin-Siegler, Janet N. Ahn, Jondou Chen, Fu-Fen Anny Fang, and Myra Luna-Lucero, *Journal of Educational Psychology* 2016, Vol. 108, No. 3, 314-28.
2. Lin-Siegler et al., "Even Einstein Struggled," 320.
3. Vedantam, Shankar. "How Stories Told of Brilliant Scientists Affect Kids' Interest in the Field," NPR, June 7, 2016. https://www.npr.org/2016/06/07/481058613/how-the-stories-told-of-brilliant-scientists-affect-kids-interest-in-the-field.

Introduction

Epigraph: Alice Calaprice and Trevor Lipscombe, *Albert Einstein: A Biography* (Westport, CT: Greenwood, 2005), 11.

1. E. B. Stolzenberg et al., *The American Freshman: National Norms Fall 2019* (Los Angeles: Higher Education Research Institute, UCLA, 2020), https://heri.ucla.edu/publications-tfs/.
2. The US Bureau of Labor Statistics projects that "between 2016 and 2026, the number of jobs requiring a bachelor's degree will increase by 10 percent." Kyaw Khine, "A Greater Number of Jobs Require More Education, Leaving Middle-Skill Workers with Fewer Opportunities," *Stat Ch@t* (web series), University of Virginia, Weldon Cooper Center for Public Service, May 10, 2019, https://statchatva.org/2019/05/10/a-greater-number-of-jobs-require-more-education-leaving-middle-skill-workers-with-fewer-opportunities/.
3. "Men with bachelor's degrees earn approximately $900,000 more in median lifetime earnings than high school graduates. Women with bachelor's degrees earn $630,000 more." Social Security Administration, Research, Statistics and Policy Analysis, "Education and Lifetime Earnings," November 2015, www.ssa.gov/policy/docs/research-summaries/education-earnings.html.
4. Bureau of Labor Statistics, *Number of Jobs, Labor Market Experience, Marital Status, and Health: Results from a National Longitudinal Survey*. USDL-21-1567, August 2021, www.bls.gov/news.release/pdf/nlsoy.pdf.

5. "Nine in ten employers believe that it is important to achieve the learning outcomes that define a contemporary liberal education, for example, and that it is worthwhile to obtain a college degree." American Association of Colleges and Universities, "How College Contributes to Workforce Success: Most Employers View Liberal Education as Essential for Workforce Preparation," *Liberal Education*, web exclusive, April 1, 2021, www.aacu.org/article/how-college-contributes-to-workforce-success#:~:text=Responses%20show%20that%20employers%20think,necessary%20for%20their%20new%20roles.
6. In 2019, 44.4 percent of high school graduates or GED recipients had begun a four-year college by the fall of that year. National Center for Education Statistics, Digest of Educational Statistics, table 302.10, "Recent High School Completers, and Their Enrollment in College, by Sex and Level of Institution: 1960 through 2019," July 2020, https://nces.ed.gov/programs/digest/d20/tables/dt20_302.10.asp.
7. According to a recent international survey, "Roughly 1/3 of first-year students in 19 colleges across 8 countries who participated in a self-report survey screened positive for at least 1 common DSM-IV anxiety, mood, or substance disorder." *Journal of Abnormal Psychology* 127, no. 7 (2018): 623–38.
8. A survey conducted in October 2020 by the Jed Foundation, which is devoted to supporting the mental health of young adults, found that "a high proportion of students are dealing with anxiety (82%), followed by social isolation/loneliness (68%), depression (63%), trouble concentrating (62%), and difficulty coping with stress in a healthy way (60%)." "Survey of College Student Mental Health in 2020," Jed Foundation, October 22, 2020, https://jedfoundation.org/news-views/survey-of-college-student-mental-health-in-2020/.
9. Terrell L. Strayhorn, *College Students' Sense of Belonging: A Key to Educational Success for All Students* (New York: Routledge, 2018). See also Leslie R. M. Hausmann et al., "Sense of Belonging and Persistence in White and African American First-Year Students," *Research in Higher Education* 50, no. 7 (2009): 649–69.

Chapter One. Learning How to Learn

Epigraph: Albert Camus, *Notebooks,* trans. Philip Thody and Justin O'Brien (New York: Knopf, 1963), 28.

1. Rachael N. Blasiman, Donald Larabee, and Dianah Fabry, "Distracted Students: A Comparison of Multiple Types of Distractions on Learning in Online Lectures," *Scholarship of Teaching and Learning in Psychology* 4, no. 4 (2018): 222–30, https://doi.org/10.1037/stl0000122.
2. See Study Report of the National Academies of Sciences, Engineering, and Medicine, *How People Learn II: Learners, Contexts and Cultures* (Washington, DC: National Academies Press, 2018); Peter C. Brown, Henry L. Roedinger III, and Mark A. McDaniel, *Make It Stick: The Science of Successful Learning* (Cambridge, MA: Harvard University Press, 2014); and Terry Doyle and Todd Zakrajsek, *The New Science of Learning: How to Learn in Harmony with Your Brain* (Sterling, VA: Stylus Publishing, 2013).

3. "Respiration Concept Map," November 18, 2008, https://www.slideshare.net/dhmcmillan/respiration-concept-map-presentation.
4. Scholars who have studied learning processes have defined metacognition in various ways. See Jennifer A. Livingston, "Metacognition: An Overview," Educational Resources Information Center, US Department of Education, 2003.
5. David N. Perkins, *The Mind's Best Work* (Cambridge, MA: Harvard University Press, 1981), 52.
6. James M. Lang, "What Will Students Remember from Your Class in 20 Years?" *Chronicle of Higher Education* (September 30, 2018), www.chronicle.com/article/what-will-students-remember-from-your-class-in-20-years/.
7. Carol S. Dweck, *Mindset: The New Psychology of Success* (New York: Random House Digital, 2008).

Chapter Two. Critical Thinking 101

Epigraph: John Chaffee, *Thinking Critically* (Boston: Cengage Learning, 1985), 187.

1. In Peter A. Facione, *Critical Thinking: A Statement of Expert Consensus for Purposes of Educational Assessment and Instruction (the Delphi Report)* (Millbrae, CA: California Academic Press, 1990), critical thinking is defined as "purposeful, self-regulatory judgment which results in interpretation, analysis, evaluation, and inference, as well as explanation of the evidential, conceptual, methodological, criteriological, or contextual considerations upon which that judgment is based." Most definitions of critical thinking include "reasoning/logic, judgment, metacognition, reflection, questioning and mental processes." Susan C. Fischer, V. Alan Spiker, and Sharon L. Riedel, *Critical Thinking Training for Army Officers, vol. 2, A Model of Critical Thinking* (Santa Barbara: Anacapa Sciences, 2009).
2. Kenneth Noland, "Context" (speech, Hartford, CT, March 1988), Sharecom, www.sharecom.ca/noland/nolandtalk.html.
3. Milan Kundera, *Encounter*, trans. Linda Asher (New York: Harper, 2010), 113–14.
4. See Charles G. Lord and Cheryl A. Taylor, "Biased Assimilation: Effects of Assumptions and Expectations on the Interpretation of New Evidence," *Social and Personality Psychology Compass* 3, no. 5 (2009): 827–41, doi:10.1111/j.1751-9004.2009.00203.x; also see Raymond S. Nickerson, "Confirmation Bias: A Ubiquitous Phenomenon in Many Guises," *Review of General Psychology* 2, no. 2 (1998): 175–220. https://doi.org/10.1037/1089-2680.2.2.175.
5. David Cooper, "Raising the Federal Minimum Wage to $15 by 2024 Would Lift Pay for Nearly 40 Million American Workers," Economic Policy Institute, February 2019. epi.org/publication/raising-the-federal-minimum-wage-to-15-by-2024-would-lift-pay-for-nearly-40-million-workers/. Also see David Card and Alan B. Krueger, "Minimum Wager and Employment: A Case Study of the Fast-Food Industry in New Jersey and Pennsylvania," *American Economic Review* 84, no. 4 (September 1994): 772–93.
6. S. S. Iyengar and M. R. Lepper, "When Choice Is Demotivating: Can One Desire Too Much of a Good Thing?" *Journal of Personality and Social Psychology* 79, no. 6 (2000): 1004. https://doi.org/10.1037/0022-3514.79.6.995.

7. After stating that he definitely did not believe in flying saucers, ancient astronauts, the Bermuda Triangle, or life after death, Asimov explained what he would believe in. From Isaac Asimov, "Don't You Believe?" *Isaac Asimov's Science Fiction Magazine*, January 18, 1982. Collected in Isaac Asimov and Arthur C. Clark, *The Roving Mind* (Buffalo, NY: Prometheus Books, 1983), 43.
8. See M. John Close and Thomas J. Bergmann, "Dogmatism and Attained Educational Level: A Field Study," *Psychological Reports* 44, no. 2 (1979): 671–73, https://doi.org/10.2466/pr0.1979.44.2.671. Also see Irvin J. Lehman, "Changes in Critical Thinking, Attitudes, and Values from Freshman to Senior Years," *Journal of Educational Psychology* 54, no. 6 (1963): 305–15, https://doi.org/10.1037/h0045302.
9. Camila Domonoske, "50 Years Ago, Sugar Industry Quietly Paid Scientists to Point Blame at Fat," *The Two-Way* (blog), NPR, September 13, 2016, https://www.npr.org/sections/thetwo-way/2016/09/13/493739074/50-years-ago-sugar-industry-quietly-paid-scientists-to-point-blame-at-fat.
10. Ivan Oransky, "Journal retracts 16-year-old paper based on debunked autism-vaccine study," *Retraction Watch Database*, October 16, 2018, https://retractionwatch.com/2018/10/16/journal-retracts-16-year-old-paper-based-on-debunked-autism-vaccine-study/.
11. Alfred North Whitehead, *The Aims of Education & Other Essays* (New York: Macmillan, 1929), 6.
12. Yeming Wang et al., "Remdesivir in Adults with Severe COVID-19: A Randomised, Double-Blind, Placebo-Controlled, Multicentre Trial," *Lancet* 395, no. 10236 (2020): 1569–78. https://www.thelancet.com/journals/lancet/article/PIIS0140-6736(20)31022-9/fulltext..
13. Steven Levitsky and Daniel Ziblatt, *How Democracies Die* (New York: Crown, 2018).

Chapter Three. What Am I Doing in This Class, Anyway? An Introduction to Disciplinary Thinking

Epigraph: Stephen D. Brookfield, *Teaching for Critical Thinking: Tools and Techniques to Help Students Question Their Assumptions* (San Francisco: Jossey-Bass, 2012), 28.

1. "A Science Checklist," *Understanding Science*, University of California Museum of Paleontology, https://undsci.berkeley.edu/article/whatisscience_03.
2. Ohm's law says that for a fixed voltage, an increase in resistance causes a decrease in current flowing through the circuit.
3. Daniel L. Schwartz, Jessica M. Tsang, and Kristen P. Blair, *The ABCs of How We Learn: 26 Scientifically Proven Approaches, How They Work, and When to Use Them* (New York: W. W. Norton, 2016), 14–24.
4. Schwartz, Tsang, and Blair, *The ABCs of How We Learn*, 44–59,
5. "1.1B: Scientific Reasoning," General Biology, Boundless, 2020, https://bio.libretexts.org/Courses/Chemeketa_Community_College/Cell_Biology_for_Allied_Health/01%3A_The_Study_of_Life/1.01%3A_The_Science_of_Biology/1.1B%3A_Scientific_Reasoning.

6. "1.1C: The Scientific Method," *The Study of Life*, Boundless, 2021, https://bio.libretexts.org/Courses/Chemeketa_Community_College/Cell_Biology_for_Allied_He alth/01%3A_The_Study_of_Life/1.01%3A_The_Science_of_Biology/1.1C%3A_The_Scientific_Method.
7. Steven M. Carr, "Redi Experiment (1665)," Memorial University of Newfoundland, 2018, www.mun.ca/biology/scarr/4270_Redi_experiment.html.
8. Scientific hypotheses must be able to be disproven by an experimental result. Claims that are not falsifiable cannot be scientific hypotheses.
9. "The Controversy Journey," FutureLearn, University of Wollongong, www.futurelearn.com/courses/homo-floresiensis/0/steps/15867.
10. Dan Falk, "The 7 Biggest Unanswered Questions in Physics," *Mach*, NBC Universal, 2017, www.nbcnews.com/mach/science/7-biggest-unanswered-questions-physics-ncna789666; Brian Greene, "Why String Theory Still Offers Hope We Can Unify Physics," *Think Big! Smithsonian Magazine*, 2015, www.smithsonianmag.com/science-nature/string-theory-about-unravel-180953637.
11. Jeffrey Williams, "The New Humanities," *Chronicle Review*, www-chronicle-com.stanford.idm.oclc.org/interactives/20191113-TheNewHumanities.
12. Of course, college is not the only context in which a person can develop these traits.

Chapter Four. How Am I Supposed to Do This Assignment?

Epigraph: Abigail Adams to John Quincy Adams, March 20, 1780. *The Adams Papers: Adams Family Correspondence, vol. 3, April 1778–September 1780*, ed. L. H. Butterfield and Marc Friedlaender (Cambridge, MA: Harvard University Press, 1973), 310–13. Abigail Adams (1744–1818) served as first and second lady of the United States.

Chapter Five. Reading 2.0: How to Read the Words That Aren't on the Page and Really Understand the Ones That Are

Epigraphs: "Quote by Swedish Proverb," *Goodreads*, www.goodreads.com/quotes/949306-in-a-good-book-the-best-is-between-the-lines. Hosseini Khaled, "Khaled Hosseini on *And the Mountains Echoed*," Interview with Lois Alter Mark, *Huffington Post* (May 2013), www.huffpost.com/entry/khaled-hosseini-on-and-th_b_3304518.

1. In the case of reading fiction or plays, it may be the identity of the character, as much as the author, that you want to attend to.
2. "Tobacco Industry Research Committee," *Tobacco Tactics*, University of Bath, https://tobaccotactics.org/wiki/tobacco-industry-research-committee. Eva C. Creutzberg et al., "Systematic Effects of Smoking," *Chest* 131, no. 5 (2007): 1557–66, https://doi.org/10.1378/chest.06-2179.
3. In many contexts, especially scientific publications, authors are expected to disclose if they have any personal or financial relationship to the subject they are writing about. It's a way of putting readers on notice that there might be a bias or slant to this work.

4. Nelson Mandela, *Conversations with Myself* (New York: Farrar, Straus and Giroux, 2010), 112.
5. Women's Rights Convention. "The First Convention Ever Called to Discuss the Civil and Political Rights of Women." Elizabeth Cady Stanton, *A Declaration of Sentiments and Resolutions* (Seneca Falls, New York, July 19–20, 1848). Available at https://liberalarts.utexas.edu/coretexts/_files/resources/texts/1848Declarationof Sentiments.pdf.
6. Fran Landesman, *The Collected Poems* (New York: Permanent Press, 2015).
7. John B. Taylor, from his blog, https://economicsone.com/2019/11/21/congressional-testimony-on-the-costs-of-rapidly-growing-government-debt/. Cited with the author's permission.
8. Vladimir I. Lenin, *A Letter to American Workers, 1918* (New York: International Publishers, 1934).
9. Malvina Reynolds, *Little Boxes and Other Handmade Songs* (New York: Oak Publications, 1964).
10. Rachel A. Wattick, Rebecca L. Hagedorn, and Melissa D. Olfert, "Relationship between Diet and Mental Health in a Young Adult Appalachian College Population," *Nutrients* 10, no. 8 (2018): 957, doi:10.3390/nu10080957.
11. Gerald Gribbon, "Steve," March 15, 2012. Photograph available at https://500px.com/photo/5890333/Steve-by-gerald-gribbon/.
12. Key studies of this issue have been produced by the Stanford History Education Group. See, in particular, "Evaluating Information: The Cornerstone of Civic Online Reasoning," Stanford History Education Group, https://purl.stanford.edu/fv751yt5934; and Sam Wineburg and Sarah McGrew, "Lateral Reading and the Nature of Expertise: Reading Less and Learning More when Evaluating Digital Information," *Teachers College Record* 121, no. 11 (2019): 1–40, https://cor.stanford.edu/research/lateral-reading-and-the-nature-of-expertise/.
13. See Raymond S. Nickerson, "Confirmation Bias: A Ubiquitous Phenomenon in Many Guises," *Review of General Psychology* 2, no. 2 (1998): 175–220, https://doi.org/10.1037/1089-2680.2.2.175. Also see Joshua Klayman, "Varieties of Confirmation Bias," in *Decision Making from a Cognitive Perspective*, ed. Jerome Busemeyer, Reid Hastie, and Douglas L. Medin (San Diego: Academic Press, 1995), 385–414.

Chapter Six. Writing Well Is Thinking Well

Epigraph: John C. Bean, *Engaging Ideas: The Professor's Guide to Integrating Writing, Critical Thinking and Active Learning in the Classroom, 2nd ed.* (San Francisco: Jossey-Bass, 2011), 4.

1. Gerald Graff and Cathy Birkenstein, *They Say/I Say: The Moves That Matter in Academic Writing* (New York: W. W. Norton, 2009), 125.
2. A play on the saying "vote early and vote often," a cynical expression about political corruption that has been attributed to a number of different individuals, mostly connected with Chicago politics.

3. See Keith Oatley and Maja Djikic, "Writing as Thinking," *Review of General Psychology* 12, no. 1 (2008): 9–27, https://doi.org/10.1037/1089-2680.12.1.9; Nancy Arapoff, "Writing: A Thinking Process," *TESOL Quarterly* 1, no. 2 (1967): 33–39, https://doi.org/10.2307/3585751; and F. Peter Woodford, "Sounder Thinking through Clearer Writing," *Science* 156, no. 3776 (1967): 743–45, https://www.science.org/doi/10.1126/science.156.3776.743.
4. There may be times when you are asked to write something that is purely a self-reflection or opinion piece, without reference to what anyone else has said about this subject. But the vast majority of college writing is argumentative in nature, meaning that you are being asked to make a claim and back it up in some way that is typical of that discipline.
5. Linda Flower, *Problem-Solving Strategies for Writing* (New York: Harcourt Brace Jovanovich, 1981), 31.
6. Bernard Malamud, Ben Belitt Lectureship Series (speech, Bennington, VT, October 30, 1984), *New York Times* Archive, www.nytimes.com/1988/03/20/books/reflections-of-a-writer-long-work-short-life.html.
7. Graff and Birkenstein, *They Say/I Say*, 118.
8. Flower, *Problem-Solving Strategies*, 45–46.
9. For examples of how to solicit useful feedback, see https://writingcenter.unc.edu/tips-and-tools/getting-feedback/.
10. See, among other studies, Erkki Kronholm et al., "Trends in Self-Reported Sleep Problems, Tiredness and Related School Performance among Finnish Adolescents from 1984 to 2011," *Journal of Sleep Research* 24, no. 1 (2015): 3–10.
11. See "It Takes More Than a Major: Employer Priorities for College Learning and Student Success," a research study conducted by Hart Research Associates for the Association of American Colleges and Universities, April 10, 2013, www.aacu.org/sites/default/files/files/LEAP/2013_EmployerSurvey.pdf.
12. Peter Elbow, *Writing with Power: Techniques for Mastering the Writing Process* (New York: Oxford University Press, 1981), 302.

Chapter Seven. Knowing How to Count What Counts

Epigraphs: Marilyn Vos Savant, *Growing Up: A Classic American Childhood* (New York: W. W. Norton 2002), 192. John Naughton, "Steven Pinker: Fighting Talk from the Prophet of Peace," *Guardian*, October 15, 2011, www.theguardian.com/science/2011/oct/15/steven-pinker-better-angels-violence-interview?newsfeed=true.

1. QR builds on, but transcends and is distinct from, mathematics: "The application of basic mathematics skills, such as algebra, to the analysis and interpretation of real-world quantitative information in the context of a discipline or an interdisciplinary problem to draw conclusions that are relevant to students in their daily lives." Susan Elrod, "Quantitative Reasoning: The Next 'Across the Curriculum' Movement," *Peer Review* 16, no. 3 (2014): 4–8.

2. Other metrics of central tendency (mode, median) can be used to report the "center" of a data distribution without being affected by outliers, but they have their own limitations.
3. As with central tendency, there are other metrics for measuring the spread of a dataset. One you may have encountered in high school is the interquartile range (IQR), which is usually paired with the median.
4. Liz Roth-Johnson, "Introduction to Inferential Statistics," Visionlearning, 2016, www.visionlearning.com/en/library/Math-in-Science/62/Introduction-to-Inferential-Statistics/224.
5. Note that bias in statistics has a different meaning and connotation than in everyday use. Here, bias refers to when the results of your sampling are significantly different from the hypothetical "actual" results from sampling all data points in the population of interest.
6. Confidence intervals are reported at a particular confidence level expressed as a percentage. For example, the 90 percent confidence interval for average fish weight might be 3.5–4.5 lbs. This means that if we were to collect ten similar samples from the same population, we would predict that nine of them would produce confidence intervals containing the population mean.
7. The type of analysis we illustrate here can also be extended to other combinations of variables: quantitative versus quantitative, categorical versus categorical, quantitative versus categorical, and so on. The details of these types of tests are beyond the scope of this book, but all provide us with a p value that is then compared to a significance level.
8. Of course, if we were looking at all smokers and all nonsmokers in a population, then this difference would automatically be significant. The uncertainty arises because we are only sampling from each group.
9. Here are some questions one might consider to assess the real-world significance of this difference: How much, on average, does an additional doctor's visit financially cost patients? Does it affect quality of life in other ways (time away from work, family, etc.)?
10. This skepticism does not, however, mean that we can never derive valuable insights from observational studies. The discovery that smoking is bad for your health, as an example, is the product of decades of careful observational study (since we cannot ethically recruit people to begin smoking). The fact that these studies were not experimental meant that more sophisticated math and much more data were required for the scientific community to reach a consensus on the causal role of smoking in disease. We now have a mechanistic understanding of how chemicals in cigarettes interact with our cells to cause disease.
11. The quote is of unknown origin, though it was popularized in the United States by Mark Twain.

Chapter Eight. Doing Research: From Consuming Knowledge to Creating It

Epigraphs: Alice Calaprice and Trevor Lipscombe, *Albert Einstein: A Biography* (Westport: Greenwood, 2005), 11. Zora Neale Hurston, *Dust Tracks on a Road: An Autobiography*, ed. Robert E. Hemenway (New York: Arno Press, 1942), 91.

1. George Kuh, *High-Impact Educational Practices: What They Are, Who Has Access to Them, and Why They Matter* (Washington, DC: Association of American Colleges and Universities, 2008), e-book.
2. For example, Newtonian physics was overturned in the twentieth century by quantum mechanics, and nineteenth century "scientific" views about race and intelligence have been debunked.
3. Wayne C. Booth, Gregory G. Colomb, and Joseph M. Williams, *The Craft of Research*, 2nd ed. (Chicago: University of Chicago Press, 2003), 52. (The fourth edition, published in 2016, was updated by Joseph Bizup and William T. FitzGerald).
4. There are some online tools that will manage your citations for you, making sure that they conform to the style required for your document. These require paid subscriptions, but if you are involved in a major project with lots of citations, they can save you a lot of time. See, for example, NoodleTools and EasyBib.
5. "Annotated Bibliography Samples," Purdue Online Writing Lab (OWL), Purdue University, https://owl.purdue.edu/owl/general_writing/common_writing_assignments/annotated_bibliographies/annotated_bibliography_samples.html.
6. For some examples of this, see the brief discussion of the digital humanities in chapter 7.
7. I am grateful to my colleague Shana Sippy (Centre College) for sharing this assignment with me.

Conclusion. The Final Frontier: Becoming an Educated Person

Epigraphs: John Dewey, *My Pedagogic Creed* (New York: E. L. Kellogg, 1897), 7. Julie Lindquist, "Hoods in the Polis," *Pedagogy* 1, no. 2 (Spring 2001): 267.

1. The Social Security Administration reported in November 2015 that "men with bachelor's degrees earn approximately $900,000 more in median lifetime earnings than high school graduates. Women with bachelor's degrees earn $630,000 more." Research, Statistics and Policy Analysis, Social Security Administration, November 2015, www.ssa.gov/policy/docs/research-summaries/education-earnings.html.
2. Julie Lindquist, as quoted in Gerald Graff, *Clueless in Academe* (New Haven, CT: Yale University Press, 2003), 24: "When people learn, they don't take on new knowledge so much as a new identity."
3. *It Takes More Than a Major: Employer Priorities for College Learning and Student Success* (Washington, DC: Hart Research Associates on behalf of The Association of American Colleges and Universities, 2013), https://dgmg81phhvh63.cloudfront.net/content/user-photos/Research/PDFs/2013_EmployerSurvey.pdf.
4. I am grateful to Professor Riv-Ellen Prell, a friend and colleague at the University of Minnesota, for her help in developing this metaphor.

Printed in the USA
CPSIA information can be obtained
at www.ICGtesting.com
JSHW021059290824
69013JS00003B/30

9 781635 767957